THE PHILADELPHIA PHILLIES

WRITING SPORTS SERIES
Richard "Pete" Peterson, Editor

The Cleveland Indians
Franklin Lewis

The Cincinnati Reds
Lee Allen

The Chicago White Sox
Warren Brown

Dreaming Baseball
James T. Farrell

My Greatest Day in Football
Murray Goodman and Leonard Lewin

The Detroit Tigers
Frederick G. Lieb

The Philadelphia Phillies
Frederick G. Lieb and Stan Baumgartner

THE PHILADELPHIA PHILLIES

by

Frederick G. Lieb

and

Stan Baumgartner

Foreword by William C. Kashatus

The Kent State University Press
Kent, Ohio

Library of Congress Catalog Card Number 2008053739
ISBN 978-1-60635-012-6
Manufactured in the United States of America

First published in 1948 by A. S. Barnes and Co. Inc.

Library of Congress Cataloging-in-Publication Data

Lieb, Fred, b. 1888.
The Philadelphia Phillies / by Frederick G. Lieb and Stan Baumgartner ; foreword by William C. Kashatus.
p. cm. — (Writing sports series)
Originally published: New York : A.S. Barnes and Co., 1948.
Includes index.
ISBN 978-1-60635-012-6 (pbk. : alk. paper) ∞ 1. Philadelphia Phillies (Baseball team)—History. I. Baumgartner, Stan. II. Title.
GV875.P45L5 2008
796.357′640974811—dc22

2008053739

British Library Cataloging-in-Publication data are available.

13 12 11 10 09 5 4 3 2 1

Contents

Foreword

William C. Kashatus

"I love baseball," admitted Frederick Lieb near the end of his illustrious career as a writer for *The Sporting News*. "I could watch it every day, every year. And to think I get paid for doing it!"

Lieb, who was born in Philadelphia in 1888, must have loved the game tremendously in order to survive the foiled heroism and hapless play of his hometown Phillies. No other major league team suffered more losses in its history (10,000+), or experienced as many last-place finishes (26). Even on those extremely rare occasions when the Phillies reached the World Series, they found a way to go down in flames. After winning the first game of the 1915 Fall Classic against the Red Sox, the Phillies dropped the next four contests, all by one-run margins. In 1950, just three years before this book was originally published, the "Fightin' Phillies" were swept in four straight games by the mighty New York Yankees, who were in the throes of still another championship dynasty.

Indeed, the Phillies were busy elevating losing to an art form while Lieb came of age, first as a fan and later as a writer for the Philadelphia News Bureau. At the same time, the Phillies served as an important benchmark in his life. As a boy, Lieb saw his first professional game from the right field bleachers at old Philadelphia Park, later Baker Bowl. His first hero was star slugger Ed Delahanty, a future Hall of Famer whose niece Lieb would later date. As a young baseball writer, he became well-acquainted with club president Horace Fogel, who once released 100 pigeons with free tickets strapped to their legs in a desperate attempt to attract fans. Unfortunately, Lieb died in June 1980, four months before the "Fightin' Phillies" captured their first—and only—world championship. If not for Connie Mack's Athletics, who won nine American League pennants and five World Series, Lieb may never have known what it was like to enjoy a winner in the City of Brotherly Love.

Fortunately for the reader, Lieb, in 1911, escaped to New York City where he refined his journalistic skill covering the storied Yankees for the *New York Press,* and later with other newspapers in the Big Apple, including the *Post,* the *Morning Sun,* and the *Telegram.* He also became part of baseball's rich folklore by dubbing Yankee Stadium "The House That Ruth Built" and having his close friendship with Lou Gehrig preserved on film in the classic 1942 tearjerker *Pride of the Yankees.*

In 1935, Lieb was persuaded by J. G. Taylor Spink to join *The Sporting News* as a regular columnist. Over the next 35 years, he became perhaps the most revered baseball writer of the first half of the twentieth century. A longtime member of the Baseball Writers' Association of America, Lieb served as president of the BBWAA from 1921 to 1923. During his 68 years as a baseball writer, he covered over 8,000 major league games, including every World Series from 1911 through 1958 as well as 30 All-Star Games. Lieb capped his distinguished career with an induction into the writers' wing of the Hall of Fame in 1972.

In addition to the many accolades he achieved as a sportswriter, Lieb was also a talented baseball historian. Readers will enjoy his anecdotes that are at once descriptive and dreamlike, wry and warm, and deeply illuminating of some of the most hallowed figures in the game's history.

Of the twelve books he authored, six were team histories of the Detroit Tigers, Boston Red Sox, St. Louis Cardinals, Pittsburgh Pirates, Baltimore Orioles, and the book you hold in your hands on the Philadelphia Phillies.

Unlike his other books, this one was collaboratively written with Stan Baumgartner, a veteran sportswriter for the *Philadelphia Inquirer* and former baseball player. A three-sport star athlete at the University of Chicago, Baumgartner pitched in the major leagues for eight seasons, five with the Phillies and three with the Athletics. The great Grover Cleveland Alexander taught him how to throw a curve ball in his rookie year, and he rubbed shoulders with Gavvy Cravath, the home run champion of the Dead Ball era. But those proved to be among the few highlights of Baumgartner's pedestrian career.

Although he appeared in 16 games for the pennant-winning Phillies in 1915, Baumgartner never could catch on with the team. He pitched in one game in the 1916 season, returned to the Phillies again in 1921, and was released in 1922. Hooking up with the A's in 1924, Baumgartner would enjoy his only two seasons as a full-time player, posting a 13–6 record in 1924 and 6–3 mark in 1925. In 1926, the hard-luck pitcher appeared in just 10 games and then was out of baseball. His career record of 26–21, 129 strikeouts, and a 3.70 ERA is more of a footnote than a memorable chapter of Philadelphia's baseball history. It also serves to explain why he became such an insightful observer of that history.

Baumgartner brings with him the perspective of a former ballplayer who performed in the unforgiving culture of Philadelphia sports. The city's baseball fans, in particular, have always viewed the game through a black-and-white prism that reflects only "heroes" and "bums." They embrace ballplayers who get their uniforms dirty and show their emotions as well as their humanness, warts and all. They're reactionaries, demanding immediate gratification and, failing to get it, express their displeasure by showering players with a hailstorm of boos. Baumgartner brings a stiff dose of this reality to the team's history—some of which he observed firsthand as a player—while Lieb offers the more nostalgic, dare I say "sentimental," perspective of a fan-turned-sportswriter.

Together, Lieb and Baumgartner take readers on a spellbinding journey from the mid-nineteenth century, when Philadelphia featured a plethora of talented amateur clubs, to the lean days of the Great Depression, when the Phillies were perennial tailenders, to the heady exhilaration of the 1950 pennant clinching, when a star-studded cast of youngsters nicknamed the "Whiz Kids" looked as if they'd be a baseball power for years to come.

There are interesting chapters on how Connie Mack of the Athletics raided the roster of the Phillies in 1901, luring prized second baseman Napoleon Lajoie from the team only to be taken to court by president John Rogers; manager Pat Moran's cultivation of the 1915 National League champions led by the brilliant pitching of Grover Alexander; the club ownership's effort to avoid bankruptcy by auctioning off such star players as Alexander, Dave Bancroft, Bucky Walters, Chuck Klein, and Dolf Camilli; and the building of a contender under DuPont heir Robert R. M. Carpenter Jr.

Other chapters detail the changing landscape of Philadelphia baseball from an amateur sport to a professional industry governed by the reserve clause; from the wooden bandbox ballparks of the nineteenth century to the concrete-and-steel structures of the twentieth; and from the Dead Ball era to the Fabulous Fifties. Throughout the book, there are individual highlights of the Phillies' Hall of Famers: "Big Ed" Delahanty, a lifetime .346 hitter who died tragically when he was swept over Niagara Falls; "Sliding Billy" Hamilton, who combined raw speed, gutsy baserunning and patience at the plate to become Baseball's first great leadoff hitter; Grover Cleveland Alexander, whose 190 wins in a Phillies' uniform represented one-third of the team's total during the six year period (1912 to 1917); Triple Crown winner Chuck Klein; and Richie Ashburn and Robin Roberts, who propelled the Whiz Kids to the 1950 pennant.

But the content of the book is secondary to its central theme, specifically the need for Phillies fans to have patience with and faith in the hometown team.

Frederick Lieb and Stan Baumgartner remind readers that it's easy to root for a winner, but some of us fall in love with a team in defeat probably because of our ability to relate. Rooting for the Phillies then, is like rooting for ourselves. After all, people tend to "lose" in life a lot more than they "win." What really matters is how they rebound from the loss. Such ability makes "winning" so much more special when it finally occurs.

William C. Kashatus holds a doctorate in history from the University of Pennsylvania. He is author of ten books on Philadelphia baseball, including *September Swoon: Richie Allen, the '64 Phillies and Racial Integration* and *Almost A Dynasty: The Rise and Fall of the 1980 Phillies.*

Preface

The Phillies have had their ups and downs through the years, but with few exceptions the club never has been dull. Even their tailenders have been interesting, and have made history. The 1930 eighth place team, for instance, batted .315, second highest National League club batting average of this century. It had a slugger, Chuck Klein, who rapped out 250 hits, drove in 170 runs, and scored 158 runs, the modern National League record. A year before, a fellow Phillie outfielder, Frank "Lefty" O'Doul, established another N. L. record with 254 hits.

Yet these high marks in the game's hitting, and slugging, department need occasion no surprise. In the past, the Phillies were always a slugging team. In 1894, the Phillies possessed an outfield in which Sam Thompson batted .403, Ed Delahanty .400 and Billy Hamilton .398. And the utility outfielder, Tuck Turner, hit a mere .423. Billy Hamilton, low man of the quartet, stole 99 bases and scored 196 runs, the National League's all-time record. Three years earlier, Hamilton had stolen 115 bases for the Phillies, another National League record which should endure through the assaults of time.

The Phillies won no pennant until their thirty-third season, when Pat Moran directed the club to the 1915 championship, but Phillie teams in the early days were anything but door mats. Before sinking into the second division mire during the ill-fated William Baker ownership in 1918, the Phillies could boast of twenty-five first division teams in thirty-five years. Up to that time, only two Phillie clubs had finished last. And Philadelphia saw such a parade of stars as Charley Ferguson, Sam Thompson, Ed Delahanty, Napoleon Lajoie, Elmer Flick, Bill Bernard, Frank Donohue, Harry White, Roy Thomas, Sherry Magee, Frank Sparks, Red Dooin, Mickey Doolan, Otto Knabe, Hans Lobert, Grover Cleveland Alexander, Tom Seaton, Fred Luderus, Gavvy Cravath, Dode Paskert and Dave Bancroft.

Then came the tragic hand-to-mouth years of the Baker and Nugent regimes, when it became necessary for the club to sell stars to live. Philadelphia fans suffered and writhed as they saw strong and popular players such as Grover Alexander, Bill Killefer, Dave Bancroft, Emil Meusel, Lee Meadows, Hal Carlson, Jimmy Wilson, Bucky Walters, Dick Bartell, Chuck Klein, Dolf Camilli, Claude Passeau and Kirby Higbe sold to clubs higher in the standing.

There was a happy ending to this period when the opulent Carpenter family of Wilmington, Delaware, acquired the then sick franchise in 1943. Gone were the forlorn years when the Phillies served as a farm for wealthier clubs. With a strong treasury and an able, alert organization in back of them, the Phillies developed a bevy of new stars—Robin Roberts, Del Ennis, Curt Simmons, Richie Ashburn, Granny Hamner, Willie Jones, Stan Lopata. Three first division clubs in the last four years, including the pennant of 1950, shows the new order in fruition. The Phillie youngsters still are developing and we feel the best years of the Phillies are in the future. The bad taste of the tailenders of the twenties and thirties will be wiped out by new pennants which lie in the years immediately ahead.

We feel we are peculiarly fitted to write this story of the Phillies. Fred Lieb was born, reared and educated in Philadelphia, lived there for twenty-three years before embarking on a long and successful baseball writing career in New York and with *The Sporting News* of St. Louis. But he saw his first professional baseball from the old right field bleachers at Broad and Huntington, always has remained a Phillie fan at heart, and has made a study of Philadelphia baseball a lifetime hobby.

The first baseball word he knew was Delahanty. He still recalls listening with open-eyed awe as a young man living across the street told of the great Del hitting four home runs in one game. Later, the first girl Lieb took to parties was a niece of the great Delahanty. He also can recall older boys telling of the arrival of the graceful Napoleon Lajoie to Philadelphia, and of his boyhood distress when the mighty Frenchman jumped to Cleveland during the American League war. One of the young fellows he grew up with won luster by taking pitching lessons from Phillie pitcher Frank Sparks at $50 a session. As a young baseball writer, he was well acquainted with Horace Fogel, sports writer-president of the so-called Phillie "Live Wires," who had the doubtful distinction of being the first of two Phillie presidents drummed out of baseball. Lieb's late father-in-law was in the Phillie Park at the time of the tragic accident on August 6, 1903, when some 500 fans were plunged from a broken left field balcony into Fifteenth Street.

Stan Baumgartner came to Philadelphia as a rookie left-handed pitcher shortly after Fred Lieb moved from Philly to New York. He came direct from the University of Chicago campus to the old Phillie clubhouse at Broad and Lehigh in the late spring of 1914, pitched a shutout against the Giants in his first starting assignment, and became a junior member of the Phillies' first pennant winners, Pat Moran's historic champions of 1915. With the exception of a few years, Stan's subsequent career as a ball player and as baseball writer for the *Philadelphia Inquirer* has been wrapped around Philadelphia baseball, particularly the Phillies. He pitched for the Phillies in 1914-15-16, again in 1921-22, and for the Athletics in 1924-25-26. His sports writing career started in Florida in the early spring of the latter year when he doubled as an Athletic pitcher and training camp reporter.

Stan knew the Phillies from the inside when they were good and bad, from the 1915 pennant winner when he was a fresh busher, to the 1950 champions when he still loyally wore a Phillie cap in the press stand. The great Grover Cleveland Alexander taught him how to throw a curve; Bill Killefer caught his first game; he learned lots of inside baseball under the canny Pat Moran, rubbed shoulders with Gavvy Cravath, the mighty home run man of the pre-Ruthian era, and was hazed by the obstreperous Sherry Magee. He suffered—and laughed—with some of the joke Phillie teams he covered for the *Inquirer* during the long years in the second division wilderness, and thrilled when the Carpenter dynasty again made the Phillies a power in baseball.

In preparing this story of the Phillies, we give grateful acknowledgment of the help tendered by George Reach, octogenarian son of Al Reach, first Phillie president; Lowell Reidenbaugh of *The Sporting News;* Al Lang, former Mayor of St. Petersburg, Florida, where the Phillies trained in 1915-16-17-18; and Seymour Siwoff of the Elias Baseball Bureau. We also were aided by the late George Moreland's useful book, *Balldom,* and the Spalding, Reach and latter-day Spink baseball guides.

THE AUTHORS.

THE PHILADELPHIA PHILLIES

CHAPTER 1

Early Philadelphia Baseball

1

PHILADELPHIA baseball goes back for well over a century. The Quaker City originally showed a fancy for Town Ball, fashioned on what then was the New England Game, as contrasted to the New York Game. Philadelphia's Olympic Club was organized to play Town Ball in the early 1830's. But the Olympics were an exclusive set; two teams within the club played each other. No boys from Kensington, Darby or South Phillie—other than Spruce, DeLancey and Pine—would have been admitted.

Two decades later, the New York Game, which is more like our present-day baseball, started to catch on, and Philadelphians gradually were weaned away from their early baseball fare. Some diehards, however, held out to the Civil War before they would capitulate. They said derisively: "Why should we be copy cats, and ape the New York clubs?" But eventually the copy cats won the day. The main difference between the two early forms of baseball was that in Town Ball, you retired the runner by hitting him with the ball, whereas in the New York Game, you threw to the base ahead of the runner.

By the late 1850's, such smart baseball clubs as the Athletics, Olympics, Winonas, Uniteds and Benedicts were part of the city's sports and social life. They had their ball fields and club-houses in West and North Philadelphia, and the teams were manned by Philadelphia socialites, young men who practiced law and medicine or were well established in the city's banking and commission houses. Many of them also played cricket; if not, they were the sons of cricketers. Baseball had not yet become a game for the hoi polloi.

One of Philadelphia's early big baseball events came in 1860, the year before the Civil War, when New York's crack Excelsior Club played a picked Philadelphia team, recruited from the best players in the city. It was the year the Excelsiors made the first trips ever undertaken by a ball team, one into upper New York State and another into Pennsylvania, Delaware and Maryland. There was quite a howdy-do as to who among the Philadelphia stars should represent the Quaker City; a number of the athletes had most vociferous partisans. Eventually the five leading clubs were all included in the line-up, and the game was played at the Camaco Woods cricket grounds on July 24, 1860, before what a Philadelphia newspaper described as a "vast crowd." The Philadelphians did quite well, too, losing to the Excelsiors by a score of 15 to 4. That was considered a moral victory for the Quaker All-Stars since fifteen runs was one of the smallest scores made by the Excelsiors all year. Only two days before, they had beaten a picked team of Baltimore stars, 51 to 6, and 50 runs was an average day's output for the mighty Excelsiors. "You played well —exceedingly well," Pitcher Jimmy Creighton of the Excelsiors complimented a group of Philadelphia stars after the game. That was real praise, coming from a master. Everyone was pleased.

2

The Civil War gave the young game of baseball a big shot in the arm. It was played by soldiers in camps, and by workers in back of the lines. Nowhere did it mushroom faster than in Philadelphia. In fact, there was such rivalry between the city's various clubs that in 1863, the Athletics engaged the first out-and-out professional player, Alfred J. Reach, second baseman of the Brooklyn Eckfords and then the mightiest batsman in the game. The name was to be an important one in Phillie baseball history. What's more, there was spirited bidding for Al Reach's services.

Arthur Gorman, later United States Senator from Maryland, tendered Reach a flattering offer to play in Baltimore. But Colonel Fitzgerald, of the Philadelphia *Item*, topped this bid and won the player for the Athletics and Philadelphia. One inducement which helped win Al for Philadelphia was Fitzgerald's willingness that Reach continue to live in Brooklyn and engage in his New York trade of silversmith. Al journeyed to Philadelphia on days that the Athletics were scheduled for their wartime matches, as games still were called at that time.

Al Reach's sturdy son, octogenarian George Reach, was kind enough to let us see scrapbooks of Philadelphia games of 1864 and 1865, in which Al Reach appeared in the Athletic line-up at second base. In game after game, Al was credited with two, three and four hits.

"Yes, my father was quite a batsman," said George proudly. "He once told me there never was a time that he couldn't hit. Among the baseball pioneers, Al Spalding was the greatest pitcher and Al Reach the greatest batter. It is odd that both of them should have become famous sporting goods men."

Al Reach eventually brought his family from Brooklyn to Philadelphia, settled in Frankford and soon started the famous sporting goods house which for years was to bear his name. His name still is on the American League balls of today.

Following the Civil War, most of Philadelphia's top "gentlemen" baseball clubs became semi-pro organizations with paid players interspersed with the gentlemen. Pitcher James Dickson McBride and Third Baseman Lip Pike, a notable long-distance hitter, joined Reach as pros on the Athletics. The early A's, the Olympias and a new club, the Keystones, were the city's outstanding teams. Eddie Cuthbert of the Keystones is credited with being the first player to steal a base, stealing third on the surprised Brooklyn Atlantics in a game in 1865.

In 1866, the only clubs to beat the Athletics were the Unions and Atlantics of Brooklyn and in 1867, this crack Quaker City club had a record of 43 games won and only 3 lost. In 1869, in one of Philadelphia's early epic struggles, the Athletics lost to the Brooklyn Atlantics by the close score of 51 to 48. In the same year, when the all-professional Cincinnati Reds had their undefeated season, they encountered three of their toughest games in Philadelphia. They defeated the Olympias, 22-11, the Athletics, 27-18, and the Keystones, 45-30. All Philadelphia enthused over what was termed "the splendid showing of the home teams."

A year later, the Athletics won a late season game from the great Reds, and termed themselves national champions when they won four games out of five from the Brooklyn Atlantics, the club which had stopped the Reds' great run of victories at 79 straight in June, 1870.

3

In 1871, Philadelphia entered the Athletics into the newly formed National Association, baseball's first professional league and the forerunner of the present-day National League. The Athletics won the pennant in the first year of the new League's existence with 22 victories and 7 defeats. The club played at 25th and Jefferson Streets, which then was practically Philadelphia suburbs. Dick McBride did nearly all the pitching, as his record of 20 victories and 5 defeats was almost the same as that of his club. Al Reach, hitting .371, as usual was the clubs's leading hitter. In his later years in the National Association, Al shifted from second base to the outfield. George Reach recalls sitting against the outfield fence with his father while the Athletics were at bat. George then was a lad of six or seven. Commented George: "Dad said to me, 'I'll have to leave you now, son. I'm the next hitter, but I'll hit one for you.' Sure enough he did just that, hitting the ball on the ground almost to where I was sitting."

In some lean years of the last quarter of a century, when Philadelphians choked on their steady second division diet, there was some undeserved criticism—in New York and elsewhere—of Philadelphia as a two-team major league city. It is interesting, therefore, to recall that Philadelphia was such a baseball hotbed eighty years ago that it was the first city considered worthy of supporting two major league clubs. In 1873, the third year of the National Association, the Quaker City was granted a second club. It was officially known as the Philadelphia Club, in contrast to the Athletics, but was early nicknamed the Quakers. Most baseball historians look upon these National Association Quakers as the first Phillies. Surely, they are at least great-great-grandpappies of the present National League Phillies.

Some baseball-minded politicians of the Fifth Ward got the idea that it would be a good idea to get up a team to buck the Athletics and furnish the Quaker City with baseball on such days as the Athletics were not using the field at 25th Street and Jefferson. The politicos were followers of United States Senator Nagel, and the Senator supposedly took a lively interest and was the financial angel. Anyway, the club was launched in McGarrity's saloon on a cold, blustery day in early 1873. The Nagel-financed smaller politicians grabbed as many stars as then were available. Players of that period were not reserved from one season to another, but it was a general practice for clubs to rehire the same players. However, the new Quakers raided right and left on the older clubs. Even though they were in a sense tenants of the Athletics at the Jefferson Street grounds, the early Phillies made their most damaging raids on the A's, snatching Catcher Fergy Malone, Levy Myerle, hard-hitting third baseman, and Dave Cuthbert, crack outfielder, from the rival Philadelphia team. George Zettlein, one of the National Association's best pitchers, was lured from the Brooklyn Atlantics, and Charley Fulmen was brought east from the crack Forest City club of Rockford, Illinois. The club was directed by a non-playing manager, George Young, who did everything from looking after the baggage on the road to counting the day's receipts.

The nickname of Quakers was richly deserved. It was less than a decade since the Cincinnati Reds had discarded their long pants and gone in for knickers, and oddities in the way of uniforms were not uncommon. The Quakers wore gray shirts and pants, white stockings, and low-crowned gray hats with a brim that went all the way around. Fans of rival cities would try to ride them with remarks, "Didst thee score a run in thee's last game?" and "Between me and thou, art thou really a ballplayer?"

They were ball players, all right, and in 1873 they put up a splendid fight, finishing second to George Wright's Boston Red Stockings. The National Association now played a heavier schedule than when the Athletics won in 1871. Both the Bostons and early Quakers lost the same number of games, 16, but the Red Stockings won 43 games to 36 for the Philadelphias.

Actually the early Phillies, or Quakers, might easily have started off with a pennant. The club was red hot in midsummer, when its political sponsors blew the team to an August vacation in the popular New Jersey resort of Cape May. The Quakers played a few exhibition games there but found plenty of time for recreation and fun. And splashing around in the south Jersey surf was one of their lighter forms of amusement. By the time the team got back to its Jefferson Street grounds, it had cooled off perceptibly. The Phillies ceased to click, went into a September tailspin, and the crack Boston club, with Al Spalding, the Wright brothers, Cal McVey, Ross Barnes and other early headliners, won their first of four straight National Association flags.

Nevertheless, Philadelphia fans felt the Quakers had done very well to finish second in their first season. The Lord Baltimores of Baltimore were third and the Athletics fourth. An early rivalry had sprung up between the two Philadelphia teams, and Quaker partisans chortled when their team fared better than the still formidable A's. Other teams in the league were the Mutuals of New York, Atlantics of Brooklyn, Nationals of Washington, and the Resolutes of Elizabeth, New Jersey.

In 1874, George Young's Philadelphia team finished on the baseball equator. They won 29 games and lost as many for a .500 percentage. That was good enough to give them fourth place, the position behind the Athletics. Fourth later was to become a favorite Phillie resting spot. In 1875, the last year of the National Association, the Phillies came home fifth with a respectable showing of 37 victories and 31 defeats. The Association survived a rough season, with thirteen clubs being members of the circuit at one time or another. It was a time of open gambling and pool selling at all ball parks. A few charges of open crookedness were proved; much more was implied. Games were manipulated to conform with the odds of the professional pool sellers. Drunkenness and rowdyism, among both players and spectators, was an everyday occurrence. Many fights broke out in Philadelphia in games between the Quakers and Athletics. The gentlemen and social registerites, who had attended the early matches of the Olympias, Benedicts and Athletics only fifteen years before, almost quit baseball. The class of the audience deteriorated badly. A few lovers of the fast-growing sport among Philadelphia's better citizenry still came out for league games, but they had to rub elbows with thugs, plug-uglies, welchers and sorehead losers who shouted their vulgar insults and imprecations from the stands.

During the winter of 1875-76, a go-getting, far-seeing Chicagoan, William A. Hulbert, aided by Al Spalding, reorganized the National Association into the present-day National League. The venerable National came into being in New York at a historic meeting on February 2, 1876, with G. W. Thompson of the Athletics representing Philadelphia. Under the new deal in baseball, many of the thugs, gamblers and questionable characters were weeded out, but of the most interest to Philadelphia was the fact that the Athletics were taken into the National League as a charter member and the Quakers dropped. The revised league had room for only one club in Philadelphia, with the Athletics, Mutuals of New York, Boston and Hartford holding forth in the east and Chicago, St. Louis, Cincinnati and Louisville in the west.

Feeling themselves superior to the rest of the league, the Philadelphia and New York Mutuals refused to make their last 1876 western trips. They took the stand, "The National League needs us more than we need it." However, the new league met this misconduct with plucky and summary action. Even though everyone realized that Philadelphia and New York then were the country's two greatest centers of population, the National League expelled these powerful clubs, and seven years were to pass before these great eastern cities again would see National League baseball.

CHAPTER 2

Quaker City Gains Worcester Franchise

⚾ 1 ⚾

IT WOULD be difficult for a present-day fan to recognize the National League of 1882. There had been numerous changes since 1876, and the 1882 clubs were strung along the New England coast and the Great Lakes. Boston, Providence, Worcester and Troy, New York, held the eastern franchises, and Chicago, Cleveland, Detroit and Buffalo made up the western ring. It was a compact snug league, with transportation charges held down to a minimum, especially in the east.

In 1882 the original American Association was launched as a second major league and a rival to the National League. It awarded franchises to cities which had been booted out of the National League or had dropped out of their own accord, Philadelphia, New York, Cincinnati, St. Louis and Louisville. With the addition of Pittsburgh, Baltimore and Columbus, Ohio, it made a pretty good league. The Athletics, who had operated as an independent club following their National League expulsion in 1876, drew the Philadelphia franchise; these early A's, the Metropolitans of New York and the St. Louis Browns were the Association's leading breadwinners.

To complicate matters for the National League, their able president and the loop's early savior, Will Hulbert, died early in the 1882 season, and his place was filled in November of that year by Col. A. G. Mills, a New York attorney, a prominent G. A. R. man and an early baseball player and enthusiast.

As an eastern man, Mills had no delusions about a major league without New York and Philadelphia. "We've got to get these big cities back into our league," he observed, soon after taking over. "Both New York and Philadelphia have tremendous futures, and some day their populations will be in the millions. If we permit the American Association to entrench itself in these cities, the Association—not we—soon will be the real big league."

Mills didn't twiddle his thumbs or go in for wishful thinking. He quickly started things rolling, and early in 1883 he moved the little Troy club down the Hudson River to the great metropolis at its mouth, New York. Next he was interested in seeing a club in Philadelphia. "We've moved Troy to New York," he told a group of Philadelphians, "and now we're going to shift the Worcester franchise. They're not big enough up there to support National League ball. I'd like to see that club in Philadelphia. And, don't tell me there already is a club in your town. Philadelphia is big enough to support two clubs. You did it back in the days of the old National Association when you had both the Athletics and the Quakers, and you can do it again."

Mills interested Alfred James Reach, first pro, the old hitting second baseman of the Athletics and by now doing well in his sporting goods venture. He had a big downtown retail store on Market Street, as well as a growing factory in Kensington. Two years before, he had entered into a partnership with Ben Shibe, a former horsecar driver and expert on leather who had gone from manufacturing whips to the manufacture of baseballs and gloves. Mills had known Reach since pre-Civil War days, when the Colonel played for the Nationals of Washington and Al was the star of the Brooklyn Eckfords. "You get the backing, build a ball park, and I'll move the Worcester franchise into Philadelphia," Mills told him.

It didn't take much of a sales talk to sell Reach on the idea of a Philadelphia National League club. Though Al was English born, the son of a London cricketer, he was baseball all the way and loved the game with real fervor. "I'm in," he told Mills, and he was in to stay for two decades as Phillie president and the club's leading stockholder. Al Spalding, who like Reach was a baseball pioneer and a successful sporting goods manufacturer, was president and a leading stockholder of the Chicago White Stockings, so Reach welcomed the opportunity of resuming friendly rivalry with the other great Al in National League competition.

Associated with Reach was Col. John I. Rogers, a lawyer with a flair for Pennsylvania politics. His title was political, as he won his colonelcy by being named to the staff of a Keystone State governor. In the early years of the Reach-Rogers association the Colonel was overshadowed by the more glamorous and better-known Reach, but in the nineties Rogers threw his weight around, frequently differed with President Al, and became the more militant member of the partnership.

Big league ball parks were no mammoth structures of steel and concrete in the 1880's, requiring the expenditure of millions. A ball park could mushroom up almost overnight. The new Phillie president leased a large field in what then was the northeastern section of the city, a district later known as Brewerytown. The field was irregular in shape and was bound by 24th Street, Columbia Avenue, 25th Street, and Ridge Avenue. The field promptly was named Recreation Park. Al Reach had the field leveled off; a small wooden grandstand and bleachers were hastily erected, and by May 1, 1883, Al was ready for business. By general consent, the new team came to be known as the Phillies, one of the most natural and spontaneous of all big-league nicknames. It was easily understood, as any oaf could recognize a Phillie as a player from Philadelphia. However, the nickname of the old National Association Philadelphias—the Quakers—persisted, and for years a number of Philadelphia dailies preferred to refer to the new ball team as the Quakers.

The club made a good impression in its first game, losing to the Providence Grays, one of the National League's better teams, by the close margin of 4 to 3. And, they lost to one of the game's greatest, Charley "Old Hoss" Radbourne, the Rhode Island team's Hall of Fame immortal. It was the first of the Old Hoss's 49 victories that year; he was to soar to 60 in 1884. Yet, the

Phillie pitcher, John Coleman, gave Radbourne a good battle, each giving up only six hits. The Phillies started well, getting to Radbourne for two runs in their first National League inning. They pushed over a third run in the seventh, making the score 3 to 0 and promising a happy afternoon for the skimpy opening crowd of twelve hundred. But these fans learned early that Phillie pitchers could not be trusted in the late innings. Providence shot up Coleman for four runs in the eighth, with Radbourne contributing a telling two-bagger to the Gray rally, and the Phillies were off to their first defeat. Unfortunately it was the forerunner of many more, as the 1883 club started hopelessly in the cellar with the horrible record of 17 victories and 81 defeats for a dismal percentage of .173. On August 21, 1883, the Providence Grays really poured it on, defeating the Phillies, 28 to 0, for the worst shutout defeat in the annals of big league ball.

In view of Philadelphia's frequent occupancy of the National League basement in the twenties and thirties, one might think that this horrendous tailender of 1883 set the pattern for years to come. Actually, however, the Quakers didn't have another last-placer until 21 years later, 1904, and they had only two in the first 36 years of the club's history.

It was a trying year for Reach and such friends who had put money into the new venture. To make matters worse, while the Phillies burrowed through the National League cellar almost to China, the rival Athletics won the American Association pennant. Naturally, they were the toast of the town. But, even while the Phillies were down, some fans who said they didn't fancy the superior airs of the early Athletics patronized the lowly National Leaguers at Recreation Park. Whether they got any recreation is still a moot question.

Reach's first manager was Bob Ferguson, an early associate of Al's in Brooklyn's pre-Civil War baseball. He also had been president of the National Association, when its rules required a player president. Before Col. Mills shook up the National League, Ferguson had been the manager in Troy. When Reach and

Rogers took over the Worcester club, they got nothing but the franchise, as the defunct New England team's worth-while players already had been gobbled up by other clubs. It meant Reach and Ferguson had to start from scratch in building up the club. A battery, John Coleman, the opening day pitcher, and Catcher Frank Ringo, was snatched from the Peoria club of the Northwestern League after they already had signed 1884 contracts. A second catcher, Emil Gross, a Chicagoan, also was engaged. He had been a regular for three years in Providence, but was an eccentric fellow and was foot-loose that spring. A second pitcher, Arthur Hagen, a fellow from Lonsdale, Rhode Island, had a record commensurate with the Phillies' 1883 showing. Arthur had recorded exactly one victory, against seventeen defeats, when he was shunted off to Buffalo.

The club's first baseman, Sidney Douglas Farrar, was a product of Paris Hill, Maine, and Sid remained the Phillies' regular first sacker for a decade. He was a pretty good fielder and is best remembered for having sired Geraldine Farrar, the famed opera singer, and as perhaps the only regular first baseman who batted ninth. It was no tribute to Sid Farrar's prowess with the stick; he was no Jimmie Foxx of the eighties. In Philadelphia's first National League game, Manager Bob Ferguson played second; Bill McClellan appeared at shortstop, and a fellow who missed being the namesake of American League president William Harridge by one letter—William Harbridge—rounded out the infield at third. The outfield was made up of Bill Purcell, John Manning and Fred Lewis, though later Harbridge shifted to the outfield and Purcell went to third.

2

There was considerable discouragement in the Phillies' camp after the .173-percentage season of 1883. Some doubted the wisdom of going on, and challenging the popular Athletics for the city's baseball patronage. They argued in favor of tossing in the sponge, and there was a feeling in the Quaker City that after its brief National League return, Philadelphia again would fade from the N. L. picture.

President Al Reach was not one of the disbelievers. He definitely decided to carry on. "We spent a year finding ourselves," he insisted. "Of course, it was expensive; we made mistakes, but

BOX-SCORE OF PHILLIES' FIRST GAME IN THE NATIONAL LEAGUE AT RECREATION PARK, PHILADELPHIA MAY 1, 1883

PROVIDENCE (N. L.)

	A.B.	R.	H.	O.	A.	E.
Paul Hines, C.F.	4	1	1	3	0	0
Joe Start, 1B.	4	0	0	10	0	1
John Farrell, 2B.	4	0	2	3	5	1
Arthur Irwin, S.S.	3	0	0	1	4	0
John Cassidy, R.F.	4	0	0	2	0	0
Cliff Carroll, L.F.	4	0	0	2	0	0
Chas. Radbourne, P.	3	1	1	1	1	0
Jerry Denny, 3B.	3	1	1	2	1	2
Bernie Gilligan, C.	3	1	1	3	1	1
	32	4	6	27	12	5

PHILADELPHIA (N. L.)

	A.B.	R.	H.	O.	A.	E.
Bill Purcell, L.F.	4	1	2	2	0	0
Bill McClellan, S.S.	4	1	1	1	2	0
John Manning, R.F.	4	0	1	1	0	1
Bob Ferguson, 2B.	4	0	0	1	3	1
Ferd Lewis, C.F.	4	0	0	0	0	0
Will Harbridge, 3B.	4	1	1	0	5	0
John Coleman, P.	4	0	0	0	6	1
Frank Ringo, C.	3	0	1	5	2	0
Sid Farrar, 1B.	3	0	0	17	0	0
	34	3	6	27	18	3

Providence	0	0	0	0	0	0	0	4	0 – 4
Philadelphia	2	0	0	0	0	0	1	0	0 – 3

Two base hits–Manning, Ringo, Radbourne, Hines. Bases on Balls–off Coleman, 2. Struck out–by Coleman, 2; by Radbourne, 1. Double plays–Denny and Start; Coleman, Ringo and Ferguson. Left on base–Providence, 4; Philadelphia, 4. Umpire–Odlin. Time–1:30. Attendance–1,200.

we learned from our experiences. Philadelphia has the population and interest to support a second club, and some day the Philadelphia National League club will be famous—more famous than the Athletics."

He started to rectify mistakes by firing the 1883 manager, Bob Ferguson. Ferguson later managed the Pittsburgh Alleghanies and New York Metropolitans, became an umpire and died in Brooklyn in 1894. Reach felt he had made a ten-strike in the man he selected to replace Ferguson, and told Philadelphia fans he had engaged the greatest manager in the country—Harry Wright.

Like Reach, William Henry "Harry" Wright was English born and a cricketer before he became a baseball player. Harry managed the first out-and-out professional team, the fabulous early Cincinnati Reds, who went for a season and a half in 1869 and 1870 without losing a game. Harry later shifted to Boston and was manager of Boston's four-time winner in the old National Association, and then brought his genius to Boston's National League clubs, winning pennants in 1877 and 1878. Following the 1881 season, Harry Wright moved on to Providence, where he managed second place teams in 1882 and 1883. Is it any wonder that Al Reach felt engaging the capable Wright was a solution to all of his problems?

Today Harry Wright often is confused with his younger brother, George, a greater player but no greater as a baseball pioneer. On the victory-crazy Cincinnati Reds of the post-Civil War period, Harry was the manager-center fielder, and George, twelve years his junior, was the team's slugging shortstop. After the Wright brothers transferred their talents and red hosiery to the Boston Red Stockings, Harry played the outfield and shortstop, and pitched when Spalding took the day off. He didn't call it quits as a player until he was in his early forties. George continued to serve him as shortstop, and later as team captain. George Wright long since has been awarded a plaque at the Cooperstown Hall of Fame, but they say he is lonesome up there without Harry. Certainly the early Phillie manager, one of the real greats of the sport, deserves wall space in Cooperstown with such immortals of his day as brother George, Al Spalding, Old Hoss Radbourne and Cap Anson.

Harry Wright raised the Philadelphia club's position two notches in 1884, finishing ahead of Cleveland and Detroit. He retained the battery of Coleman and Ringo, also Purcell, Manning and McClellan. George Andrews was procured from Toledo to fill Bob Ferguson's shoes at second, and a green rookie, Joe Mulvey, was pressed into service at third base. But the club's main acquisitions that year were two players who quickly won their way into the hearts of Philadelphia fandom, Charley Ferguson, pitcher and all-around player, and Outfielder Jim Fogarty. Unfortunately, both had comparatively short careers, death striking them down in their very prime—Ferguson in 1888 and Fogarty in 1891.

Ferguson, a native of Charlottesville, Virginia, did most of the team's pitching after he joined the Phillies, but he also was the club's best hitter, best base runner, and could fill in anywhere. He was too valuable a man to sit on the bench, and when he wasn't pitching he usually took over a post in the outfield. Later he alternated between the pitcher's box and second base.

How good was Charley Ferguson? The late John K. Tener, former Governor of Pennsylvania, ex-president of the National League and big leaguer of the 1880's, ranked Ferguson at the very peak of baseball stars. "With due respect to Wagner, Cobb and Ruth, I believe Ferguson would have been recognized as king of them all had he lived another ten or fifteen years," Tener once said. "Had he lived longer, people would have recognized his genius. Potentially, he had more than any ball player I ever saw. He was a player without a flaw or weakness, as he could do everything equally well. He could hit, pitch, run or field, and it made no difference where they played him. He had the elusiveness of King Kelly, and was one of the smartest players of his time. If he was pitching, he constantly was outguessing the hitter; if he was at bat or on the bases he outsmarted his pitching rival with equal ease."

George Reach echoes Tener's sentiments. "Ferguson was a really great player," he said. "I'll go even further than that, and say he was wonderful. He could do everything required of a ball player. Ferguson was great as a pitcher, but on account of his hitting, running and fielding, George Wright and my father began to think of him more as the team's second baseman. It was like Ed Barrow, years later, playing Ruth, a fine pitcher, in the outfield to utilize his home run hitting. I still vividly recall Charley's speed in getting to first, and around the bases. He could get down to first as fast as the best of them, and I've seen them all. Ferguson was a long strider, and for that reason deceptive. Some people didn't realize how rapidly he actually got over the ground. What a pity his great career should have been snuffed out after only four years! Otherwise, he would have written things into the records that still would endure."

Fogarty wasn't as great a player as Ferguson, but he was a hard hitter and a good rangy outfielder. With a big black handlebar mustache, he was an early favorite with Al Reach's Irish constituents. Jim was a distinct personality, a player of the swashbuckling type, and as a native San Franciscan he was the vanguard of a great parade of Golden Gates boys to reach the big leagues—Bill Lange, George Kelly, Harry Heilmann, Lefty O'Doul, Willie Kamm, Frankie Crosetti, the three DiMaggios, Gerry Coleman and many others.

Al Reach's observations in countering the evil forebodings of his 1883 friends, that all the Phillies needed was a little patience and a few good ball players, came true in 1885 when the National League Phillies gave Quaker City fans their first taste of first-division ball. They wound up their third season in proud possession of third place, and it was years before Phillie fans again would know the miseries and pitfalls of the second division. For that matter, neither Al Reach nor George Wright were men who thought in terms of the second division.

After losing 64 more games than they won in 1883, the 1885 performance of 56 victories against 54 defeats was most encouraging. Only the champion Chicago White Stockings and the New York Giants came in ahead of the Philadelphia entry. Two pitchers, Ferguson and a dashing Providence, Rhode Island, boy—Ed Daily—won 52 of the 54 games. Oddly enough each pitcher scored 26 victories; Fergy's record was 26-19 against Daily's 26-22. One of Ferguson's victories was a 24-0 job against the Indianapolis club. Phillie fans got a big kick out of that one, for it took the curse off that 28-0 loss to Providence two years before. Daily was acquired from the Harrisburg club of the Eastern League. Like Ferguson and Fogarty, he also was short-lived, dying in 1891.

Wright hired a new shortstop from Kansas City, Charley Bastian; and a catching newcomer, left-handed John Clements, saw service behind the plate. John, a native Philadelphian, was one of the few southpaw catchers in big league history, but throwing with his left arm never curbed his style. He threw with the best of them, and played big league ball until 1900, most of it with the Phillies. Clements got his start the year before with the Philadelphia Keystones of the outlaw Union Association. When the Keystones gave up the ghost in the late season, Wright snatched up their able young catcher. John caught eight late season games, and then handled Ferguson and Daily during most of the successful 1885 season. Unlike some of his short-lived associates, Clements lived until 1941. Wright came up with another Union Association catching refugee in Charley Ganzel, who had played with St. Paul. He was released to Detroit early the next season, and like Clements was to have a long and worthy big league career, catching for National League champions in Detroit and Boston.

3

"Our final position looks rather silly when contrasted to our percentage," Harry Wright commented to Reach, his boss, after a fine 1886 season. "In 1883, we win only two more games than we lose and finish third. This year we win thirty-eight more than we lose, and have to be satisfied with fourth. That's crazy! But, I'll tell you one thing, Al; we now really have a ball team, and definitely are on the way up. It's now only a matter of time before I can give you a championship. I make you that promise."

Yes, that 1886 Phillie percentage of .622, netting only a fourth-placer, is silly in view of what has happened in the subsequent six decades. It still is the all-time percentage high for the club. One reason why it didn't lift the Phillies any higher is that the Chicago White Stockings and the Detroits, the two top contenders, battled for the pennant in the stratosphere with percentages of .726 and .707, respectively. Mutrie's third-place Giants, with a percentage of .630, beat out the Reach-Rogers-Wright team by eight points. "I should have beaten out Jim Mutrie," Wright remarked ruefully.

George Wright was justified in his feeling of optimism for the future. The club had come a long way in its four years, and everyone respected the new Phillies. They were an attraction wherever they went, and at home their patronage had advanced well ahead of that of the rival Athletics, who had slumped to sixth place in the American Association. Young Ferguson was the hero of the town; he was better than ever, winning 32 games and losing only nine. Eddie Daily saw more service in the outfield than on the pitching mound this season, while a Detroit acquisition, Danny Casey, took up the slack on days when Fergy wasn't pitching. Danny did all right, too, winding up with a 25-19 record. Providence dropped out of the league after the 1885 season, and Wright made another constructive move in grabbing Arthur Irwin, the Grays' erstwhile captain-shortstop. Arthur, a native Bostonian, had played shortstop for the Grays in the Phillies' inaugural game in 1883. He was a shrewd, aggressive player, and the first infielder to wear a glove. He invented and patented it, and Irwin gloves soon were manufactured at a tidy profit in the Reach-Shibe factory. As a player-captain and later as manager, Arthur Irwin was to figure prominently in early Phillie history.

Irwin's acquisition made it possible to shift Charley Bastian to second base. Other valuable acquisitions were Outfielder George Wood and Catcher Jim McGuire. Both came from Detroit, along with Pitcher Casey, in the deal for Charley Ganzel. McGuire, nicknamed the Deacon, then was a youngster in his third year of big league ball. Jim was to stick around in a fabulously long career which was to see his name entered in big league box-scores for 27 seasons.

Late in the 1886 season, the Phillies visited Washington with all intentions of mopping up against the tailenders. In the game of September 11th, Washington inserted a rookie catcher, Cornelius McGillicuddy, into its line-up. No one paid much attention to the string bean receiver, but as Connie Mack he was to figure big in Philadelphia baseball and at the turn of the century he was to be a painful thorn in the Phillies' side. Wright's team lost the game in which Mack made his debut, 4 to 3, but the Phillies closed the season in high, winning thirteen of their last fifteen games, not counting three ties.

CHAPTER 3

Runners-up to Detroits in 1887

1

AL REACH was well pleased with the way his National League investment was going. "Some people wanted me to quit after our bad 1883 season," he chuckled. "They said with the Athletics in town, we'd never draw. Not enough people would come to see us play to make it worth while operating a National League club! Well, we outdrew the Athletics by a big margin, and our only difficulty was finding space for all the people who wanted to pay to see us play. Our Ridge Avenue park isn't big enough to handle our crowds. We've got a real team now, and we've got to get a park worthy of our team."

In looking for a site for a new park, Reach selected a dump-like lot on north Broad Street, bounded on its other sides by Lehigh Avenue, north 15th Street and Huntington Streets. It was next to the Reading Railroad tracks, where they crossed Broad Street, and seemed a most unlikely location for a ball field. Yet, Reach was to convert this dump into one of the show-places of baseball in the 1880's and 1890's.

George Reach tells of the first time his father took him to the site of the new ball park. "We then lived in Frankford, and father asked: 'How would you like to take a drive?' I was quite agreeable and we drove over Nicetown Lane to Broad Street and south on Broad to Huntington. There dad stopped the buggy, and said, 'George, what do you think of that for a ball ground?' I thought he was joshing me, as the field was covered with tin cans and other debris, while a dirty stream ran through it. I began to laugh, and I said: 'I know, father, you are joking and having some fun with me.' 'Not at all,' he replied. 'What's more I intend to erect a ball park here of which we all may be proud.' Well, he surely made good that boast."

The first wooden stands soon were burned down, and it gave Al Reach and Col. Rogers the opportunity to build a ball park which was the predecessor of all modern ball parks. Years before other big league clubs abandoned their wooden ball parks, Reach built a park of steel and brick which was the talk of baseball. Sightseers were brought to Philadelphia just to see this ornate palace for old King Baseball. At the start, it had pavilion seats for 5,000 and right and left field bleachers accommodated another 7,500. The clubhouse and the club's offices were in deep center field at Broad and Lehigh. However, the main entrance was at 15th and Huntington, and though the official name of the new structure was The Philadelphia Baseball Park, for years Philadelphians referred to it as "the Huntington park" or "the Huntington Street grounds."

Though Reach's Phillies were playing to substantial business and had taken much of the play from the American Association Athletics, businessman Al had to think of other ways to get revenue for his new expensive edifice. Bicycles then were the rage, and bike races most popular. So, a quarter-mile bicycle track 15 feet wide ran around the edge of the field. It had banked turns, and for years thereafter Phillie outfielders had to race up the banked turns in pursuit of long fly balls or hard-driven grounders. When the Phillies were on the road, the ball park was taken over by the bicycle racers and their fans.

The first wooden park at Broad and Huntington had its baptism on April 30, 1887, and with standees packed like canned sardines behind outfield ropes, the opening day crowd was estimated at 20,000. Philadelphia newspapers called it the greatest crowd that had seen a ball game anywhere up to that time. A holiday spirit prevailed, and before the game the Phillies and their opponents, the New York Giants, were paraded in open barouches up Broad Street to the new ball park. The Phillies made it a gay and gala afternoon for their joyful fans; for years it remained a red-letter day in Philadelphia baseball. The first nine Phillies to go to bat in the first inning, from lead-off man George Wood to ninth man Sid Farrar, hit safely, and this opening barrage paved the way for a stunning 19 to 10 victory over the New Yorkers. The crowd herded behind the outfield ropes surged forward at regular intervals, forcing the outfielders to play on the backs of the infielders. As a result, many of the hits were ground-rule doubles. However, that blistering first game attack at the Huntington Street grounds set the pattern for years to come—the slugging Phillies. Regardless of where they finished, they were the boys of the big bludgeons, and the very words, Phillies and sluggers, were synonymous.

During the previous winter, Reach had a hot piece of baseball news to turn over to George Wright. Calling his manager to his office, Al was all excited as he remarked, "George, I've just had the most wonderful piece of news from Chicago. Spalding has sold King Kelly to Boston. Without Kelly, the White Stockings won't be nearly so dangerous. I think we can beat them; what's more I think Spalding selling Kelly will mean the pennant for us."

Wright was equally enthusiastic. "Yes, that should eliminate Chicago," he agreed. "I know I've got a better team than Mutrie in New York. The club we've got to beat now is Detroit. If we can finish ahead of them, we'll celebrate our new park with a pennant."

The two baseball pioneers had the situation figured out perfectly. Without King Kelly, the Babe Ruth of that day, the White Stockings, champions of 1885 and 1886, dropped to third; the Phillies beat out the dangerous Giants, but the Detroits, another slugging aggregation of that period, couldn't be shaken off. Yet it was a wonderful race all season, with first the Phillies and then the Detroits setting the pace. Actually, it was a five-team race most of the way, as the Boston Beaneaters, strengthened by Kelly, also finished above .500, resulting in the most profitable season the National League enjoyed up to that time. All of the first five teams, especially the Phillies, made substantial profits.

At the finish, the Detroits had a 3½ game advantage; their record was 79-45 to the 75-48 of the Phillies. Oddly enough, the champion Detroits and runner-up Phillies had lower percentages than when these two clubs finished second and fourth, respectively, the preceding year. The Phillies topped the third-place Chicagos by four games and the fourth-place Giants by seven.

"I'm sorry we couldn't win, but it was a good season. And I finished ahead of Spalding," said Reach wryly.

A new experienced pitcher, Charley Buffington, had been procured that year from Boston, and he contributed a 21-17 record to the 1886 second-placer. Charley Ferguson won 21 games and lost 10, but with Buffington and Casey going good, Wright was using his ace performer more and more at second base. Fergy hit .412 that year, but it was the season bases on balls were scored as hits, and .400 hitters were plentiful.

2

Stark tragedy struck the Phillies at the very start of the 1888 season, and it was to postpone their first pennant by many years. Philadelphia's baseball idol and star of stars, Charley Ferguson, died on April 29th, nine days after the season started and twelve days after his twenty-fifth birthday. He had contracted typhoid fever while the Phillies were in training. When Charley first was stricken, his teammates were not too concerned and felt it wouldn't be long before formidable Fergy would be back with the club. "Fergy is big and strong; he'll lick this sure," the men commented on the bench and in the clubhouse. "He'll be back with us before we know it." But Charley never came back. Day after day the fever burned deeper into his once fine physique. The skill of the doctors of 1888 was far below what it is today, and a stunned city heard that Ferguson had lost his last—and most important—game.

Not only Philadelphia but the entire baseball world grieved at the passing of this splendid athlete. It was years before radio brought baseball into the homes, but women and children wept unashamedly when they heard the sad news. The news spread like wildfire, and men went around Philadelphia streets saying with awed, hushed voices, "Charley Ferguson is dead! Charley Ferguson is dead! Isn't that a terrible blow for the Phillies?" His fellow players, wearing their black arm bands, were grief-stricken. Apart from the personal loss, they knew what a blow the club had suffered, but they tried to keep up their courage by assuring themselves: "We've got to win now—just for poor Charley's sake."

But winning without Charley was no easy matter. Clubs then employed a three-man pitching staff, and when a team lost its ace, it was a tough blow. When it lost a Ferguson, such a pitcher was irreplaceable. Casey and Buffington carried on, and in an effort to fill Ferguson's shoes, Wright signed a fighting gamecock from the Camden, New Jersey, water front—William J. "Kid" Gleason. He was termed "the Kid" because of his size, as he was only five feet, seven inches, but Gleason was as tough as nails and could lick a man twice his size. And the truculent Camdenite was ever ready for a fight! In 1887, he had pitched and played the outfield for Mt. Carmel, Pennsylvania, Williamsport and Scranton. Gleason was just twenty-two when he was signed by Wright. He was to stick in the big leagues as a player for twenty years in a career that started and ended in Philadelphia. Another pitcher, Ben Sanders, also was signed to help fill the gap. He came from the Canton team of the Ohio State League, and was just the opposite of Gleason, a six-footer with a long, loose, rangy frame.

Sometimes in baseball, a team will lose a top-ranking star and then spend years trying to find an adequate replacement. Something like that happened to the modern Yankees when their great first base star, Lou Gehrig, was stricken with a fatal disease in 1939. In 1953, they still were trying to find a suitable replacement. At other times, clubs have been most fortunate in finding a quick successor to a super-star. The 1888 Phillies were in the latter category. Wright had started the season with his old infield: Farrar, first; Bastian, second; Irwin, shortstop; and Mulvey, third. But on the eve of the new season and before the seriousness of Ferguson's illness was appreciated, Harry had announced. "Ferguson will play second base in any game that he doesn't pitch. We're always stronger with Charley at second; he is the best second baseman in the league."

Perhaps Bastian realized he had lost his manager's confidence, or he tried too hard to offset Ferguson's loss. He tied himself into knots by pressing; his batting average slumped to .192 and his fielding became erratic. The Phillies were in the first division in midseason and still in the race for the pennant, when Wright told Reach, "We've got to get somebody in there for Bastian. He's losing too many games for us at second base."

Clubs then had no full-time scouts, but alert club presidents and managers kept themselves posted on the better minor league players. "There's a fellow playing for Wheeling in the Tri-State League that's going very well," said Reach. "They tell me he is quite a hitter. His name is Delahanty—Ed Delahanty."

"Well, you better get him quick. We need somebody who can hit," shot back Wright. Wheeling wanted a lot of money for its prize, $1,900, which was a sizable amount for a lower class minor league player in 1888 dollars; but Reach took the gamble, and in July, big brawny Ed Delahanty was installed at second base in place of the slumping Bastian.

That was not Delahanty's position when he later took Charley Ferguson's place in the hearts of Philadelphia fans. His greatest fame was won as a slugging left fielder, though his managers constantly were calling him in for stints at first base. He was one of the famous Cleveland baseball family which produced five brothers, all of whom played big league ball at some time or another. Edward James was the oldest; the others were Tom, Frank, Jim and Joe. Though Edward later became known throughout baseball as "Big Ed," he was not the physical giant many present-day fans imagine. Actually, the first and greatest Delahanty was only five feet, ten inches tall, and his playing weight was 170 pounds. But he was stockily built, had powerful arms and shoulders and a bull-like neck, and as he developed he could hit a baseball with terrific power and for amazing distances.

Like many Irishmen, Delahanty had two sides to his nature: he could be a fun-loving chap who liked his beer and the other diversions so common to the ball player of his day, but at other times he would fall into moods of depression and surliness. He liked to set them up for his friends at his favorite saloon at 12th and Market streets, and knew all the sports fraternity from heavyweights Bob Fitzsimmons, Tom Sharkey and Peter Maher to the madams of Vine and Buttenwood streets.

Though the great Delahanty later led both the National and American Leagues in batting, twice batted .400 and compiled a record studded with brilliant batting feats, his 1888 start with the Phillies was no blaze of glory. Surprisingly, in his first major league season he was known more for his speed on the bases than for his batting power. While "Del" left a .408 batting average behind him in Wheeling, his Phillie stick-work wasn't much better than that of the benched Bastian. Ed could show only an average of .227 for 74 games. His extra-base power was not yet in evidence, for in 290 times at bat he produced only eleven doubles, one triple and one homer. Also, he was no Ferguson—not even a Bastian, at second base, chipping in 47 errors for half a season. But he could get over the ground, and stole 38 bases.

"I thought I would get more hitting out of the big fellow," Wright confided to Reach. "He meets the ball well, but he can't keep it away from the fielders. But he really can run! Some day he may be a champion base runner. And he loves to play ball."

With Kid Gleason, Ferguson's pitching replacement, showing no better than an 8-16 record, and young Delahanty still in the rookie stage, the 1888 Phillies did well to finish third. Only the new champions, the Giants, and the Chicago White Stockings came home ahead of them. Al Reach took pleasure in again winning the year's series from the team of his sporting goods rival, Al Spalding, the Phillies winning their Chicago series ten games to eight. But the showing with Mutrie's New Yorks was a nightmare, the Phillies having a 5-14 record against the new titleholders. At the Polo Grounds, the Phillies won only one game and lost eight. "George, our showing in New York was horrible," Reach said to his manager. "How do you account for it?"

"Those Giants always seemed to finish with the most runs," was Wright's annoyed rejoinder.

It was about this time that Al Reach took Mrs. Reach and their son George for a swing around the National League circuit. "It was fun, and quite an adventure," recalled George Reach many years later. "Lady patrons of baseball were rare, and many of the male fans were rather careless about their language. Their comment to umpires and players would not be tolerated in present-day baseball. Frequently father would be about the club's business, and leave mother in my charge. He would sit us in a box in back of the home plate, where we would be as far away from the tough bleacher element as was possible. Of course, the fans in the grandstand weren't exactly saints, either. However, mother had grown up in baseball; she had married father when he played for the Brooklyn Eckfords, and she just closed her ears to some of the remarks. But baseball then already had pleasant, well-equipped parks. This especially was true of our new park in Philadelphia, Spalding's West Side grounds in Chicago, and New York's Polo Grounds."

3

The 1889 season was one of disappointment. The Phillies came home fourth, but with 64 defeats against 63 victories, they had their first season under .500 since their second year—1884. And they repeated their wretched showing at the Polo Grounds, again winning only one game and losing eight in the home of the New York champions. Reach, Rogers and Wright felt a little better at the showing on the Huntington Street grounds, where the Phillies won six out of ten from the already hated New Yorkers.

Outstanding reason for the disappointment was that the Phillies did not capitalize more in the way of victories on the sizable cash outlay to the Detroit club for the mauling outfielder, Sam Thompson. Sam was one of baseball's outstanding sluggers of the 1880's and 1890's. A broad-shouldered Hoosier, Sam had been the powerhouse of Detroit's championship team of 1887, when he hit .408 in the year of the inflated batting averages. His nickname was "Big Sam" or just "Big" Thompson.

The Detroit National League club went out of existence at the end of the 1888 season, but before giving up the franchise, the Detroit owners—Druggist Fred Stearns and Charles Smith—peddled their stars to the other clubs of the league. And Reach felt he got away with the biggest fish when he snared the clubbing Thompson for Philadelphia.

Sam did all right, though not as well as he was to do in later years, hitting .296. But the Phillies suffered other aches and pains, especially in the infield. A whole raft of guys played second base and shortstop. Delahanty started the season at second but met with a series of injuries, and other mishaps, which limited his play to only 54 games. However, when "Del" did get into Wright's line-up, there was a marked improvement in his hitting, as he jacked up his average from .227 to .292. But Ed still hadn't found his real power, failing to connect for a homer. Before "Del's" injury, Bastian had been released to Chicago. There were mutterings of discontent between Wright and his shortstop-captain, Arthur Irwin. First Arthur was benched, and then in June he was released to Washington, where he took over the management. Billy Hallman, a Pittsburgher, succeeded Irwin at shortstop, while Fred "Piggy" Ward and Albert Myers were other infield replacements.

CHAPTER 4

Year of the Triple Somersaults

1

THERE WERE mutterings of a baseball revolt all during the 1889 season. Trouble between the mustachioed gladiators and their National League bosses had been brewing for several years. The late eighties were the most prosperous period baseball had known up to that time, with the Philadelphia club and its fine plant being considered especially opulent. However, only stars who were playing managers or player-captains drew over $2,000, and most players drew less. They felt they weren't getting their share of baseball's new prosperity.

Many of the game's leading players took part in the 'Round-the-World tour of Al Spalding's Chicago White Stockings and the National League All-Stars in the winter of 1888-'89. While cruising along the waters of the Pacific, Indian and Atlantic oceans the stars had plenty of opportunity for discussing their grievances. Three players who were to be ringleaders of the revolt, John Montgomery Ward of the Giants, Ned Hanlon of the Pirates, and John Tener of Chicago, were prominent members of the party. Two Phillie outfielders, Jim Fogarty and George Wood, made the trip as members of the All-Stars and were thoroughly indoctrinated. "We've got to get more money out of this game," Fogarty remarked on his return. "We attract the fans, but the owners pocket all the profits."

The players had a tight labor organization at the time, termed the Baseball Brotherhood. Ward was president, and Tener, secretary-treasurer. Following the 1889 season, most of the National League players seceded from the old league and enlisted in a new independent circuit, the Players League, which had fairly responsible backing, and which promised the players better salaries and a share in the profits. Actually the eight Players League franchises were awarded to the player representatives of the various teams, and that in Philadelphia went to Pitcher Charley Buffington. The National League, in its turn, appointed a strong war committee to fight the Brotherhood and the Players League. It was headed by the Chicago veteran, Al Spalding, with barrister John I. Rogers, Al Reach's Philadelphia partner, and John B. Day, president-owner of the Giants, as his associates. Rogers, veteran of many political feuds and skirmishes, was particularly aggressive, and vehement in denouncing the jumpers. "We'll fight these ingrates with everything we have," he declared. "And it won't be long before we have our jumpers crawling home."

Approximately 80 per cent of the National League players went over to the new league. The Phillies did not fare as badly as some of the other clubs, but Reach and Rogers saved a number of players by lavish use of ready cash. Players who signed early Players League contracts but were induced to return to the Phillies were the two catchers, the left-handed John Clements and Pop Shriver, Second baseman Al Myers, and the slugging outfielder from Detroit, Sam Thompson.

The irreconcilables were: Charley Buffington, the Brotherhood agent on the Phillies; another pitcher, Alex Sanders, known as the Virginian; First baseman Sid Farrar; Shortstop Billy Hallman; and the outfielders who made the world tour, Jim Fogarty and George Wood. They were 100 per cent Brotherhood men and rebuffed all efforts to induce them to jump back. In fact, Fogarty became the manager of the Philadelphia Players League team in 1890, and with his Irish imagination painted vivid pictures of the riches to be made in the new league.

Reach wasn't as vehement in denouncing the jumpers as was his partner, Rogers, but he was deeply hurt over what he regarded the desertion of Sid Farrar, his ninth slot-hitting first baseman, at a time when Al felt his baseball investment was in deadly peril. "Sid had been with us from the start, ever since those tough days in 1883," said Reach. "He always was a good first baseman, but he never hit much; yet year after year, we kept him on. Of all my players, I thought Sid would be the one to remain loyal."

Not only were Reach, Rogers and Wright confronted with the problems of jumpers and double jumpers, but also of the triple jumpers, Ed Delahanty, the fine young second base prospect from Cleveland, and Third baseman Joe Mulvey. Both signed Players League contracts early in the revolt, but forgot all about their loyalty to the Brotherhood when Rogers offered them cash and better contracts to sign with the Phillies. But the Players League agents weren't through, and they induced the pair to take a third jump, Mulvey to the newly constructed Players League park at Broad and Dauphin streets, several blocks north of the Phillie park, and "Del" to his home town of Cleveland. Some of the Players League big brass decided it would be a good piece of business to have the budding young star play before the fans of his native city.

"The scalawag!" roared Rogers, when told of Delahanty's run-out to the Players League for a second time. "I thought he was a man of honor."

One Phillie who remained loyal during all the excitement was the chunky little scrapper from Camden, Bill "Kid" Gleason. "George Wright gave me my big chance two years ago, when I was just a fresh kid playing the coal towns, and I'm not running out on him now," said the Kid. In a weakened league, Gleason was largely responsible for the Phillies' third place finish in 1890 by winning 38 games and losing 16. He won practically half of the team's 78 victories. With Buffington, Casey and Sanders gone, Gleason was the bellwether of the staff as Wright recruited pitching odds and ends from minor and semi-pro fields to see him through the season. With just one more even fair pitcher, the Phillies might have won their first pennant during that hectic war season. The new Brooklyn club, playing the same team that had won the 1889 American Association pennant, beat them out by eight games, while Chicago nosed out the Phillies for second place.

The baseball strife had its compensation for the Phillies, one being the purchase of the human rocket, Billy Hamilton, greatest of all National League base runners. Though Hamilton was an easterner, a product of Newark, New Jersey, he was acquired from the Kansas City club to fill one of the big outfield holes. Billy quickly established himself in center field and became the team's crack lead-off man. Though this was the era in which the great batsman and base runner King Kelly immortalized the expression, "Slide, Kelly, slide!", Sliding Billy Hamilton quickly surpassed the King in wholesale larceny of bases. Billy holds the National League record with 797 stolen bases for twelve seasons. Ty Cobb, holder of the major and American League record, stole only 95 more in a career lasting twenty-four years. Hamilton was fast as a deer, and he could wriggle around a baseman—waiting with ball in hand—like a slippery eel. Billy was such a remarkable base runner that his hitting often is overlooked, but in six seasons with the Phillies his average never dropped below .324, rising as high as .398. Surely Billy Hamilton is another Phillie who belongs in the Hall of Fame.

A second Billy—Billy Sunday—also a flash on the bases, saw service with the Phillies in the year of the Brotherhood War. Billy and Bill Sowders, a pitcher, were the only Pittsburgh National League players who did not jump to the Players League team in that city. However, the Pittsburgh club soon was in deep financial trouble and was pleased to trade Sunday to the Phillies for $1,000 and some lesser players. It was Billy Sunday's last year of professional ball. He embarked soon afterwards on the career which was to win him international fame as an evangelist.

The National League had good reason to be proud of Philadelphia that year. While National League clubs played second fiddle in the important turnstile department to the Players League in New York, Chicago, Boston and Pittsburgh, the Phillies were a pillar of strength for the old major. Philadelphia actually tried to support three major league teams that season, as the American Association Athletics still were in business at

25th and Jefferson. But they had a bad season, finishing last; Fogarty's Players League team fared little better, coming home fifth. With their third place contender, the Phillies got the cream of the town's baseball patronage.

At a time when crowds were streaming into the Huntington park, with National League parks almost deserted in Pittsburgh and Cleveland, many said the Phillies saved the National League. With Rogers spurring on Spalding and Day, the National League's war committee brought their Players League foes to their knees. By buying out some of the league's backers and putting pressure on others, they forced the Brotherhood-sponsored loop to call it quits after one disastrous and expensive season.

"I knew they couldn't last," said the belligerent Rogers. "All we had to do was stand firm, and see the Players League collapse from its own inherent weakness."

2

When the Players League collapsed, the National League and American Association declared a general amnesty to jumping players, and their names were restored to the reserve lists of the clubs with which they had played in 1889. Most of the clubs welcomed back their jumpers, but there was no "Welcome" mat out for them in Philadelphia. Reach might have been more lenient with the so-called deserters, but Rogers wanted no truck with them.

Only two of the jumpers were retained, Jim Fogarty and young Ed Delahanty. Fogarty's health had deteriorated in 1890, and in the latter part of the season Buffington had relieved him as manager of the Philadelphia Players League team. "Jim's a sick man; he's repentant, and I don't think we should dump him," said Reach.

"All right, be sentimental," snapped Rogers. "Fogarty stays on the payroll, but I don't want any of the others, Buffington, Wood, Farrar, Casey—above all, not Buffington."

There was a touch of pathos to Reach's regard for Fogarty. Jim died of tuberculosis before playing another game in a Phillie uniform. He faded like a lily in the spring of 1891, the end coming May 20th, when the once handsome San Francisco boy was only twenty-seven years old.

There was no sentiment in the retention of the triple jumper, Ed Delahanty. Ed had come fast in his year in the Players League and won national distinction by getting six hits—three singles, two doubles and a triple—in six times at bat off Mark Baldwin of Chicago, one of the game's better pitchers, on June 2, 1890. "Del" had batted .296 for Cleveland, and there was a substantial pick-up in his extra-base hits—24 doubles, 15 triples, 3 homers. In Cleveland, they had shifted him to the outfield, where he showed to better advantage than at second base. Ed soon became the Phillies' regular left fielder, in a great outfield of Delahanty, Hamilton and Thompson. Delahanty, however, remained versatile, and Wright frequently played him at first base. He liked to play there, saying, "It's fun to be right in the middle of the game. In the outfield, you've got to wait too long for a fly ball, and when you get a bad pitcher in there, you run until your tongue hangs out."

The Phillies now were to enter the period which the militant Col. Rogers was to term "the fourth place rut." For five straight seasons, in the early nineties, that was to be their final position. "By crimetty, are we anchored there? Can't we ever get out of this fourth place rut?" he once demanded irately of Reach.

These fourth-placers varied considerably, and the 1891 team fell one game under .500, winning 68 games and losing 69. More and more, the Phillies were to be known as a club with power hitters but inferior pitching. Wright used no less than eleven pitchers in 1891, an unusual number for that period, but Kid Gleason (24-19) and Charley Esper (20-14) were the only dependables. Esper came from the south Jersey town of Salem, and after an early fling with the Athletics, he had developed during the Brotherhood war year. Late in the season Reach and Rogers, in an effort to help their battered staff, purchased Timothy Keefe from the Giants. This supposedly was a hot piece of news for Phillie fans. Tim had been one of the great stars of the 80's with the New York Mets, and later with the New York Giants, and in 1888 had run off a winning streak of nineteen straight. But the staff missed Buffington, who was permitted to drift to Arthur Irwin's Boston American Association team, where he helped Art win the flag with 28 victories against nine defeats.

"If the club hadn't been so stiff-necked about taking Buffington back, and Buff had won those 28 games for us, that would have won the pennant," said some disgruntled Phillie fans.

If the 1891 Phillies failed to advance above fourth place, it wasn't because of the failure of their lead-off man, Billy Hamilton, to get on, or advance himself into scoring position. Billy was the Phillies' first National League batting champion with an average of .338. A year before, he hung an even greater record into the National League book, one which grows brighter with each succeeding year. He stole the magic number of 115 bases in 133 games, the all time N. L. record. Ty Cobb, the American League titleholder, stole his 96 bases in 1915 in 156 games. With few present-day clubs stealing 115 bases a season, Billy's record may last to the end of time.

3

There was a big shake-up following the 1891 season. After the National League and American Association had been at loggerheads all through the 1891 season over two former Athletic jumpers, Louie Bierbauer and Harry Stovey, the two circuits merged into a twelve-club organization as the National took in the American Association cities of Baltimore, Washington, St. Louis and Louisville. The Athletic owner, George Wagner, was awarded the Washington franchise. That was a good break for Reach and Col. Rogers. It meant that for the first time since the Phillies entered the field in 1883, they had the Quaker City exclusively to themselves. It also meant that when the club wound up in its chronic fourth spot, only three clubs topped the

Phillies; eight trailed the Quakers. It meant good first division ball, well-patronized ball, but a brand which was unsatisfactory to both the owners and the fans.

In 1892, first year of the twelve-club league, the National played a split season. Cleveland won the first half; the Boston Beaneaters took the second half and ran away with the playoffs. The Phillies battled hard in both halves, but in the final standings John Ward's Brooklyns slipped in ahead of the Phillies in third place. Col. Rogers was disgusted with the showing of the club on the road and felt road defeats cost the club the pennant. The club lost five, won none in Brooklyn, and in Boston, they won only two and lost four. But what especially irked Rogers was the showing in St. Louis, where Chris Von Der Ahe's Browns celebrated their entry into the National League with an eleventh place club. Bad as the Browns were, in Sportsman's Park they drubbed the Phillies five games out of seven.

"Harry, why are we so terrible on the road?" Rogers demanded of Wright. "Once the team gets away from Broad and Huntington, it acts like a bunch of stray befuddled cats. And what was the matter with the club in St. Louis? Why didn't we do better against Von Der Ahe's clowns? Were the players out all night carousing?"

"The home team always has the edge," insisted Wright. "And in St. Louis, I guess it was Gleason. The Kid took great joy in beating us."

Yes, the faithful Gleason, who had stuck so loyally to the Phillies during the Brotherhood war, found himself an 1892 Brownie. There was considerable hocus-pocus following the National League-American Association merger. Gus Weyhing, for years star pitcher of the A's, Catcher-third baseman Lave Cross, and Joe Mulvey, the triple-jumping third baseman, came to the Phillies from the disbanded Athletics. So did Wilfred "Kid" Carsey, ace pitcher of the 1891 Washington A. A. club. Everybody owed somebody a player, and when the trading was over the Camden kid landed with Von Der Ahe in St. Louis. Lave Cross had the unique distinction of playing in the uniforms of four Philadelphia major league clubs, the old American Association Athletics, the Philadelphia Players League team of 1890, the Phillies, and later with the modern Athletics of the American League.

Though Gleason was a tough nut to crack in his new brown socks, the winter deals brought fruit. Weyhing, a Kentuckian from Louisville, was then one of the game's top-ranking pitchers and broke in with the Phillies with a 30-victory season. Carsey also did well, 19-16, and Tim Keefe, at the age of thirty-six, had one more good year, winning 20 games and losing 16. A young Staten Islander, John Budd Taylor, who had a tryout with the 1891 New Yorkers, was procured from the Giants and soon developed into a winning pitcher. Under a sort of lend-lease arrangement, the Phillies had the use of Roger Connor, the Giants' all-star first baseman, before returning him to New York in 1893. The sturdy biscuit-panted man from Waterbury hit .285 in his lone season in Quaker toggery, one of the few seasons in Roger's eighteen-year major league career that he fell below .300.

4

Jack Boyle, known as Honest John—a St. Louis Brownie before the consolidation—was the Giant first baseman in 1892, but in 1893 the former Giant captain-shortstop, John Montgomery Ward, switched his managerial talents from Brooklyn to New York. Meeting Harry Wright, he told him, "I surely would like to have Roger Connor back with me on the Giants. Why, it wouldn't seem like the same team if I didn't have Roger at first base."

"Well, that former Brown player, Boyle, would look all right in a Philadelphia uniform," said Harry. "Give us Boyle, and I think I can talk my bosses into returning Connor."

So Honest John came to Philadelphia as the new first baseman. He stuck at the post for six years. Boyle put off his 1893 Fourth of July celebration by two days, but when he broke loose on July 6th, he put on quite a pyrotechnic display. In six times at bat in an 11-inning game with Chicago, John fired five singles and a double off Pitcher Bill Hutchinson.

However, the pride and delight of the Philadelphia crowds continued to be the crack outfield of Delahanty, Hamilton and Thompson. "Del," now twenty-six, had reached his prime and developed into the league's foremost slugger. After reaching the .300 class for the first time in 1892, Big Ed now exploded for a .370 average and an extra-base total of 31 doubles, 20 triples and 19 homers. The latter was one of the best home run crops of the gay nineties and made Delahanty the 1893 home run king. Sliding Billy Hamilton soared to .395 in his fourth season in Philadelphia and Big Sam Thompson hit a robust .377. Despite all this power, Boston, Pittsburgh and Cleveland finished ahead of the Phillies in the twelve-club standing.

"We have the best club in the league, and still we don't win," muttered many of the fans. Whether or not it was justifiable, there was a prevalent feeling in and around Philadelphia that man for man, the Phillies had it over any club in the National League.

Col. Rogers had the same idea. In a conference with his partner Al Reach, he brought up the matter. "Harry Wright now has been the Philadelphia manager for ten years," he said. "Only once in that time has he done as well as second, and now we're stuck in that fourth place rut. We've been liberal in spending money for Harry; have gotten him the best players that were available and still we don't win. I do not think he is getting the best out of our splendid material. I'll swear we have a better team than the Pittsburgh club, which finished second."

"I would hate to let Harry go," replied Reach. "He's so loyal —and has been so long in the game."

"That may be the trouble," shot back Rogers. "Maybe you've put your finger right on it; Harry has been too long in the game. He goes back to those Cincinnati Reds of the sixties. We're now playing a different brand of baseball in the nineties."

Rogers won his point, though it wrenched Reach's heartstrings when he told Harry his managerial contract would not be renewed. At the suggestion of Reach and Rogers, the National League created a special office for old Harry—chief of umpires. He did not hold it long, dying on October 3, 1895, at the age of sixty. Some friends seemed to think that losing his job on the Phillies contributed to his demise.

The man selected to replace the old war horse was Arthur Irwin, shortstop-captain before the Brotherhood war. Irwin always was a smart player and a man well grounded in his baseball. After leaving the Phillies, he managed Washington and the Boston 1891 American Association champions. He also coached a famous team at the University of Pennsylvania, where his giant left-hander, George Reese, was one of the greatest pitchers in the country, amateur or professional.

It seemed almost unbelievable, but despite some sensational ups and downs and another great slugging team, Irwin's first team finished exactly one point better than Wright's last club. The two clubs were as alike as peas: 1893—Won 72; Lost 57. Per. .558. 1894—Won 71; Lost 56. Per. .559.

The latter season was one of heartaches for the fans, headaches for Irwin and the owners, and one which left all in a state of nervous prostration. The Phillies always promised so much, and fizzled just as they seemed about to capitalize on their power. They spent the early months bobbing in and out of second place. Then from June 18th to July 30th, they took a nose dive that dropped them from second to seventh. Just when they seemed in danger of falling right through the league, Irwin righted his craft and the Phillies started up again, putting together a ten-game winning streak from August 15th to 25th. That lifted them to fourth, and they seemed pointed higher, when their hopes were dashed on their last western trip, on which they won only six games out of seventeen and dropped their last five in St. Louis and Cleveland. As they came home in their usual fourth place slot, a dark horse—the Baltimore Orioles—batted, ran, stole, browbeat and scratched their way to the first of three pennants.

"I always thought when Boston was stopped, we'd be the club to stop them," said the disconsolate Rogers. "Now the pennant goes to an upstart team of rowdies."

Yet Philadelphia had its bright spots during this dizzy season, and some of their 1894 deeds still blaze brightly in today's record books. There was the day in Louisville, on August 17th, when the Phillies humiliated Barney Dreyfuss' Colonels by the outlandish score of 29 to 4. The Phillies set a record for most hits in a nine-inning game, 36. All were made off the same pitcher, Wadsworth. How he lived through that shellacking must remain a mystery. The Phillies scored in every inning but the second, but they made up for that by tallying six runs in both the first and third. All eleven players used by Irwin broke into the hit column. The big boss thumper was Sam Thompson, with a homer, triple, double and three singles in seven times up. Billy Hamilton, Shortstop Joe Sullivan and Catcher Mike Grady each whacked out five hits; Delahanty had only four singles but scored five runs. Hamilton stole only one base, but Honest John Boyle filched three.

Delahanty had his second "six for six" game, getting five singles and a double off Pfann and McGuire of the Cincinnati Reds on June 16th. Only Delahanty and the latter-day Cardinal first baseman, Jim Bottomley, cracked out "six for six" twice in their respective careers.

We've heard much of the great outfields of the game: Babe Ruth, Earle Combs and Bob Meusel of one famous Yankee team; Tommy Henrich, Joe DiMaggio and Charley Keller of another New York American outfit; Duffy Lewis, Tris Speaker and Harry Hooper of the Red Sox World's Champions of 1912 and 1915; Bobbie Veach, Ty Cobb and Sam Crawford of the Tigers; and Stan Musial, Terry Moore and Enos Slaughter of the Cardinal World's Champions of 1942. But if you really want baseball's top all-star outfield, you've got to go back to the Phillies of 1894. The low man on the regular trio was Billy Hamilton with an average of .398. But Billy stole 99 bases and scored 196 runs. Delahanty came next with .400, and Thompson was top man with .403. And now hold your hats: the utility outfielder to this mighty trio, George "Tuck" Turner, hit a meek .423. What's more, Tuck saw considerable service. With injuries limiting Thompson to 102 games and Delahanty to 114, Turner participated in 77 contests, scored 94 runs and rang up 147 hits. He didn't fatten up, either, in that 36-hit joust over Louisville, in which he drew only one hit in five attempts. Like Pitcher John Budd Taylor, Turner was a Staten Islander.

For a spell, the 1894 Phillies had two Delahantys on the payroll, as Big Ed talked Irwin into giving his brother Tom a trial. He played in only one game at second base, but later saw service in the National League with Cleveland, Pittsburgh and Louisville.

5

"We have the hitting; now if we can get a little better pitching, I think we can make it," said Arthur Irwin before the 1895 season.

Under his coaching the year before, Taylor and Carsey had good seasons, winning 26 and 24 games respectively. Gus Weyhing had some good days, but his work wasn't up to its former high standard. It took some hard hitting behind Gus to keep him above the .500 mark with 19-17. In his six former seasons, Gus had averaged 28 victories. Among the pitching rookies tried out by Irwin in 1894 was an aggressive kid from Fitchburg, Massachusetts, Jimmy Callahan. He was too green to stick under Irwin, but the boy had a lot of stuff and confidence and later won his spurs as a front-line pitcher with the Chicago Nationals and as a pitcher, outfielder and manager of the Chicago White Sox of the American League.

If Weyhing hadn't collapsed completely in 1895, Irwin might have led the team to its first pennant. The indifferent 19-17 season was a precursor of what was to come. The Kentuckian suffered from a lame arm and was a total loss. Nineteen victories from Gus, or even fifteen, would have meant the championship, but he took part in only two games and was charged with one defeat. It saddled the pitching burden on Taylor and Carsey and a bunch of youngsters hastily recruited to fill the breach. Yet the Phillies' terrific power lifted the club out of its fourth place rut—into third place. This time they trailed the scrappiest two clubs in the league—the Baltimore Orioles and Cleveland Spiders. But, considering the loss of Weyhing, their record of 78 victories against 53 defeats for a .595 percentage was most satisfactory.

In an effort to stay in the race, a whole raft of young pitchers were brought in: Willie McGill, Tom Smith, Bill Beam, George Hodson, Henry Lampe, Con Lucid, Al Orth and Frank White. Orth proved the jewel of the lot. A Hoosier from Danville, Indiana, Al was purchased from the Lynchburg club of the Virginia League for $1,000. Orth had a slow, deliberate delivery but possessed a winning touch from the start, breaking in with an 8-1 record. In his first National League game he helped Carsey and Taylor bring in a 23 to 9 win over the Giants. Following this relief job, Al clicked off eight straight victories, followed by a tie against the Baltimore champions. It wasn't until his last game of the season that he suffered a 6 to 3 defeat at the hands of the Brooklyn Dodgers.

Again the Phillies' all-star outfield shattered the fences, and at the finish only five points separated the mighty maulers: Delahanty—.399; Thompson—.394; Hamilton—.393.

CHAPTER 5

Larry Lajoie Tossed into Geier Deal

⚾ 1 ⚾

BALL CLUBS constantly are trying to improve. Their owners get fidgety and nervous, and think something should be done. They get tired looking at the same line-up, and think changes are advisable—and necessary. Too often these changes backfire and leave the club far worse off than before the owner started tinkering with his personnel. Something like that happened on the 1896 Phillies.

As Al Reach devoted more and more time to his sporting goods venture, Col. Rogers gave more time and attention to the ball club. And the Colonel could be most domineering and fault-finding. Frequently he and Irwin hadn't seen things eye to eye. With the Phillies' terrific club batting average, Rogers wasn't satisfied with Irwin's two-year showing and felt a lot of games were frittered away in late innings as Arthur experimented with untried pitchers. But Irwin couldn't call on Taylor and Carsey every day.

Perhaps Arthur could have stayed, but Andy Friedman, the new Giant owner, gave him a substantial offer to come to New York. Reach and Rogers might have matched this offer, but they decided not to stand in Irwin's way. As it was, Arthur soon learned that he was working for a far more cantankerous boss than his former Philadelphia employers.

The managerial vacancy was filled by advancing Secretary William J. "Billy" Shettsline to the post. Bill, a kindly lovable soul, easily could have been called Mr. Phillie. In a long sojourn with the Phillies lasting nearly four decades, he was to be everything on the club—secretary, manager, president, business manager. A big portly man, he bubbled with good humor, good cheer and a kindly philosophy on life. No one ever made more friends for the club than the genial "Shetts." A native Philadelphian, he lived in the suburb of Glenolden, where he raised chickens when he wasn't trying to raise ball players for the Phillies. Though Shettsline never got past sand-lot ball as a player, nobody ever knew more about the intricacies of the baseball business. He first became interested in pro ball when he helped put a Philadelphia club into the outlaw Union Association in 1884. After his experience as a baseball outlaw he made a connection with the Phillies, first as handy man and ticket taker, subsequently graduating to bookkeeper and secretary.

After giving the managerial job to Shettsline, the club pulled one of its worst boners. Billy Hamilton wanted a moderate salary increase, and in a penny-pinching deal Rogers traded the popular batsman and speedboy to the Boston Beaneaters for Third baseman Billy Nash. The idea was to install Nash as team captain, a sort of assistant manager under Shetts. Team captains then had a far more important role than they have today. On many clubs they changed pitchers and directed strategy on the field. Such outstanding player managers as Cap Anson, Charley Comiskey and John Montgomery Ward were manager-captains, but managers such as Jim Mutrie, "Watty" Watkins and Pat Powers had their captains look after matters on the diamond.

Nash had a good background when he was brought to Philadelphia. He had sparkled on the Boston infield on the champions of 1891-2-3 and enjoyed a reputation for being a smart, cagey player. But unfortunately, by the time the stupid Hamilton-Nash trade was perpetrated, Billy was pretty well washed up. He played in only 64 games, hitting .242. On July 29th, he was demoted and the captain's commission turned over to Jack Boyle, who in 1896 served as a part-time catcher. Roger had procured the old slugger and Hall of Fame immortal, Dan Brouthers, to play first base. Alas, it was the redoubtable Dan's eighteenth and last big league season. With Shettsline as manager, and Nash and Boyle as team captains, Col. Rogers had no worries about a fourth place rut. The Phillies slipped from their satisfactory third of 1895 to a dismal eighth.

2

If the season of 1896 brought disappointment, heartaches and the first second-division club in twelve years, it saw the Phillies gain their greatest player outside of the pitching box. The player was Napoleon "Larry" Lajoie, peerless second baseman and generally regarded as the most graceful of ball players.

What's more, the acquisition of the brilliant Lajoie came as a windfall. The Phillies were shot with luck in obtaining this master workman. Almost overnight the club had developed trouble in what was its leading department, the outfield. Hamilton had been sacrificed to Boston; Thompson, at thirty-six, suddenly was cracking up; and Delahanty frequently was needed at first base to spell out the aging Dan Brouthers. After Turner's uncanny .423 in 1894, and .388 in 1895, Tuck suddenly pooped out and was hitting a paltry .231 when released to St. Louis. The club hastily picked up such outfielders as Joe Sullivan, Dick Cooley and Sam Mertes.

The Fall River club of the New England League had an outfielder by the name of Phil Geier, whose exploits were written up in Frank Richter's old *Sporting Life*. Rogers sent a scout to Fall River to look up Geier, and the outfielder immediately caught his fancy. Charley Marston, the Fall River owner, was willing to sell, but there was some haggling over the price.

"Tell you what I'll do," said Marston. "Give me fifteen hundred dollars for Geier, and I'll throw in the big Frenchman, Lajoie."

The deal was authorized by Rogers, and Lajoie, the throw-in, became Philadelphia property. Geier was a fair ball player but soon was outdistanced by the graceful Lajoie.

Lajoie, son of French parents, was the town cabby in Woonsocket, Rhode Island, a neighboring town to Fall River. He acquired a local reputation, and Marston signed him to an 1896 contract on the back of an envelope. Before the Phillies acquired Lajoie, Arthur Irwin of the Giants had sent an idle player to Fall River to scout Lajoie. The oaf turned in an adverse report, a lucky break for the Phillies. How any one could be so wrong is still hard to comprehend, as Lajoie was hitting .429 for 80 games when tossed into the Geier deal. What's more, he looked every inch an athlete, all of the six feet, one inch of him. His best playing weight came to be 195 pounds.

The season was two-thirds over when Lajoie joined the Phillies. Delahanty was playing first but talked the newcomer into taking a fling at the position. Nap hit .328 in 39 games. He was within a fortnight of his twenty-first birthday when he reported but already had developed much of his power. Fans and fellow players marveled at the extra-base hits that rippled off his bat. His 57 hits in his first brief big league season included eleven doubles, ten triples and four home runs. What a find! He was destined to remain a star big-time performer for another score of years.

Before long all Philadelphia was singing the Rhode Islander's praises. Author Lieb was only eight years old when Lajoie came to Philadelphia, but he distinctly recalls older kids telling of the Frenchman's great deeds. Lajoie soon became the apple of our eyes, greater even than Delahanty. The small fry never referred to him as anything else than La-joy. Our elders also spoke of him as La-Joy. It wasn't until Lieb graduated to the big league press boxes that he knew the accepted pronunciation of the great player's name was Lazh-o-wah. And even though the whizz from Woonsocket was to jump to the new American League five years later, Philadelphia always considered Lajoie as one of its own and a player dear to the Quaker City's heart.

As for the player we soon came to revere as King Larry, he was an odd type. Lajoie never was a mixer, and while he had a small circle of friends, few ever knew the Frenchman intimately. As a young player in Philadelphia, he was tall, dark and handsome, and had his share of temptations and adventures. Several times Col. Rogers had "Frenchy" on the carpet on matters of discipline, but Larry always was careful to protect his physical condition, particularly his eyesight. Even later in his career, as Cleveland's playing manager, he rarely read newspapers and magazines and had little use for the early flickers. He felt reading newspapers on trains and attending movies might dim his batting eyes. After he retired from baseball as Indianapolis manager in 1918, he practically severed all of his former baseball connections. In the last quarter of a century he has lived in various places in Florida, and closed his door to sports writers. The friendly Bill Corum and Lieb were among the many who were rebuffed while trying to get an interview from Larry. The only time he appeared at a baseball gathering was at the dedication of the Cooperstown Hall of Fame in 1938, which he attended with the other then living immortals, Hans Wagner, Ty Cobb, Connie Mack, Grover Alexander, etc.

If the arrival of Lajoie in 1896 put a new star in the Phillie firmament, it didn't dim the older star, Ed Delahanty. He hit .394, led the league in doubles with 42 and homers with 13. Four of the homers were made in an unforgettable game at the old West Side Park in Chicago on July 13. For good measure, Del threw in a single. The "Four Homers a Game Club" has grown to six during the present home run era, but for many years it was an exclusive two-man organization—Bobbie Lowe, who first turned the feat in 1894, and Delahanty. After Del's Chicago carnival, thirty-six summers elapsed before a third man, Lou Gehrig, blasted four homers out of Shibe Park in 1932.

Despite Delahanty's five hits for 17 bases, Cap Anson's Chicagos beat the Phillies, 9 to 8. Both starting pitchers, Bill "Adonis" Terry of Chicago and Virgil Garvin of the Phillies, stuck out the full nine innings. However, outside of Delahanty, the Phillie offense was tame, as the Quakers got only four other hits. Big Ed started blasting in the first inning, when he hit the first pitch for a two-run homer over what was termed the "inner right field fence" at the Chicago park. On his second attempt, Eddie limited himself to a puny single. His real gem came in the fifth, when with Hullen and Mertes on base, he again hit a first pitch and sent the ball over the center field scoreboard and the canvas screen behind it. A Chicago *Tribune* reporter termed it "the longest hit of the year at the local grounds." It landed in a yard across the street.

His third homer in the seventh was a drive to left center, which bounced by Center fielder Bill Lange. It was the only one of the four homers which stayed in the park. Del came up for the fifth time with two out in the ninth and the usually partisan Chicago crowd took up a cry, "Line it out, Del," and "Make it four, Del." Big Delahanty followed instructions and drove another ball over Lange's head. It eventually landed on the roof of the clubhouse in left center and then bounced over the fence. According to Frank J. Roberts, the *Sporting News'* Chicago correspondent, "Pitcher Terry shook hands with the batter at the home plate and complimented him on his great feat." Roberts further reported: "The 1100 fans in attendance followed Delahanty to the players' bus and gave the glad hand to the hero of the game."

3

Reach and Rogers went into a huddle at the end of their ignoble eighth place season. "We've got the players, but we've got to get somebody who can fire the club," said Rogers. "Somebody who can make our players play ball." Al readily consented to the Colonel's diagnosis of the Phillies' ills.

They felt the answer to their problem, the man who could put a charge of dynamite under the Phillies, was a fiery Georgian, George Tweedy Stallings, and one of the real Dr. Jekylls and Mr. Hydes of baseball. Nearly two decades later he was to become the famous Miracle Man of the Boston Braves. The son of a Confederate general, Stallings was graduated from the Virginia Military Institute and took two years of medicine at the College of Physicians and Surgeons in Baltimore. He was a college catcher, had an early tryout with Harry Wright on the 1887 Phillies, and it was Harry who induced him to give up medicine in favor of baseball. With the exception of a spell with Brooklyn during the 1890 Brotherhood career, George's playing career was mostly in the minors and in 1896 he had won recognition as the fighting, domineering manager of the Detroit club of the then minor Western League, forerunner to the present-day American League.

Reach and Rogers brought Stallings, then aged twenty-eight, to Philadelphia under a three-year contract. He was a man of many contradictions. No man in baseball ever fitted out a dinner jacket to better advantage. A suave Southern gentleman in a drawing room, he was a veritable demon on the ball field, especially on the bench. No slave driver on his father's plantation ever drove General Stallings' field hands any harder than son George drove his ball players. Despite his education and breeding, he was as superstitious as a native Haitian, and his profanity and terms of derision for thick-skulled ball players never have been matched in baseball.

Ball players in the nineties were not genteel characters. It was an era of roughnecks and umpire fighters as exemplified by the Baltimore Orioles and the Cleveland Spiders. Some boys with good family connections worked their way into the game, but it was no game for fastidious, thin-skinned young men. The Phillies had their share of fellows from the wrong side of the tracks; when anyone got rough—or vulgar—they could take it and dish it out. But even these hardened Phillies couldn't stand Stallings' profanity and brainstorms. From the start, they didn't like George, and no one tried to pretend the club was one happy family. Explosions were frequent, and a disgruntled team dropped to tenth. Reach and Rogers hung their heads in shame when only Dreyfuss' Louisville Colonels and Von Der Ahe's Browns trailed the Phillies in the 1897 standings.

The antagonism between Stallings and the players reached a fever heat in the late spring of 1898, when the Phillies were the first big league team to go on strike against their manager. The feeling of dislike which the so-called "Cry Baby" Cleveland Indians felt for Ossie Vitt, their 1940 manager, was mild compared to the virulent hatred which these Phillies of the Spanish American War year felt for their manager. They hated Stallings' guts and wanted all the world to know it.

A committee of players, headed by Outfielder Dick Cooley, called on Reach and Rogers and insisted they no longer could play for Stallings. In fact, Cooley made it even stronger; he said they wouldn't. In a statement to the public, given to the city's newspapers, Cooley said: "We are fed up with the way Stallings has been riding us and decided we had enough of him and would regard him as our manager no longer. For weeks he's been handling us like a lot of cattle. We may not be the best team in the league but we don't intend to put up with Stallings' tactics."

Stallings' contract had a year and a half to go, but Rogers and Reach bought it up on June 18th, sent Big George on his way, and again turned the reins of the club over to Billy Shettsline. The players were satisfied; they perked up in their play almost as soon as Stallings left. They won six more games than they lost for a percentage of .523, the bottom rung in the first division of the twelve-club standing.

Before Stallings was dethroned, the Cincinnati Reds exposed a cute little trick which no doubt helped Phillie batting averages at the Philadelphia park. We've talked before of the Phillies' ability to win at home, whereas so often they were pushovers on the road. It always had been a sore spot with Col. Rogers. Anyway, in an early 1898 game in Philadelphia, Tommy Corcoran, Red infielder, was coaching at third base and kicking dust around, when the spikes of his shoes caught in something which at first seemed to be a thick vine. Tommy looked down at his feet and on closer inspection found it was no vine, but a wire. He gave it a good yank, and several yards of wire came out of the ground.

Corcoran halted the game, kept tugging away at the wire, and with players of both teams at his heels, traced the wire across the field right into the Phillies' locker room. There they found Morgan Murphy, a reserve catcher who rarely did any catching, sitting with a telegraph instrument beside an open window. Murphy tried to hide the instrument, also a pair of strong opera glasses that completed his equipment. But the cat was out of the bag. It eventually was learned that Murphy spied on opposing catchers and relayed their signals, via the wire, to the Philadelphia third base coach. A sort of a buzzer was under the dirt, and by keeping his foot on it, the coach knew one buzz meant a fast ball, two a curve, three a change of pace. The coach signaled his information to the batsman, who usually knew just what to expect.

It is possible that the Phillies used this device before Stallings, but it sounds very much like one of the Big Chief's machinations. Twelve years later, as manager of the New York Yankees, he got himself into Ban Johnson's American League doghouse with a similar scheme, when he had an observer with opera glasses hidden in an opening in the New York scoreboard.

Yet the Stallings years were not without their good facets. One of George's last constructive moves was to take Lajoie off first base and shift him to second. It was from this position that he became the peerless King Larry, the player without a weakness. With a little better judgment on the part of Con Lucid, a secondary Phillie pitcher, the 1897 Phillies might have had the immortal shortstop Hans Wagner as a running mate to Lajoie in a second base double play combination.

Col. Rogers and Shettsline had heard glowing reports of slugging Hans Wagner, infielder on the Paterson, New Jersey, team of the Atlantic League. Pitcher Lucid was temporarily disabled, and to make him earn his keep he was dispatched to Paterson to get a line on Wagner. Lucid happened to look in on a Paterson-Richmond game.

"Wagner can hit, but he's too clumsy for the National League," was Lucid's report. "But Richmond has a shortstop, Norman "Kid" Elberfeld, that caught my eye. He fields like a demon. I believe that boy will go far, and that you can't go wrong in investing some money in him."

On the strength of this report, Rogers passed up Wagner and bought Elberfeld. A few weeks later, Barney Dreyfuss bought Wagner for his Louisville National League club for $2100. Elberfeld developed into a famous little shortstop, though he remained only briefly in Philadelphia. Wagner, of course, became one of baseball's supermen, bracketed with Ty Cobb and Babe Ruth as the game's three greatest.

Rogers and Reach spent money lavishly in these two off years, and players picked up included men who were to figure prominently in Philadelphia and big league baseball for the next decade: Pitchers Frank Sparks, Bill Duggleby, Wiley Piatt and Frank Donohue; Catchers Ed McFarland and Bill "Klondike" Douglas; Infielders Monte Cross, Ed Abbaticchio, Billy Lauder and Kid Elberfeld; Outfielders Elmer Flick and speed demon Dave Fultz. Lauder and Fultz gave the Phillies some culture, as Billy was a former Columbia University baseball captain and Fultz came from the University of Virginia. Abbaticchio, shortened to Abby in the box-scores, was the forerunner of the great Italian invasion which hit big league baseball in this century. Shortstop Montford Montgomery Cross was no relative of Third baseman Lave Cross, though the pair played on the same infields on the Phillies and later-day Athletics. Sparks stayed only for the 1897 season, but after the turn of the century he returned as one of the Phillies' most dependable pitchers. Elmer Flick, a steel-wristed young fellow from Bedford, Ohio, took over the right field post from the slipping Sam Thompson. Elmer was a .300 hitter from the start, a batting champion in the making, but unfortunately Philadelphia soon would be deprived of his brilliant services.

4

After three years in the doldrums, the Phillies again came up with a crack club in 1899, one of which the entire town was proud. The Quakers were in the fight all the way, but a Brooklyn club, strengthened by an infusion of Baltimore Oriole blood—Ned Hanlon, Willie Keeler, Joe Kelly and Hughie Jennings, won the pennant, beating Shettsline's Phillies by four and a half games. Boston barely nudged out the Phillies for second place by a single game and a percentage of .625 against .618. That .618 still remains the second best percentage in the team's history. And to show how quickly the club snapped back, it won

39 more games than did Stallings' tenth place crew of only two years before.

In the *Sporting News Register,* this 1899 Philadelphia club was termed the greatest of all Phillie teams, greater than the club's two subsequent champions. The team had everything, hitting, pitching, fielding and base-running. Charles "Chic" Fraser, a sturdy native-born Scotsman and a 21-game winner, and capable, clever Bill Bernard, were added to the pitching staff, and Roy Thomas moved from the outfield of the University of Pennsylvania to the center field post on the Phillies with the ease of a man walking across his living room. Thomas was a natural born lead-off man, an expert bunter, and a man who could drive a pitcher crazy by standing at the plate and fouling off balls as long as it suited his fancy. Roy once fouled off 22 pitches before working a pitcher for a base on balls. In fact, it was because of the ability of Roy Thomas and John McGraw of Baltimore to stand at the plate and foul off balls practically at will that the present foul strike rule was adopted shortly afterwards. Thomas came from the neighboring town of Norristown, and had one of the oddest sidelines ever taken up by a ball player. When the Phillies took the road, Roy was salesman for an undertaker supply concern.

With Delahanty in left, Thomas in center and Flick in right, the Phillies again had an outfield that matched the great Delahanty-Hamilton-Thompson trio of a few years earlier. Big Ed soared to .408 this year to win his first batting title; Thomas broke in with a tidy freshman average of .324, while Flick's second year average was .343. Lajoie, out of the game a good deal with injuries, hit .379 for 72 games. Philadelphia fans comforted themselves with the thought that if King Larry had played the full season, the club would have won the pennant.

Lajoie took part in 102 games in 1900 and hit .346, but that still wasn't enough to give the Phillies their coveted first pennant. Following the 1899 season, the National League again streamlined down to eight clubs. With a slogan, *Cut off the dead wood,* Andy Friedman, the New York owner, induced the league to lop off Baltimore and Washington in the east and Cleveland

and Louisville in the west. Under this new setup, the 1900 Phillies, with their biff-bang line-up, repeated their 1899 third place finish. It was the old story. The Phillies thrilled the town by capturing the lead at the getaway and holding it until June 18th. This, at last, was to be the year! They slipped to second place for a couple of days, but regained first base June 20th. Unfortunately that was the last time Philadelphia fans would see their club head the list for many a year. After the Fourth of July, the club slumped off; Brooklyn again took the flag and a revamped Pittsburgh club, strengthened by Barney Dreyfuss' old Louisville stars—Wagner, Clarke, Phillippe, Ritchey—beat out the eastern Pennsylvania team for second place.

After experimenting with catchers Douglas and McFarland at first base, Shettsline again moved in big Delahanty to that corner of the infield. This move became feasible after the acquisition of Jimmy "Shorty" Slagle from the disbanded Washington team. Jimmy was in Roy Thomas' class for mulcting bases on balls from unwilling pitchers, and he could steal bases like a Billy Hamilton. Shorty hit .299 as a 1900 Phillie. Lave Cross was released to Brooklyn, and Fighting Harry Wolverton was acquired from Chicago to play third base. Though Wolverton was born in Mt. Vernon, Ohio, he developed his baseball talents on the Coast and had all the mannerisms of a westerner, even to wearing a wide-brimmed hat. Harry was an aggressive character, and Shettsline made him captain of the team. Fred Jacklittch, a Brooklynite, won a locker as a spare catcher.

CHAPTER 6

American League Raids Tear Team Asunder

1

ANDY FRIEDMAN, the Tammany brave who owned the Giants, was the evil genius of the National League. He cooked up a fantastic scheme whereby the National League would be changed into a gigantic syndicate, with a well-paid president and treasurer, and eight league-hired managers to get the same pay—$5,000. Worse than that, Friedman proposed that he and three clubs associated with him would get the lion's share (66 per cent) of the common stock: New York, 30 per cent, and Boston, St. Louis and Cincinnati each 12 per cent. Of the anti-Friedman clubs, Philadelphia and Chicago each were to get 10 per cent; Pittsburgh, 8; and Brooklyn, 6.

Rogers and Reach were livid with rage at this outrageous proposal. "Only a blackguard could think up such a thing," protested Rogers. "Why, we're a better franchise than New York."

In a long deadlock to elect a president in 1901, the Phillies, Chicago, Pittsburgh and Brooklyn supported Reach's old friend, Albert Spalding, and the pro-Friedman faction stuck by the incumbent, Nick Young. After 25 futile ballots Friedman and his cohorts left the room, but the Giant Secretary, Fred Knowles, remained behind as an observer. Col. Rogers, who was in the chair, immediately asked for a roll call. Though Knowles refused to respond when New York was polled, Rogers ruled that the Giants were represented and that a legal quorum was in attendance. The four anti-Friedman clubs, with Reach voting for

Philadelphia, then proceeded to elect Spalding president. The courts later threw out this Rogers steam-rolled election, but the Friedman syndicate scheme was dead.

Another Friedman-sponsored move, the lopping off of the loop's so-called "dead wood"—Cleveland, Washington, Baltimore and Louisville—after the 1899 season, also worked badly for the National League, especially for its Philadelphia club. It furnished Ban Johnson, live-wire young president of the Western League (changed to the American League in 1900) with his golden opportunity. In 1901, he moved into the vacated National League territory of Cleveland, Washington and Baltimore; he already was in Detroit, abandoned by the National League some years before. He kept Milwaukee for a season, and put rival American League clubs in Philadelphia, Chicago and Boston. At first, Ban thought he might spread eastward and blossom into a major by peaceful means. But when the National League voted to battle the "invaders," Johnson fought a bitter no-holds-barred baseball war. The American League threw the reserve clause out of the window; contracts meant nothing; and Johnson's managers, Connie Mack, Clark Griffith, John McGraw, Jimmy McAleer, Jim Collins, Hugh Duffy and George Stallings, raided the National of most of its outstanding talent.

In Philadelphia, the situation was further complicated by the fact that Johnson procured Ben Shibe, Al Reach's sporting goods partner, as a backer for the new American League Athletics. While the National League had used the Spalding ball for years, the Reach ball had been the official sphere for the old major American Association and later of Johnson's Western League. Ban called on Al Reach in Philadelphia, offering to make the Reach ball the official pellet for his new major in return for certain considerations. Reach turned Ban over to his partner Shibe, and old Ben was interested. It produced the paradoxical situation where one partner, Shibe, became president of the new Philadelphia American League team, while his associate, Reach, retained the presidency of the Philadelphia Nationals. If these were not complications enough, Al's son George had married Ben Shibe's daughter Mary. Yet, despite these close business and domestic relations, the two clubs immediately were locked in deadly combat. It need not be surprising, however, that in the bitter Philadelphia internecine baseball fight, Col. Rogers was more aggressive and vituperative in trying to fight off the invaders than Reach, whose signature was on the new American League ball. In fact, Rogers blamed Reach for not battling harder, and there were strained relations between the partners in their latter years of operation.

"It's the Players League fight of 1890 all over again—only worse," said the Colonel. "But we licked the Brotherhood, and we'll lick this upstart, Ban Johnson, if we all hold together."

Shibe's manager in Philadelphia was the tall lanky New England catcher, Connie Mack, who had made his National League debut with Washington against Harry Wright's Phillies in 1887. Mack later managed the Pirates but became a Ban Johnson stalwart in Milwaukee. Johnson gave him a quarter interest in the new Athletics as a bonus for coming to Philadelphia.

Connie immediately cast covetous eyes on the two outstanding stars of the Phillies, Nap Lajoie and Ed Delahanty, and the crack Phillie pitchers, Bill Bernard, Chick Fraser and Wiley Piatt. Mack and other American League raiders were helped by a parsimonious rule passed by the National League in 1893, making the league's top salary for a player $2,400. There were some violations, as minor league clubs today violate salary limits by slipping money under the table, and other subterfuges. In 1900, Delahanty and Lajoie had made a secret agreement not to sign unless they did better than the $2,400 limit. Eventually Del wangled a $3,000 salary out of Col. Rogers, but Lajoie bettered the limit by only $200, agreeing to take $2,600. Rogers had told him $2,600 was all the club was paying Big Del. Later, when Lajoie learned Delahanty was getting $3,000, he hit the ceiling, stormed into Col. Rogers' office and demanded the other $400. Rogers refused.

As a consequence, when Mack offered Lajoie $4,000 to play in 1901 at his new Athletic park at 29th Street and Columbia Avenue, the big Frenchman readily consented to jump. However, Nap played it with all the caution of his French forbears;

he insisted that all the money be deposited in the Northwestern National Bank of Philadelphia in the name of Frank Hough, sports editor of the Philadelphia *Inquirer*, and a man named Johnson with whom Larry boarded. On pay day, Hough and Johnson drew checks against the amount and paid off Lajoie.

Mack made Delahanty a similar offer, but Rogers matched the figure, and the big clouter remained one more season with the Phillies. Rogers eventually had to tear up contracts to retain other players, but when the new season started his losses were Lajoie, Fraser, Bernard and Piatt. Early efforts to restrain the jumpers in the lower Philadelphia courts were of no avail.

All National League clubs were weakened by the American League raids, and the 1902 Phillies did surprisingly well despite their jumpers. They finished second to the Pirates, their first runner-up position since 1887. While it was Pittsburgh all the way, for the greater part of the season the Phillies made a good fight of it, winding up only seven games in arrears. In the first season of the American League in Philadelphia, Rogers easily held off Connie Mack and Al Reach's partner, Uncle Ben Shibe.

Though Rogers refused to give King Larry that extra $400 the year before, he now spent money freely. Delahanty started the season at first base, but on June 24th, he put through a fairly big deal with Brooklyn, purchasing Hugh Jennings, the old Oriole shortstop, for $3,000. The American League also had been trying to get Hughie, and there was a general feeling around Philadelphia that Jennings would be named Phillie manager. But that part of the deal never did jell. Hughie's arm had gone back on him, and by this time he was a first baseman. As he took over at first, Delahanty returned to left field, and Jimmy Slagle was released to Boston. Another outfielder, George Browne, was engaged. Joe Dolan was a stopgap filler-in at second base for Lajoie. Late in the season, when Rogers learned that Harry Wolverton had signed a 1902 contract with the Washington Americans, he was suspended for the balance of the season.

The most amazing thing about the 1902 second place club was how it survived the loss of Pitchers Bernard, Fraser and Piatt. However, Al Orth, Bill Duggleby and Frank Donohue took on the added burden, and the club was fortunate enough to dig up two promising youngsters, Happy John Townsend, a right-hander from Townsend, Delaware, and Guy Harris White, a stylish southpaw and off-season dentist from Washington, D. C. "Doc" White was destined for a career of stardom; but alas for Philadelphia fans, most of it was with the Chicago White Sox.

2

If Rogers and Reach felt they had trouble with their 1901 Phillie jumpers, 1902 was the year of their travail and desperation. With the exception of Roy Thomas, the true-blue little gent from Norristown, practically every worth-while player on the Phillies cast his lot with the young American League. Connie Mack again reached into the rival park and plucked the hard-hitting right fielder, Elmer Flick, Pitcher Bill Duggleby and Shortstop Monte Cross. The new St. Louis Browns snatched Frank "Red" Donohue, who had become the club's pitching mainstay with a 21-14 record for 1901. But the biggest blow came when Ed Delahanty jumped to Washington. With him went Pitchers Al Orth and Jack Townsend and Third baseman Wolverton.

The American League was not destined to enjoy the prestige and power of Big Del's bat for long. After Eddie had won the 1902 batting title, his earth life came to a tragic end on July 2, 1903, at the age of thirty-five. A few days before, Del had been suspended for drinking by Tom Loftus, his Washington manager. Ed remained on his spree in Detroit and took a train for New York. He continued drinking on the train and kicked up such a rumpus that the conductor had him put off near the Canadian end of the international bridge at Fort Erie, Ontario. Ed moved across the bridge, and either fell, jumped or was pushed into the Niagara River below, where swift currents carried the body of the great slugger over Niagara's famed Horseshoe Falls.

Early in the 1902 season, Col. Rogers had a few moments of joy. He then thought everything would come out all right. On

April 21st, a few days after the start of the season, the Pennsylvania Supreme Court handed down a far-reaching decision. It upheld the validity of the option clause in the Philadelphia National contracts and reversed a decision of the lower Philadelphia court which had refused to grant an injunction restraining Lajoie, Bernard and Fraser, the 1901 jumpers, from playing with the Athletics. It ordered those players to return to the Phillies. While the court action did not mention Flick, Duggleby and Cross, the 1902 jumpers, they naturally came under the same category.

"This is just what we needed," said Col. Rogers, waving a news flash of the court's finding. "Now we'll see whether the Athletics and our deserters will defy the courts."

Many felt it was a knock-out blow for the young American League, and might set a pattern for courts in other states. But Ban Johnson acted quickly, and remained full of fight. If Lajoie, Flick and Bernard could not play for the Athletics, Johnson assigned the formidable trio to the league's Cleveland club. For the full 1902 season, the three players had to remain out of Pennsylvania jurisdiction. Of the Phillies who jumped to the A's, only pitchers Fraser and Duggleby obeyed the court's order and again took up their lockers at the Broad and Huntington grounds. Wolverton jumped back to the Phillies after playing 59 games for Washington. For some reason, Col. Rogers did not bother about Shortstop Monte Cross, a good fielder but mediocre hitter. Monte became the Athletics' regular shortstop.

The fate of a Philadelphia team without Lajoie, Delahanty, Flick, Bernard, Orth, Donohue and Cross may well be imagined. The club plunged from a respectable second to a dismal seventh. It was a horrible season for the National League, its line-ups riddled by desertions. Pittsburgh, which suffered less from American League raids than any other club, won the pennant with a 27½ game lead over second place Brooklyn. Where the Phillies trailed the 1901 Pirate champions by only seven games, this year they wound up 46 games in back of the team from western Pennsylvania. And to increase Col. Rogers' bed of thorns, Connie Mack won his first American League pennant as the Phillies wallowed in the National League mire. The A's took over the better part of the town's baseball business, and at one time Barney Dreyfuss had to advance a sizable sum to the Phillies so that the war-scarred club could carry on.

Yet even a season of great adversity had its few bright spots. They were the signing of two aggressive kids from the Cincinnati district, Catcher Charles Sebastian "Red" Dooin and Shortstop Rudy Hulswitt. Red came from Cincinnati, and Rudy from across the river in Newport, Kentucky. The pair had played some semi-pro and minor league ball, and were signed for the Phillies in the St. Louis *Sporting News* office by editor A. J. Flanner at the request of Al Reach.

Dooin, an Irish carrot-top, became one of the Phillies' best and most aggressive players, and one of the team's most beloved personalities. Red was a comparatively small man for a catcher, five feet, nine and a half inches tall and weighing 165 pounds, but he was all hustle. A little iron man, bubbling with Gaelic wit, sarcasm and fight, he caught in the National League for fifteen years, and in the five seasons from 1904 to 1909, Dooin caught over 100 games. Though Roger Bresnahan generally was credited with being the first catcher to wear shin guards, Red Dooin actually was the first. He wore them under his stockings two years before Bresnahan displayed his shin guards publicly. Mike Murphy, the old Pennsylvania trainer, gave Charley the idea. Dooin had a fine tenor voice, sang frequently in Philadelphia's Roman Catholic churches, on the stage with his vaudeville partner Pat McCool, and in the early days of radio. Red even sang and whistled his complaints to umpires, usually homemade little ditties about blind mice, arbiters who couldn't keep on their toes, and uncomplimentary references to their background. Sometimes Charley got by with it, but on other occasions he was summarily tossed out on his ear. "How can you throw a man out of a game just for singing?" Red would demand indignantly. Many Philadelphia fans still rate Red Dooin as the team's all-time No. 1 catcher.

Baseball peace eventually came over the land in January, 1903, with the National League granting full recognition to the

American League as a full-fledged major. But before the peace pact was signed, the forlorn Phillies were to lose another of their crack players, the skillful left-handed pitcher, Doc Harris White, who jumped to the White Sox and who in 1904 was to pitch five successive shutouts for the Comiskey team. Another young 1902 pitcher, Bill Wolfe, signed with the new New York Highlanders, and Shortstop Rudy Hullswit, who was so pleased to sign a Phillie contract in Flanner's editorial sanctum, also inked an American League contract. However, the peace commissioners, in considering the cases of a dozen disputed players, ordered Hulswitt returned to the Phillies. It was a little sop for the Quakers but contrasted feebly with the great stars lost to the American League, most of whom were to shine in the Johnson loop for years to come.

CHAPTER 7

Socialite Potter Buys the Club

1

THE Reach-Rogers regime came to an end a few weeks after the termination of the devastating baseball war. They had operated the club through twenty seasons of woes and heartaches. They had built the best park then in baseball, had had some great teams, and great players. The treasured pennant often seemed so near, but some impish gremlin always tore it from their grasp, whether it was through the untimely death of Charley Ferguson, the upsets of the Brotherhood war, the mutiny against Stallings, or the jumping of the great stars, Lajoie, Delahanty, Flick, Bernard, Donohue and White, to the American League. Yet both the first pro ball player and the sometimes irascible Colonel severed connections with the club with heavy hearts. They had been through so much together! The National League showed some appreciation of the brave fight Reach and Rogers waged, electing them to honorary membership in the league on March 6, 1903, shortly after the club changed hands. In the league's 77-year history, only twelve men have been accorded this honor.

The fiery little Pirate owner, Barney Dreyfuss, who advanced money to the Phillies during the grueling American League fight, engineered the deal whereby Reach and Rogers sold the property to a Philadelphia syndicate headed by James Potter for $200,000. Jimmy Potter, the new president, was a Philadelphia socialite, and a prominent alumnus and former athlete of the

University of Pennsylvania. While he knew more about squash and indoor tennis than about baseball, he was sports-minded, and notwithstanding his own blue blood, Potter had countless friends among Philadelphia plebeians. He was in the brokerage business, and enlisted a number of his friends in the venture. With the baseball war over, and the Phillie property badly run down, it looked like an excellent buy for the price. Dreyfuss' machinations were further in evidence when he had one of his catchers, Charley "Chief" Zimmer, named as 1903 manager. Billy Shettsline moved back into the business office.

Chief Zimmer's reign lasted only one unhappy season. The Phillies repeated their seventh place finish of the preceding season, and suffered five more defeats than the forlorn 1902 entry. Adding to the club's bad luck was one of the worst accidents to befall an American baseball club, major or minor. On August 6, 1903, the Phillies were entertaining a fairly sizable Saturday afternoon crowd. The Quakers weren't much to look at in those days, and when a fire broke out on Fifteenth Street, across from the western boundary of the park, most of the left field bleacherites showed more interest in the fire than in the ball game. They converged on the outer rail of the balcony to be in a better position to see the fire, and with the usual crowd psychology fans from the same section moved to the balcony to be sure they would not miss anything. We already have called attention to this balcony, a carry-over from the days when the park did double duty as a bicycle track. While the balcony supports were of iron, they had rusted and were not built to withstand such concentrated pressure. There was the noise of crunching metal, followed a moment later by agonizing shrieks of horror and terror. The balcony had given way, precipitating some 500 fans into the street below. The fans in the grandstand and right and center field felt sickening feelings in the pits of their stomachs as the tragedy unfolded before their eyes, the collapsing balcony and the fans plunging out of sight.

The carnage on Fifteenth Street was terrible. Ambulances and patrol wagons from all parts of the city were rushed to the scene. Men and boys with bleeding skulls and broken legs and arms fought to disentangle themselves. Those who fell first suffered death or were badly injured as they cushioned the fall of those that came immediately after them. Broken pieces of the balcony pinned down others. When the police and hospital attendants separated arms and legs, they found 12 persons dead. Another 232 maimed were rushed to Philadelphia hospitals. It was a grim episode of a grim season.

Yet the 1903 season had a few bright spots, the return of Bill "Kid" Gleason and Pitcher Frank Sparks, and the hiring of Outfielder John Titus. Gleason, winner of 62 games for the Phillies as a pitcher in 1890-91, had shifted to second base in St. Louis in 1895 and become one of the best second sackers in the league. He next moved to Baltimore and New York, and six seasons with the rowdy Orioles and a team of Giant toughies taught him fresh tricks in aggressiveness. Gleason jumped to the Detroit Tigers in 1901, but came back to his first love, the Phillies. Tully Frank Sparks, a soft-spoken Southerner from Monroe, Louisiana, who was briefly with the Phillies in 1897, was another bullfrog during the baseball war, as he jumped back and forth to the Milwaukee A. L. club, the Giants, the Red Sox and landed with the Phillies just before the peace. Sparks was a smooth, easy worker, with good control and lots of mound savvy. Fans always liked to see him pitch; win or lose he always gave a good account of himself, and rarely was knocked out. Even with that poor 1903 team behind him, Frank had a satisfactory 11-15 record. Sparks, Fraser and Duggleby accounted for 36 of the team's 49 victories.

Titus was a native Pennsylvanian from St. Clair who could hit baseballs for surprising distances considering his comparatively small stature. John did most of his talking with his bat, as loquaciousness was not one of his faults. Both his fellow players and Philadelphia fans dubbed him Silent John. "He doesn't even make any noise when he spits," observed Kid Gleason. Unlike the boisterous Kid, who had a standing feud with all rival players and umpires, John Titus rarely disputed an umpire. He went to bat with a toothpick clenched tightly between his teeth, and wore a little straw-colored mustache. He and Monte Cross, who jumped the Phillies in 1902, were the last mustachioed warriors in the big leagues. Titus walked with his thighs close together, and Philadelphia's undecorous right field bleacherites called him "Tight Pants" or something even less flattering. But the fans grew to like and respect Silent John, who did a lot of execution from third or fourth place in the batting order. The youngster, Silent John, and the thirty-seven-year-old Kid hit practically the same that season—.286 and .284 respectively.

The Phillies hit bottom in 1904, their first tailender since the sorry season of 1883. And with the league increasing its schedule to 154 games, the team also suffered the ignominy of being the first Phillie team to lose 100 games. Hughie Duffy, the chap who holds the highest National League batting average—.438 with the 1894 Bostons—relieved Zimmer as manager, as the Chief joined the National League staff of umpires. The appointment of Hughie showed that war hatreds and bitterness already had subsided, as Duffy was one of the American League's busiest raiders in 1901 and 1902 and all but ruined the Boston National League club.

While playing on the Boston Beaneaters, Duffy, the team's center fielder, and a fellow outfielder, Tom McCarthy, were inseparable and known as the Heavenly Twins. Hughie truly must have been blessed with a heavenly disposition. Author Lieb, then a high school boy, sat in the two-bit right field bleachers during a hot summer double header with the Reds in Duffy's first season in Philadelphia. The club operated on a thin budget, and Hughie had to do his own utility outfield chores. On this occasion, he was filling in right field for injured John Titus. At intervals of every five minutes, a loud-mouthed bleacherite cupped his hands and yelled for all the park to hear: "Hughie Duffy, you are a lousy manager! Hughie Duffy, you are a lousy right fielder! Hughie Duffy, you are a louse!" The bleachers then were right next to the actual playing field, and as Duffy ran near the foul line he often was no more than ten feet from his tormentor. He would have been justified in jumping over the rail and punching this roughneck in the nose, but not once in the long afternoon did Duffy talk back, nor even take any notice of the lout's presence in the ball park.

A seventh and eighth place season convinced Jimmy Potter he didn't belong in baseball. After all, this was different from racquets. Also, there were a lot of suits as an aftermath of the August 6th tragedy of the year before. Some of Potter's friends wanted out. There was a reorganization of stockholders in which Potter withdrew as president, and Bill Shettsline, the man of many talents, was called to the presidency.

2

Something good came to Heavenly Twin Duffy in 1904, despite his tailend finish. In trying to strengthen Duffy's outfield, Billy Shettsline reached no farther than the Pennsylvania town of Clarendon to snatch an uninhibited, hard-running, strong-hitting semi-pro, Sherwood Robert Magee. Charley Dryden, then the ace baseball writer of the Philadelphia *North American*, called the youngster Sherwood Nottingham Magee, and that middle name stuck years thereafter. The boy from Clarendon wasn't quite twenty when he reported to the Philadelphia ball park and Magee was the same kind of bargain as was Lajoie eight years before, when Larry was tossed into the Geier deal. In 1903, Magee had played independent ball for Carlisle, Pennsylvania, and Allentown, and "Shetts" had to pay him little more than his train fare to bring him to Philadelphia.

Sherry Magee showed something from the day Duffy injected him into the line-up. He could get over the ground, and had a natural knack of meeting the ball. What's more, he met it with terrific power. Like Ed Delahanty before him, Magee gave one the impression of being a much bigger man physically than his five feet, ten inches and 175 pounds. Sherry was a blithesome, carefree spirit, with little respect for authority. He found training irksome and never paid much attention to it. Magee was in his share of scrapes and once, allegedly while sleepwalking, he walked through an open second-floor French window in his Philadelphia home to the ground below. And got out of it with only a few bruises. But Sherry was the type of player a manager could build a ball club around. In 1905, Magee's first complete season, he hit .299, bagged 24 doubles, 17 triples and 5 homers, scored an even 100 runs and stole 48 bases. That helped Duffy hoist the Phillies out of the cellar into fourth place with a percentage of .546 and a gain of 31 victories over the previous season. It was quite a comeback for the prostrate team of 1904, and quite a feather in Hughie Duffy's cap.

Phillie fans again found themselves with quite an outfield to get excited over. Magee was in left, Roy Thomas continued in center, and Tight Pants Titus played right. Among 100 game players, Roy ranked fourth in hitting with .317 and second in scoring with 118 runs. Silent John batted .308 and scored 99 runs. No other outfield in either major league that year could boast of scoring 317 runs.

The hard-hitting of clean-up man Sherry Magee wasn't the only factor in a one-year gain of .204 points in Phillie percentage. Shettsline and Duffy swung other shrewd deals. Perhaps the most far-reaching was a trade involving First baseman William "Kitty" Bransfield with the usually astute Pirate skipper, Barney Dreyfuss. The Phillies had a young first baseman, Del Howard, in their organization, and Barney was so anxious to get him that he not only traded Bransfield, regular first baseman on the Pirate champions of 1901-2-3, but also threw in Outfielder Harry "Moose" McCormick, and Otto Krueger, a dwarf of a utility player who filled in either the infield or outfield. Bransfield had been in a mental and physical slump in his last year in Pittsburgh, but he snapped out of it as soon as he exchanged his Pirate regalia for the Quaker toggery of Broad and Huntington. Kitty played a strong first base for the Phillies for the next six years.

Bransfield's nickname was Kitty, but there was nothing kittenish about this new Quaker. A couple of gamblers sent a message to Bransfield and Red Dooin that if the pair called on the third floor of a house on Columbia Avenue, near Broad Street, they would hear something to their advantage. It was the address of a gambling house. When Dooin and Bransfield heard the "advantageous" bit of news from the two gamblers, the catcher kicked the sure thing boys from the third floor down to the second, where Kitty took over and kicked them down another flight of stairs to the street.

Another most beneficial deal was the trading of Third baseman and team captain Harry Wolverton to Boston for Pitcher Charley Pittinger. Pittinger had a whale of a season with the 1905 Phillies and was a horse for work, winning 23 games and losing 17. Some of the ruder Phillie fans called him "Horse Face", and Horace Fogel, the Philadelphia baseball writer, once referred to him as "the horse-faced Mr. Pittinger." He received an angry letter from a girl fan, who wrote: "It was most unkind of you to write what you did about Charley Pittinger. I think he is beautiful for a man." In his next day's column, Horace commented: "A beautiful pitcher, but hardly a beautiful man."

Frank "Fiddler" Corridon, another winning right-hander, was acquired from the Cubs, and "Shetts" signed another fine pitching prospect from Philadelphia's Girard College, Johnny Lush. Lush was a good hitter, helped out at first base and the outfield, but never quite lived up to his early promise. And in July, Shettsline really had a thrilling piece of news for Philadelphia fans. The Cardinals had fired Kid Nichols as pitcher-manager, and he had been signed by the Phillies. Next to the great Cy Young, Kid Nichols was the game's greatest pitcher at the turn of the century. He had seven successive seasons in Boston in which he won over 30 games. The redoubtable Kid did his best to live up to his extravagant press notices. He won ten out of sixteen games for the Phillies in three months, but it was Nichols' last real effort, as he did a complete fadeout in 1906.

The 1905 club also came up with two new players on the left side of the infield, Third baseman Ernie Courtney and Shortstop Mickey Doolan. Courtney, an early American Leaguer in New York and Detroit, had good power at the plate but was an ordinary workman in the field. The new shortstop, Doolan, made up for any of Ernie's deficiencies as he ranged far to his right or left. Mickey Doolan was one of the outstanding shortstops in Phillie history, and as a defensive player he compared favorably with two of his great contemporaries, Hans Wagner and Joe Tinker. Doolan was tall and lanky, had a great arm, could throw standing on his head, and resembled Marty Marion, the Mr. Shortstop of four Cardinal championship teams. And, like Marion, Doolan was only a fair batsman. In nine seasons with the Phillies, his batting high was .263.

Doolan came from the mining town of Ashland, Pennsylvania, and was purchased from the Jersey City club. He studied dentistry, and during his early Phillie career practiced in the off-season. Perhaps the practice of dentistry made him so deft with his fingers and hands. His real name was Michael Joseph Doolittle, but even before coming to the Phillies he had changed it to Mike Doolan. It never would have done to have a Dooin and a Doolittle on the same team.

The trading of Harry Wolverton made Kid Gleason captain of the team. And Camden Bill took his captaincy seriously. He was a staunch and sturdy assistant for Duffy, and still proclaimed he could lick any man on the club. If he couldn't, the Kid would have felt he was a heck of a captain. As a symbol of his authority, he kept an old leather belt in his locker. He used it as a strap and if any one misbehaved, the culprit could expect the worst. It was part of his job to keep young players in line, and on several occasions the young slugger, Sherry Magee, felt the Captain's wrath.

3

Horace Fogel, Billy Weart, Jim Nasium (Edgar Wolfe) and other Phillie sports writers fed Philadelphia fans some hot copy in the spring of 1906. If the 1905 team gained 200 points in percentage, what if the 1906 club gained another 100? they speculated. Again they were talking of the Phillies as a contender, a club with a real pennant chance.

Hopeful Philadelphia fans were quite willing to believe these optimistic forecasts, and early season interest was whetted by the first visit of McGraw's New York Giants to the Phillie park. The fall before, the Giants had stove in the Athletics in the 1905 World Series and Philadelphia wished them no good. Besides, the

Giants were so cockily aware of their role of World's Champions; they strutted and swaggered, with John McGraw, their cockalorum manager, leading the strut. The Phillies that year acquired a new utility infielder, Paul Sentelle, a hot-tempered Latin from New Orleans. Ernie Courtney was hurt, and Sentelle was filling in for him at third.

McGraw, coaching in the third base box, pretending to talk to Doolan, asked, "Hey, Mike, who's that clown playing next to you? How'd he ever get into the big league?"

Taking the barb, Sentelle turned a flushed face to McGraw, and said, "So, you're the great Muggy McGraw? And if you didn't have Mathewson and McGinnity, you'd be in the bushes, where you belong."

Shortly afterwards, with a Giant runner on second, McGraw coached his batter: "Hit it down to this busher at third. He's so yellow, he won't even try to stop it. He's so yellow, it's running out of his back and staining the back of his uniform."

A moment later, Sentelle and McGraw were down on the ground, swinging, kicking and punching. Players from both benches ran to the scene of conflict, making threatening motions. Umpire Johnstone eventually separated the battlers and threw both out of the game, but Sentelle and McGraw resumed the battle under the stands.

Feeling during the game was intense, and it didn't mollify the home feelings when the Giants got away with the game. A near riot broke out after the contest. Baseball hadn't yet provided clubhouse facilities for visiting teams, and sweaty ball players left the park in uniform. The Giants, being World's Champions, disdained the horse-drawn buses used by ordinary teams. They came and went to the park in open barouches, drawn by black horses wearing big black and yellow blankets marked, NEW YORK GIANTS, WORLD'S CHAMPIONS. Some angry fans tried to pull the blankets off the horses, but one of the Giants grabbed the coachman's whip and began swinging right and left at the heads of the crowd.

A number of street venders were selling homemade lemonade on 15th Street. The fans reached into the lemonade cans for halves of lemons and shied them into the open barouches. Author Lieb, a kid in his middle teens, was one of the crowd. Roger Bresnahan, scrappy Giant catcher, was in the last barouche. Standing up in the rear, he was kicking away at the fans nearest him when he lost his balance and was precipitated into the street. Whether the Giants realized Roger had fallen into the hands of the enemy, Lieb never could fathom. The Giant caravan continued swiftly south on 15th Street, leaving the catcher to his fate. He quickly was surrounded by some 1,000 angry fans. By kicking away with his spiked shoes and swinging his fists, he fought his way into a corner grocery store and promptly slammed and barricaded the door. A half hour later he was rescued by a squad of police, but eventually Bresnahan was fined $10 for disturbing a peaceful Philadelphia Saturday afternoon.

Despite the spring's fancy optimism, the 1906 Phillies again finished fourth. Back in that fourth place groove again! For one thing, Horse Face Pittinger dropped from 23 victories to 8, and that hurt. In his third season, Sherry Magee belted the ball for .282, with an extra base bag of 36 doubles, 8 triples and 6 homers. Leading the Phillies at bat that year was a local infield rookie, Joe Ward, plucked by Shettsline off the sandlots of Manayunk. Joseph hit himself a flashy .295 for 30 games. Another newcomer, also a suburbanite, was Pitcher Lew Richie from Ambler, Pennsylvania. He was a tall string bean, with a cranelike neck, and when he was right, he was dubbed the "Ambler Beauty." Lew had a fair first year, winning nine games and losing eleven.

CHAPTER 8

Billy Murray Wanted No Secrets on His Club

1

Two fourth place finishes weren't good enough for Hughie Duffy. He moved on to Providence of the International League in 1907, and Billy Murray, manager of the Jersey City club of the same loop, took over Hughie's old quarters in the Phillie clubhouse. Unlike Duffy, William Jeremiah Murray had no background as a .438 hitter. He was strictly a manager in mufti. A native of Peabody, Massachusetts, Billy had achieved considerable success in the minors as a handler of men and developer of players. Friendly and likable, he went a long way with his Irish blarney. Though his temper flared up occasionally, he felt he could do more with players by kidding them, telling them how good they were, than by abusing them and belittling their talents. He loved to kid Sherry Magee, saying, "Now if I were a hitter like you, I'd feel awfully silly letting a deaf pitcher like Dummy Taylor make a monkey out of me."

Murray fetched along his Jersey City third baseman, Edward Lester Grant, of Franklin, Massachusetts. He was known as Harvard Eddie. Eddie was considered something of a freak in his day, a chap with a Harvard sheepskin who signed a professional baseball contract. Some felt he would have been a better player if someone had set a fire under him. There was plenty of fire around him when he came to the end of his trail in the Argonne forest, October 21, 1918, when as acting-Major Grant he lost his life while leading his battalion to the rescue of Col. Whittlesby's

"Lost Battalion." He played his last big league ball with the Giants, and a monument to his memory was erected in centerfield at the Polo Grounds in 1921.

Necessity brought about another change in the Phillie infield. Kid Gleason was approaching forty-one when he started the 1907 season in his usual second base spot. Though still youthful in spirit, his hair was gray, his face wrinkled and his joints full of creaks. When Gleason was sidelined by an early season injury, Murray inserted a chubby, fat-faced kid, Franz Otto Knabe, of Carrick, Pennsylvania, into his line-up at second base. The Kid never did get back, though he coached Knabe and taught him everything he knew. Otto was a bundle of aggressiveness, a splendid fielder and a good man at reaching base. He and Mickey Doolan soon made up one of the top double play combinations in the majors, not too far behind the famous Tinker and Evers of the Cubs. Otto was a character, too, in the same sense as was Gleason, the second baseman before him. He was vitally alive, and bubbled with fun and good-nature. Though Knabe was as German as sauerkraut, and the proper pronunciation of his name was "Ki-nob-ay", that was too fancy for the Philadelphia fans and kids, who called him Otto Nabe.

The 1907 Phillies got off to a real start at New York's Polo Grounds, and figured in one of the most fantastic opening games on record. An unusually heavy April snow had fallen the day before the game, and on the morning of the opener, John T. Brush, the New York owner, had a gang of workmen clearing the field of snow. Much of it was heaped in piles in foul territory and in the outfield. Fiddler Corridon was the Phillie pitcher and he further froze the Giants with his assortment of curves and shoots. After eight innings, the New Yorkers had only one hit, a single by Cy Seymour, and the Phillies were leading, 3 to 0.

By this time the New York crowd became bored with the show, especially the paucity of Giant hits. The winter before there had been a change in the New York civic administration, and the new Mayor, William Gaynor, issued a ukase: "No more city police in ball parks or other private places of amusement." Brush hadn't yet caught the idea and had no private cops on hand to police his plant. Instead of waiting for the end of the game, the bored fans poured out of the stands and marched across the field to the big exit gate in center field. To make it worse, some kids and oldsters made snowballs, and thought it great fun to pummel the ball players and umpires. Eventually, when one exploded around Bill Klem's ears and he had some 1,000 strangers on his ball field, he forfeited the game to Philadelphia, 9 to 0.

That was a good augury, as the 1907 Phillies moved up a notch to third place, beating out the Giants for that position in September. Philadelphia got a great boot out of their Phillies beating out the hated McGraw.

Murray might have done even better if he hadn't run into his share of bad luck. Bransfield was out with a crippling injury for half the season, but Courtney did a bang-up job as a first base replacement. And faithful Roy Thomas, still with the club, went into a season-long batting slump and eventually was replaced by Osborne, a player who had been with Murray in Jersey City. That moved Knabe up to the lead-off spot in the batting order.

Magee thrived under Murray's good-natured gibes, and with an average of .328 was runner-up to the perennial batting champion, Pittsburgh's mighty Hans Wagner. But as the Irishman from Clarendon reached top stardom he developed into quite a bully, with young players being the prize victims of his pranks. Much of his humor was cruel and far-fetched.

Pitcher Frank Sparks also had a terrific year. Sparks really flew from the Louisiana boy all season, as he hung up a 22-8 record. Corridon won 18 and lost 14. Murray unveiled a pint-sized righthander, Lew Moren, who threw a surprising fast ball for his size. He was the son of a well-to-do Pittsburgher. Reports had it that Lew's dad sent him a $50 check for every game he won. If he did, Lou collected $550 from his father's bonuses that year, as he won 11 games and lost 18.

Late in the season, Murray came up with a pair of pitchers who had tremendous possibilities, George McQuillan, a Brooklyn righthander, and Harry Coveleskie, a big southpaw from the Shamokin coal country. McQuillan, who first pitched under the name of Mack, broke in with four victories and no defeats. He had a great physique for a pitcher, strong powerful shoulders and arms, and his fast ball really danced. Covey was even bigger than McQuillan; he was one of four brothers who played professional ball, and Murray plucked him off the Kane, Pennsylvania, club of the Inter-State League.

Shortly after Coveleskie joined the club, a runner reached base on the big Pole. When Harry paid no attention to him the runner took a long lead and easily stole second. When Coveleskie returned to the bench, Murray remonstrated with him, and asked: "Why didn't you hold that runner on base?"

"I didn't know he was there," replied the naïve Harry.

After the game, Murray held a conference in the clubhouse with Coveleskie, Red Dooin and his four regular infielders.

"Kitty, did you know there was a runner on first and not tell Covey?" he demanded angrily of Bransfield.

When Bransfield pleaded guilty, he turned to Knabe and asked sharply, "Otto, is it also true that there was a runner on base, and you didn't tell Harry?" Then he fired the same question at Mickey Doolan, Eddie Grant and Red Dooin.

When they all admited they knew but "hadn't told Harry," Billy beat his fist on a table, and still feigning angry indignation, blurted: "From now on, we'll have no further secrets in this club. Whenever a runner gets to base on Harry, I want you men to tell him. Do you all understand?"

2

The 1908 club again had to be satisfied with the fourth place groove. There really wasn't room for the club any higher up, as the three top clubs, the Cubs, Giants and Pirates, finished between .643 and .636. But for Philadelphia it was a great season, as their young left-hander, Coveleskie, just recalled from Lancaster, knocked the Giants out of the pennant in the last week of the season by winning three games.

It was the year of the great National League play-off between the Cubs and Giants, when the two clubs played off the so-called

"Merkle game"—the one in which the unhappy Fred had neglected to touch second, on the day after the close of the season. The Cubs won the play-off, and the Giants finished a game behind, tied with Pittsburgh for second place.

There wouldn't have been a play-off, but for the Phillies and Coveleskie. The National League had a curious schedule that year, with the Phillies playing the Giants a solid week, September 28th, 29th and 30th in New York, and October 1st, 2nd, and 3rd in Philly. With a double header in each town, it meant eight straight games. Every fan in both towns realized the Phillies could boot the Giants out of the race. The Giants battled hard, won five of the games, but they couldn't solve the fast left-handed shoots of young Coveleskie. With the club only a few days, Harry turned back McGraw's strong contender three times in six days. He had had a strong season in Lancaster, winning 22 games, and Murray knew he was hot.

He started in September 27th with a six-hit shutout, as he defeated Otey Crandall, 7-0, giving the Phillies a split in a double header. Covey helped win this one with a triple. On October 1st, after Mathewson took the first game of a second double header from Corridon, Coveleskie won the second game from a fellow left-hander, George Wiltse, 6 to 3. This time he yielded only four hits. In the final game of the week, Harry caught up with the great Matty, going after his thirty-eighth victory, but the youngster from Shamokin triumphed, 3 to 2. Covey gave up six hits, or sixteen for the three historic games. Ever afterwards, he was known as Harry, the Giant Killer. Had the Giants won just one of these three jousts from the Killer, they would have won the flag with no need of postseason complications.

McGraw was furious at Murray. "What has Billy against me?" he demanded. "No manager in a tight race has a right to play favorites. It was a lousy trick of Murray pitching that young left-hander out of turn in his effort to beat us out of the pennant."

"In this game, you're out to win ball games," was Murray's rejoinder. "We played our best against the Giants, Cubs and Pittsburgh all season. We didn't do so well against McGraw with our more experienced pitchers. He won five of the games; what's he kicking about? When I found I had one man who could beat him, naturally I used Coveleskie as often as possible."

All Philadelphia applauded Murray in the controversy. Quaker City fans felt it somehow squared things with McGraw for the Sentelle fight of 1907, and other indignities. Actually, McGraw had no beef, and the Phillies really made it possible for New York to be a late September contender. The 1908 Quakers did exceedingly well against the great Cubs, 1907 and 1908 World's Champions, winning the year's series, 13 to 9. On the other hand, they won only 6 games, including Covey's 3 in the fall, out of 22 from the Giants.

If Coveleskie was an October sensation, the real Phillie pitching prince of that 1908 season was the chunky Brooklynite, George Washington McQuillan. Not only Philadelphia but the entire league was singing the praises of Billy Murray's George Washington. "He'll be Mathewson's successor as the No. 1 pitcher of the National League," his boosters insisted. No wonder! In George's first full season, he won 23 games and lost 17. Murray used the twenty-three-year-old youth as though he were a truck horse, pitching him in some 360 innings. Maybe he overworked the sturdy youngster, as "Mac" never had another season to approach 1908.

Coveleskie wasn't the only late-season pitching pick-up. Another was Earl Moore, an American League discard from Cleveland who won two of his three games. Billy Foxen, a little southpaw, also made his presence felt. Magee slipped this year from .328 to .283. High man among the Phillies was Kitty Bransfield, who rallied splendidly from his 1907 ills, and hit .304. In a year of scant .300 hitting, only the names of Wagner, Mike Donlin and Larry Doyle topped the dexterous Kitty. Faithful Roy Thomas was released to Pittsburgh, as Wilfred Osborne took over in center field.

All in all, the Phillies of this period were a picturesque, scrappy lot, colorful and aggressive. And lots of fun to watch: the peppery Dooin behind the plate; Doolan, with his high-pitched voice; the noisy Knabe; Silent John Titus; the smooth-fielding Bransfield; and the blustering Magee. They didn't play pink tea baseball. Doolan and Knabe could roughen you up around second base with the best of them, and everybody played baseball as though he lived it.

3

For several months in 1909, the Phillies were an adjunct of the city's Republican machine. And Philadelphia at that time was as Republican as Alabama is Democratic. The club was purchased by the Quaker City's two top political bosses, Israel W. Durham and James P. McNichol, and a banker, Clarence Wolf, from the syndicate which had bought out Reach and Rogers in 1903. Durham was elected president, and the versatile Shettsline, president for four years, was returned to his former post as business manager. Billy Murray also became a stockholder; the New Englander purchased the shares held by Barney Dreyfuss, who had received them as security for money advanced to the club during the American League war.

"Izz" Durham was quite a fan, had fond hopes for the club, and proclaimed: "We will save neither money nor effort to bring a first National League championship to Philadelphia."

Some of the papers poked fun at the political bosses in their baseball venture. One cartoon had Durham and McNichol cracking their political whips and demanding that Sherry Magee deliver 225 hits for his precinct, Mickey Doolan 600 assists for his, and young McQuillan, 30 victories. However, Durham already was a sick man when he bought into the club, and his occupancy of the presidential box at Broad and Huntington was brief. After a lingering illness, he died in Atlantic City on June 28, 1909, at the early age of fifty-two.

Everything considered, the politicians didn't have a happy season. Cincinnati managed to slip into the Phillies' "fourth place groove," as Murray's team slipped back to fifth, their first second-division finish since 1904. And Philadelphia didn't like it! The season's biggest disappointment was Harry Coveleskie, the Giant killer from Shamokin. Harry did no Giant killing, and after a mediocre 6-10 season he was traded to Cincinnati for another southpaw, Ad Brennan, who got much of his fame by punching John McGraw of the Giants on the chin. Covey also failed with the Reds, fell back to the minors but eventually reached stardom in the American League with the Detroit Tigers.

The wily McGraw had a big assist in bringing Coveleskie's Phillie career to a quick end. Smarting under Coveleskie's defeats of 1908, McGraw learned during the winter that Harry played the snare drum and an orchestra horn in the Shamokin town band; and that when he felt particularly sentimental, he played intimate ditties on his horn to his Shamokin sweetheart. So by the spring of 1909, McGraw was ready for him. With McGraw imitating a horn blower in the third base coacher's box, and the other coach playing a fake snare drum from first base, and the pair singing or humming Harry's sentimental tunes, they had the big fellow daffy, and in 1909, the Killer failed to last longer than an inning or two against New York.

McQuillan found it difficult to resist the good-time Charlies who like to bask in a star's reflected spotlight. George found night life both tempting and attractive, and early became one of Murray's most difficult discipline problems. To make matters worse, George came down with an attack of yellow jaundice and he slipped from 23-17 to 13-16. Corridon had a lame arm and Sparks was out of condition practically all season. At one stage, Earl Moore and little Lew Moren carried the staff. Two other pitchers who were doing little–Lou Richie, the Ambler boy, and Charles "Buster" Brown—–were sent to Boston for Center fielder Johnny Bates, a good hitter, base runner and lead-off man.

Sherry Magee played with marked indifference, and hit a poor .270. In fact, the politicos had Magee traded to the Giants for Mike Donlin, but it didn't jell. Donlin was a holdout, and at the time the trade was announced he was on a vaudeville tour with his talented wife, Mabel Hite. But Billy Murray wouldn't stand for it, and said, "That deal will only be made over my dead body. Magee is twenty-five, Donlin is thirty-one; so its a crazy trade." He also insisted on his rights as a stockholder, and that under the terms of his contract no deals could be made without his sanction. Much to McGraw's displeasure, the deal was called off.

CHAPTER 9

Horace Fogel's Live Wires

AFTER Israel Durham died, neither Jim McNichol nor Clarence Wolf, surviving members of the political trio, had any yen to go on with the ownership of the Phillies, and during the better part of the 1909 season there were frequent rumors that the Club again had been sold. When it did change hands on November 26th, shortly before the National League's annual meeting, the name of the new president and "owner" was a stunner for Philadelphia's baseball fans. It was Horace Fogel, the man who had been feeding Phillie fans with interesting sports copy in his columns in the Philadelphia *Item, Evening Telegraph* and *Evening Star.* Horace had a cronic dry whistle, and like most newspapermen—especially of that era—he lived from one pay day to the next. But an official announcement by the club had it that Horace Fogel had purchased a controlling interest in the Phillies for $350,000; and when Jimmy Isaminger, Billy Weart, Gordon Mackay and other erstwhile sports writing pals called at the club's offices, Horace, cigar in his mouth, already was sitting there with feet on the president's desk as a sign painter was putting new lettering on the door:

HORACE FOGEL, PRESIDENT
Private

"Where did you get that kind of money?" asked Weart.

"Who's backing you? Who put up the dough? Who is the real owner?" persisted the news hawk, Mackay.

But Fogel acted as though spending $350,000 for a ball club was as everyday a proceeding with him as buying a five-cent cigar. "I'm the real owner," he snapped back, "and I'm the guy who will run the Phillies from now on."

It later developed that the money in back of Fogel was Taft money from Cincinnati. Fogel was a pal of Charley Murphy, aggressive president of the Chicago Cubs and a former sports writer, and it was Murphy who swung the deal. Charles P. Taft was also Murphy's Chicago backer, and for some years thereafter Mrs. Taft held title to the Philadelphia ball park. Yet until Fogel later got himself into a mess of trouble, the Taft interests stayed completely in the background. And Fogel, as long as the league permitted him to remain, became Murphy's alter ego, supporting the truculent Chicagoan in everything he proposed, good or bad.

Fogel was a personality and a character. He came originally from Macungle, Pennsylvania, and in addition to his newspaper background he also had dabbled in running ball clubs. He was bench manager of the Indianapolis National League club of 1887 and managed the Giants briefly in 1902. He was the immediate predecessor of John McGraw. McGraw always ridiculed him as the manager who had tried to make a first baseman out of his ace pitcher, Christy Mathewson, saying the first thing he did on taking control of the Giants was to return Matty to pitching duty. Horace always resented such aspersions on his managerial acumen, saying he used Matty on first base because his first baseman was injured, that he had no bench and Matty was the best hitter among his pitchers.

Fogel was an early version of the Larry MacPhail-young Bill Veeck type of a colorful, dynamic club president. As a former sports writer, he believed in getting all the publicity for the Phillies he could get. And if the players couldn't provide enough, he believed in manufacturing it. The Quakers then were playing second fiddle to Mack's Athletics in the city's patronage scramble, and he intended to change that. His ideas were imaginative and novel—zany many persons considered them four decades ago—but Bill Veeck might ask today: "Why hadn't I thought of that?"

To begin with, he wanted to inject more fire into his players.

He felt they hadn't hustled enough in the past, and tried to change the club's well-known nickname, the Phillies. "The word 'Phillies' is too trite," he explained to Isaminger, Weart, and Tiny Maxwell. "It has come to mean a comfortable lackadaisicalness, the fourth place groove. And the word 'Quakers' stands for peaceful people who will dodge a fight. Well, we're not going to be that way. We're going to get into fights. Why don't you fellows call the club the Live Wires?" And come to think of it, it wasn't too far from the later-day appellation of Whizz Kids.

However, the unimaginative baseball writers, or their newspaper executives, didn't fall for it, and continued to call the club the Phillies. It wasn't Horace's fault—he did everything to win acceptance for the Live Wires. He ordered thousands of metal watch fobs decorated with the replica of an eagle with wires sparkling from it. Unable to get a real eagle from the Philadelphia zoo for his 1910 opening game ceremonies, he borrowed 100 pigeons from a pigeon-fancier, strapped free admission tickets to the legs of the birds, and sent them aloft as a band swung into the American Eagle March.

The late Jimmy Hagen, fun-loving South Philadelphia Irishman who joined the club as an office boy in 1902, was Horace's partner in crime. It was Jimmy's job to help think up ideas, and to whip Horace's ideas into adequate phrase-catching press releases. One day there was a memorandum on Jimmy's desk to get out a release on Fogel's latest brain child. He intended to have a lion cage wheeled to the pitcher's mound, and a wedding performed inside the cage. With a lion as one of the witnesses!

"But, what will Tiny Maxwell say to this, boss?" inquired Hagan.

Tiny was the 265-pound stuttering former All-American guard from Swarthmore, then sports editor of the *Evening Ledger*.

Horace replied, "He probably will say: 'Wh-what is that d-damn f-fool F-Fogel g-going to d-do next?' But, he'll print it."

During the Fogel regime, a boy baby was born in the ladies' room at Philadelphia Ball Park. "I guess we can't take all the credit for that," Horace told his faithful Hagen. "But it was a good stunt just the same. And I'm sure that kid will grow up to be a real Live Wire."

Shortly after Fogel took over the presidency he called a press conference. "We're going to be a live wire ball club, so we'll need a live wire organization from top to bottom," he said. "Billy Murray is a nice fellow; I like him, but he didn't put enough fight into the club. His contract will not be renewed. But I'm giving you boys a real live wire manager, Red Dooin. How do you like my selection?"

The boys liked it; the fans liked it. Everyone seemed to think it a natural that the scrappy redhead should be promoted to the management, and during Dooin's five years at the helm, the Phillies had some of their snappiest and most interesting teams.

The first year under Dooin saw only moderate improvement. Red's first club won four more games than Murray's last and moved back into Fourth Place Avenue, while Sherry Magee, with a .331 average, broke Hans Wagner's tenure on the batting throne and gave Philadelphia its first National batting champion since Delahanty in 1899. Sherry had quite a season, as he also led the loop in runs scored (110), whacked out 39 doubles, 17 triples and 6 homers, and stole 49 bases. It surely vindicated Murray's fight to nix the Magee-Donlin deal of the year before. Johnny Bates, the new man from Boston, was the only other Phillie .300 man.

Early in the season, Dooin had trouble in making some of his carefree charges realize that he intended to be a real boss. Pitchers Earl Moore and George McQuillan were caught in flagrant violations of the club's training rules and suspended. Moore, a big, handsome fellow, seemed to profit by the experience as he went on to enjoy his best Philadelphia season, winning 22 games and losing 15. McQuillan, however, refused to mend his ways, and in midseason Fogel clamped an indefinite suspension on his erring Brooklynite—only a few years before, the white-haired boy of the staff. Sparks burned out completely, and Foxen, after repeatedly getting his brains knocked out, was released to Chicago. Moren had a satisfactory season and George Ewing, purchased from Cincinnati, was a lifesaver with 16 victories.

Dooin was handicapped early in the season with a sore shoulder, yet in a way it proved a blessing in disguise. It enabled the club to get Pat Moran, who later was to figure prominently in the Philadelphia story. Fitchburg Pat had been Johnny Kling's catching assistant on the great Cubs, World's Champions of 1907-8, but Pat was getting along in years and in 1910, the Cubs brought up a fine catching youngster, Jimmy Archer. So Charley Murphy gave his pal Fogel a break by letting him have Moran in the emergency. Pat helped out by catching 56 games, and soon proved he was a handy man to have around. Murphy did Fogel a second good turn by releasing to the Phillies a husky young first baseman from Milwaukee, Fred Luderus, who, too, soon was to write history at the Huntington Street park.

CHAPTER 10

Aleck and Fourth of July Pennant

1

EARLY in 1911, the excited voice of Jimmy Hagen was on the phone when the Phillie office put in calls to all the Philadelphia newspapers. "Mr. Fogel wants you to send someone to the office right away," Jimmy said. "Something important!"

It really was quite a story. Fogel coughed a bit, and said, "Boys, I've just made a trade with Garry Herrmann and Clark Griffith of Cincinnati that I think will give the Phillies their first pennant. Isn't that right, Charley?" he asked of Red Dooin, also in the room. Red nodded in the affirmative and beamed.

"All right, Horace! All right! Let's have the trade," broke in impatient Gordon Mackay.

"It's no ordinary trade, Gordon," said Fogel, giving his voice dignity to emphasize the extent of the transaction. "Nothing retail; this is wholesale business. It's the biggest deal ever made by a Philadelphia club. It's four for four. We give up Third baseman Grant, Center fielder Bates and Pitchers McQuillan and Moren and in return we get their third baseman, Hans Lobert; their center fielder, Dode Paskert; and two good pitchers, Jack Rowan and Fred Beebe."

It was as big as Horace said it was, and fans, not only in Philadelphia and Cincinnati but all over the baseball world, discussed it for weeks. In Cincinnati, the deal eventually reacted against the manager, Clark Griffith, and had much to do with his severance of relations with the Reds and return to the American League. Red fans generally agreed with their Philadelphia brethren that Horace had outfoxed the Old Fox.

The most valuable players procured by the Phillies, of course, were Lobert and Paskert. The former with his bowed legs looked like a medium-sized edition of Hans Wagner. Lobert then was the National League's leading third baseman; he batted .309 in 1910 and was one of the fastest runners in the two majors. For years he held the old record for circling the bases, 13.8 seconds, made on October 9, 1910. Paskert was another antelope on the bases and a fly hawk in the outfield. No one in the game could go back farther for fly balls, and he belongs among the great center fielders of all time. Paskert hit an even .300 in his last year with the Reds. Dode and Hans supplied the Phillies with new speed: in 1910 the former stole 51 bases and the latter 41, and Lobert was in only 90 games. The newly acquired pitchers also seemed as good as the men Fogel gave up: in 1910 Rowan's Red record was 14-13 and Beebe's 12-14. All in all, a pretty cozy deal!

Fogel was right in thinking the deal might make the Phillies pennant-winners. Lobert and Paskert did all that was expected of them, but the ex-Red pitchers disappointed. Yet, when Fogel made his claim for the 1911 flag, the pitcher who almost made it possible wasn't even on his mind.

We'll revert to a scene in Fogel's office in the late summer of 1910. Patsy O'Rourke, a sort of unofficial scout for the Phillies, had just returned from a tour of the old Class B New York State League.

"See anything up there that caught your eye, Patsy?" asked Fogel.

"You bet, Mr. Fogel," replied Patsy. "A fine pitcher. One of the greatest pitching prospects I've ever looked at." He could scarcely bridle his enthusiasm.

Horace took a few puffs out of his cigar, and remarked: "Patsy, if you're talking about Chalmers, you can save your breath. We've already got him." (Pitching for Scranton, George Chalmers, a Scotch-born New Yorker, led the New York State League with a 25-6 record).

"No, I don't mean Chalmers. He's good, but the fellow I'm talking of, Alexander, is even better," said O'Rourke.

"Better than Chalmers?" said Fogel with a trace of scorn. "Every one tells me that Chalmers is the best in that league."

"Well, all I can say is that you better grab this Alexander before someone else does," concluded Patsy.

Fogel didn't think enough of O'Rourke's tip to buy the pitcher. Instead, he took the uncertain chance of grabbing him in the draft. Here Horace was in luck, and at the 1910 draft meeting the Philadelphia club was awarded Pitcher G. Alexander of the Syracuse club for $750. In that way, the Phillies procured Grover Cleveland Alexander, who must be ranked on even terms with the great Mathewson as the two top National League pitchers. Both closed their careers with 373 N. L. victories, and author Baumgartner has no hesitancy in saying Alexander is the greatest pitcher he ever saw perform. Grover still leads the league in shutouts with 90. The acquisition of Aleck for the $750 draft price must always be linked with the deal whereby Lajoie was tossed into the Geier deal as the greatest of all Phillie baseball bargains.

There is no greater indictment of the scouting departments of four decades ago than the fact that no big league club purchased this great youngster before his name was dropped into the draft mill. For Grover hadn't exactly hid his light under a bushel in Syracuse. He was right up there with Chalmers with 29 victories and 14 defeats. Reports no doubt already were in circulation that Aleck was inordinately fond of a corn by-product of his native Nebraska, and if Aleck couldn't get corn, well, he wasn't particular. He'd drink anything. Yet only in infrequent occasions—and mostly toward the end of his career—did he permit his drinking to affect his pitching. And he lasted in the big leagues until he was forty-three.

Alexander was born on a farm near St. Paul, Nebraska, on February 26, 1887, so he was twenty-four when he came to the Phillies. He didn't like farm life, and got a job as a telephone lineman, making a few extra bucks pitching semi-pro ball on Sunday. Out of that came an offer in 1909 to pitch for Galesburg in the Class D Illinois-Missouri League for $50 a month. Playing ball was more fun than stretching telephone wires, so Grover grabbed it. He was a quick success, winning 15 games and losing 8, but an early injury almost terminated his career. While he was at bat at Galesburg, he was felled by a fast ball which struck him on the side of the head. Young Grover spent quite a stretch in the hospital, and when he was released he was cross-eyed, as the errant pitch had injured an optic nerve. It was several years before time completely corrected the condition.

The Indianapolis club of the American Association drafted Alexander from Galesburg but never exercised its option, permitting him to go to Syracuse in exchange for a small baseball favor. A year before, this same Indianapolis club had sold Pitcher Rube Marquard to the New York Giants for the then top minor league price of $11,000. They had title to a much more valuable pitching asset than Marquard and let him slip through their fingers.

Alexander was six feet, one inch tall, weighed 185 pounds, and was a typical son of the Middlewest corn belt, freckled and sandy-haired. And, the Phillies, too, almost let this prize get away from them before he pitched a National League game. At the Phillies' 1911 training camp at Wilmington, North Carolina, Aleck showed a free and easy delivery and a good fast ball, but seemed rather indolent. Where other rookies sweated and panted, Grover took things much easier. He acted as though he was on a par with Moore and Rowan, with years of big league ball behind him.

Shortly before the club broke camp, Red Dooin made a list of the young players who would be let out. Alexander's name was on the list. Red showed it to Pat Moran, who was helping him with the pitchers, and when Pat's eyes reached Alexander's name, he scowled and muttered: "What's that fellow, Alexander's, name doing on that list, Charley?"

"Oh, you mean the big fellow we drafted from Syracuse," replied Dooin. "Well, Pat, I can't carry them all. We've got to get from under the expense of carrying all of these youngsters. I've got to release some of them."

"But not this one, Charley. Not Alexander!" insisted Moran.

"He's really got something. I could help him to become a real pitcher."

Moran was slated to manage the Phillies' second team on a barnstorming jaunt, while Dooin took the first stringers to Philadelphia for the then extended spring series with the Athletics. Dooin finally agreed to let Alexander accompany Moran's second team, and to delay his final judgment on Alexander until Moran rejoined the squad in Philadelphia.

When Moran returned, he was higher than ever on Alexander. "He looks better every time out," he insisted.

"All right, I'll start him against the Athletics, and see how he fares," replied Dooin.

It was the last Saturday game of the City Series, and Aleck blanked the A's, then World's Champions, during his five-inning stint. Dooin was satisfied, and recommended to Fogel that Aleck be retained. When the 1911 season was over, the kid Dooin wanted to release had won 28 games against 13 defeats and had an earned run record of 2.14. It was the greatest freshman record by any pitcher in this century.

2

The 1911 Phillies started on high. They opened at New York's Polo Grounds and held the Giants, favorites for the pennant and eventual winners, to five hits in two games. Earl Moore led off with a brilliant two-hit 2-0 job. For six innings New York's unlucky Leon Ames pitched a no-hitter against Earl, but the Phillies got to him in the closing innings. The next day Jack Rowan, the new man from Cincinnati, pitched a three-hitter while winning from Mathewson, 6 to 3. A Giant rally in the eighth inning was snuffed out when Dode Paskert made a catch which still is an epic in big league baseball. Fred Merkle hit a terrific drive to deepest right center, and in the evening twilight it didn't seem humanly possible for anyone to get near the ball, when far out by the old wooden bleachers the fans could see the ghoulish figure of Paskert make a last desperate leap and come up with the ball.

Lieb was a freshman writer in New York that spring, but he still ranks that catch among the three greatest he has seen in a 42-year baseball writing career. The old wooden stands at the Polo Grounds burned down that night, and wags among the Philadelphia writers said the conflagration was started in the bleachers by Paskert's sizzling catch.

From New York, the Phillies moved on to Boston, where Pat Moran's protégé, Alexander, lost to the Braves, 5 to 4, in his National League baptism. But Aleck posted a victory over Boston in a relief role on Patriots Day, April 19th, and Grover's glorious victory parade was on. Phillie fans tried to figure the days the tall Nebraskan would pitch; it always was a thrill to see the graceful freckled boy work. The Phillies bobbed in and out of first place throughout the first half of the season, when the race developed into a humdinger, with five clubs, the Phillies, Giants, Cubs, Pirates and Cardinals, in the running. The Phillies led at the proverbial Fourth of July halfway post, and as the Athletics also were first in the American League, Philadelphia fans were in a dither and speculating on an all-Phillie World Series. When the Phillies showed the way from July 13th to August 3rd, at one time leading by as much as five games, that dream seemed well on its way to realization. Then a combination of three of the worst breaks ever to hit a contender toppled the Phillies out of the race in August and September.

Oddly enough, all of this misfortune came in games with the Cardinals, who under the fiery ex-Giant Roger Bresnahan, were making their first bid for a first division berth since the American League war. The first casualty came as early as May 23rd, when Silent John Titus, enjoying one of his best years, broke a leg while sliding into Bresnahan at the home plate in a game at the Philadelphia park. John's right leg snapped like one of the toothpicks in his mouth. Furthermore, the slide into the bulky St. Louis catcher-manager was unnecessary, as the Phillies won the game easily, 12 to 4. The club survived this injury and continued winning with Harry Welchonce, Bill "Runt" Walsh, an infielder, and Fred Beck, picked up in a hasty deal with the Reds, in right field.

With the right fielder already lost, Sherry Magee's hot temper cost the Phillies their hard-hitting left fielder after Magee's assault on Umpire Bill Finneran at the St. Louis ball park, July 10th. It was in the heat of the race and the heat of a sultry St. Louis summer. Magee had been nervous and edgy, and the day before had been tossed out by Umpire Johnstone. Unquestionably he was suffering from a persecution complex, and when Finneran called him out on strikes on a pitch Magee always insisted wasn't even close, Magee hauled off and swung a potent right to the point of Finneran's jaw. It was a clean KO, as the umpire went down cold. National League Umpire Tom Lynch, himself a former umpire, suspended Magee for the balance of the season and fined him $200.

There is no doubt that Magee's offense was one of the most flagrant ever committed on the diamond, but Fogel and most of the Philadelphia fans and writers felt Lynch had been too severe in his punishment, especially as one regular outfielder, Titus, already was out and the club was making a brave bid for its first pennant. Billy Weart of the *Evening Telegraph* especially pitched into Tom. He demanded to know why Lynch had been so much easier on Bresnahan after Roger had attacked Umpire Bill Klem earlier in the season. He said Lynch never heard Magee's side, that Finneran had been carrying a chip on his shoulder in Philadelphia games all season, and that only two weeks before, Magee had served as a peacemaker when Finneran invited Charley Dooin under the stands for a fist fight.

The final straw and the knockout blow to the Phillies' pennant hopes came in the next series with those belligerent Cardinals when Charley Dooin suffered a broken leg, July 26th, at the Huntington Street grounds. This time Red was the victim as the St. Louis center fielder, Rebel Oakes, hit him hard in a slide to the plate. The bad news came shortly after Red was rushed to the hospital, and a bulletin read: *Mr. Dooin is seriously injured, and there is no chance that he will play ball again this season.*

With a patched-up outfield, the Phillies had remained in first place, but there was no replacement for the aggressive and talented Dooin. Pat Moran, the old catcher, might have helped, but he had a bad arm and could scarcely get the ball down to second. Two former American Leaguers, Ed "Tubby" Spencer and Tom Madden, were ineffective and batted little. In desperation, Fogel engaged Jack Kleinow, who had been Jack Chesbro's catcher on the early New York Highlanders—now the Yankees—but he was well past his prime. In the late season, the Phillies finally brought up a real catcher, Bill Killefer, who had been with the Browns in 1909-10, and spent the 1911 season with Buffalo. Killefer, unusually fast for a catcher and nicknamed Reindeer, later was to win fame as Alexander's great battery mate, but Bill then was a green kid and batted a paltry .188 in six games. The pitchers lost confidence in these lame-armed has-beens and immature catchers; the morale of the staff was shattered and the entire team sagged.

After the Dooin injury, Fogel clamored for the reinstatement of Magee, saying the Phillies had suffered enough. He enlisted some of his fellow club presidents, and Lynch commuted Magee's sentence to 36 days. But Tom was unforgiving. *This in no ways ameliorates Sherwood Magee's grievous offense against the game in which he makes a livelihood,* said Lynch's statement. *Under ordinary circumstances, he would serve every day of his deserved suspension. But, taking cognizance of the new loss suffered by the Philadelphia club in the serious injury to Manager-catcher Dooin, following the earlier injury to player Titus, I reinstate player Magee as of August 16.*

By an odd coincidence the Phillies again played the Cardinals on the date of Magee's return, and he gave the club a temporary shot in the arm as it scored a 10 to 2 victory. But Sherry's return was not enough to turn the tide. And Lynch no doubt would have jumped out of his skin had he known that his able assistant, Secretary-Treasurer John Heydler, later would appoint the troublesome Magee to the National League's umpire staff.

In addition to Alexander's 28 victories, there were a few bright spots in this unhappy season. The Scotch boy, Chalmers, didn't do as well as Aleck, but came through with a fine 13-10 record. The 41 games won by the two 1910 New York State Leaguers compensated for the almost complete flop of the two pitchers who came in the big Red deal, Rowan and Beebe. After Rowan pitched his three-hitter against Matty on the second day of the season, he won only two other games. Earl Moore also failed to follow up his early two-hitter, and failed to win half of his games, winding up with 15-19. Bill Burns, a left-hander procured from the Reds, showed lots of stuff but was unlucky, and dropped a number of close decisions. He is the same Texas Bill Burns who later figured prominently in the Black Sox scandal of 1919. The season also saw the development of Fred Luderus as the club's regular first baseman. Kitty Bransfield started the season at his old bag, but stepped down after playing 23 games. The Milwaukee Dutchman did so well in pinch-hitting and utility roles that he took over in May, and hit a strong .301 for his 145 games.

Oh yes, after all the fine promise, and the days spent in first place, the 1911 Phillies' finish saw the club in the conventional fourth spot. They blew their chances for third place to the Pirates in a barren six days in the last week of the unhappy season.

3

The bad breaks of 1911 were intensified in 1912. Believers of astrology insisted that the Phillies were under a bad sign from April to December. Or, as Jimmy Hagen's Irish grandmother would have it, "Some bad little people are sitting on their backs."

It started with Magee breaking a wrist in the spring series with the Athletics, putting him out of the first month of the regular season. Sherry was scarcely back before he was out again following an outfield collision with Dode Paskert. After that, trouble came thick and fast. Hans Lobert smashed a rib, after which his fill-in, Runt Walsh, promptly proceeded to snap an ankle. Lobert was back for a few weeks, when he sustained an even worse injury, a cracked kneecap, which incapacitated him for the balance of the season. Hans played only 62 games at third. Tom Downey, a Cincinnati importation, tried to give a hand, but his erratic play blew so many games that Fogel dispatched him to his friend Murphy, in Chicago. As a succession of young third basemen—Downey, Dodge, Boyle, Mangus, an outfielder—rattled in Lobert's shoes, Otto Knabe further complicated things for Dooin by breaking a bone in his hand.

There also was plenty of trouble in the battery department. Big Earl Moore had his pitching arm broken when hit by a batted ball, and George Chalmers, the promising New York kid, was practically useless after tearing some ligaments in his shoulder. Early in the season young Alexander was out of condition, and just as Lefthander Ad Brennan was developing into a winning pitcher, he was knocked out by diphtheria in August.

Charley Dooin had another difficult season. Handicapped in the first half by a lame arm, he later contracted an intestinal ailment which had him so weak he could scarcely lift a bat, let alone swing it. This wouldn't have been so bad if the promising young catcher, Bill Killefer, hadn't run into a succession of injuries, first a broken finger and then a broken bone in his hand. They said then, "Reindeer is a good young prospect, but he's too thin and his bones are too brittle for him ever to make a regular big league catcher." How wrong they were! Peaches Graham, former Brave and Cub, was another lame arm, and at one time the ancient Pat Moran was the only available catcher. His arm wasn't equal to the emergency, and in 13 games Patrick hit an anaemic .115. Despite all this bad luck, the Phillies were in the first division practically all season, dropping to fifth in September when the Reds nosed them out of their usual fourth niche by ten points.

Apart from the many breaks, the 1912 season had a few compensations. In midseason, faithful Silent John Titus was traded to Boston for another outfielder, Roy Miller. Titus never was the same player after breaking his leg in 1911. Miller was a "good hit, no field" type of ball player, who lost the 1911 batting championship to Wagner by one point, .334 to .333. It looked as though Fogel made a pretty slick deal, but Miller never hit anything like that again.

However, Horace brought up another outfielder, Clifford Clarence Cravath, from the Minneapolis club, and Cliff soon was to throw his weight around the Phillie ball park. A stocky tobacco-chewing Californian, Cravath didn't think too much of the names wished on him by his parents, especially the Clarence, and preferred his two nicknames of "Gavvy" and "Cactus." In Philadelphia, it was mostly Gavvy. Cravath already was thirty-one when he landed with the Phillies, and had been knocking around the better minor leagues for a decade. After five years with Los Angeles, he landed in the American League in 1907 and the next season and a half he was kicked around by the Red Sox, White Sox and Senators. In his two seasons in the American League, Cravath hit .256 and .154. That wasn't good, and despite a flock of Gavvy-propelled homers in Minneapolis, no big league club would gamble on the slugger until Fogel paid $3,500 for him.

Gavvy fell a victim to the sore arm brigade on the 1912 Phillies, but he hit .284 for 130 games and smacked eleven homers. That was high home run production for that era, and won Cravath an early reputation as a home run threat. Heine Zimmerman, the National League leader, had only three more, and twelve won Frank Baker of the neighboring Athletics the home run crown in the American. Baumgartner regards Cravath as the best hitter against a spit ball or any unusually breaking delivery that he ever saw. While Gavvy had a grim visage and usually was taciturn, he was a great practical joker and kept the Phillie clubhouse in constant turmoil with his pranks.

In Alexander's second season he dropped from 28-13 to 19-17. He was feeling the zest of youth, and having his fling. But the Phillies came up with a pair of young pitchers, righthander Tom Seaton and south-paw Eppa Rixey, who threatened to outdo Alexander and Chalmers, the crack rookies of 1911. Seaton, a tall, slim, wiry fellow, was acquired from Portland in the Pacific Coast League, while the six foot, five inch Rixey of Culpeper, Virginia, was a product of the University of Virginia. Bill Phelon, the late Cincinnati baseball writer, called him Eppa Jeptha Rixey so long that most persons thought the Jeptha was part of his name.

Like Alexander, Seaton was a prairie boy from Nebraska, and had won 24 games with the 1911 Portland Beavers. Tom was smart and cunning, could make his fast ball break like a snapping black snake whip, and he had an assortment of pitching tricks.

Even with erratic Phillie support, he clicked off 16 victories against 12 defeats in his freshman season.

From the start, Eppa Rixey was a character. He had been scouted and recommended by Cy Rigler, National League umpire. Fogel supposedly paid $2,000 to the tall Culpeper boy for signing, and Rigler expected to get a piece of it. When Rixey failed to pay Rigler, a coolness developed between the umpire and the pitcher. But it later developed that Eppa never did get the two grand. As the result of this Rigler-Rixey flare-up, the big league passed a rule prohibiting umpires from doing any further scouting as a side line. Though Rixey never had pitched a pro game until he joined the Phillies, he broke even in 20 games after his June graduation.

4

Bad luck to his ball players, in the way of broken legs, hands and arms, was to prove the lesser part of Horace Fogel's ill fortune in 1912. It had been a nerve-straining season for Horace. As remarked before, he belonged to the drinking type of sports writer so common in his day. As one mishap after another wrecked his fine team, it was not unnatural that he should seek comfort from his friends among the Philadelphia barkeeps. But after Horace had a few under his belt he popped off, and much of his conversation was unwise.

In the Giants' quest for a second straight pennant, McGraw's team had gotten off to a big early lead, but the Cubs put on a spirited late season drive and at one time almost caught the New Yorkers. And though the Phillies were out of the race, Horace's sympathies were all with his pal Murphy's Cubs in their battles with McGraw's hated Giants. At a time when the Cubs were trying to close the final gap, Fogel made some wild charges; (1) that the 1912 National League race was "crooked"; (2) that league president Lynch's umpires unduly favored the Giants; and (3) that Roger Bresnahan, St. Louis manager and former Giant catcher, played his weakest line-up against his former New York mates.

Fogel's bitterness against the umpires stemmed from the Finneran-Magee incident of the year before, and his feeling against Bresnahan was enhanced by the fact that both Titus and Dooin broke their legs in plate crashes in Cardinal games. Perhaps the writers of that day were to blame for printing Fogel's rash words in their full literal sense. As a former good fellow of the press boxes, he was well acquainted with the top writers of Chicago, Charley Dryden, Hugh Fullerton, Ring Lardner and Cy Sanborn; and the New York crowd, Sam Crane, Boze Bulger, Damon Runyon, Sid Mercer, Bill Hanna and others. But he was now popping off as the president of a National League club—not as a baseball writer; and as the Giants and Cubs were in a red-hot race, his remarks were a real story, and made some hot controversial copy in Philadelphia, New York and Chicago.

Following the league season, President Tom Lynch filed serious charges against the president of his Philadelphia club. And Horace's early efforts to laugh them off were of no avail, as the league, in executive session, voted that Fogel be formally tried by the seven other club presidents. The club owners sat as a court at New York's old downtown Waldorf-Astoria, with Julius Fleischmann, a former Cincinnati mayor and a minority stockholder in the Reds, as the presiding judge. Fogel was found guilty of five of the seven charges that Lynch brought against him, and he was "barred forever from the councils of the National League."

It was a sad end for the president of the Live Wires. He did a little sports writing after that, ran unsuccessfully for Congress from a Philadelphia district before the city started the practice of electing any Democratic Congressmen, and died an unhappy man on November 15, 1928.

CHAPTER 11

Start of a New Era

⚾ 1 ⚾

FOLLOWING the expulsion of Horace Fogel, Albert D. Wiler became a stopgap president of the Phillies. The Cincinnati interests that backed Fogel had their fill and wanted "out," and as speedily as possible. It gave William H. Locke, popular secretary of the Pirates, an opportunity to realize his ambition to become a major league club owner. Helped by Barney Dreyfuss, who always seemed to have his finger in the Philadelphia pie, Will got up a syndicate to buy the franchise and on January 15, 1913, he took over and was elected president. In rounding out investors, Locke went to his New York cousin, William F. Baker, a former New York Police Commissioner, and Baker subscribed to a sizable block of stock. His investment was second only to that of Locke.

Locke took over under the most favorable conditions. To begin with, he was taking over a fine ball club, despite the 1912 fifth place finish. It was a well-balanced team, with such tried veterans as Dooin, Magee, Lobert, Doolan, Knabe, Paskert, a new home run threat in Cravath, such coming youngsters as Luderus and Killefer, and four fine young pitchers in Alexander, Seaton, Chalmers and Rixey.

Will was well liked and had many friends in both major leagues. In Pittsburgh, where he had been Dreyfuss' right-hand man, he had built up a reputation as an astute baseball man. Everywhere in baseball, people were saying: "Will is a great guy, and deserving of the best. Philadelphia is lucky to have him."

Philadelphia felt the same way. After such neophyte presidents as Potter, Durham and Fogel, it felt good to have a practical baseball man heading the club. "Locke has a lot of baseball savvy; he has lots of connections, and may be just the man to bring to Philadelphia its first National League pennant," wrote Billy Weart.

Locke worked hard, day and night. There still was some stock scattered around Philadelphia from the old Potter syndicate. He tried to bring it in, necessitating much detail. He tried to improve the physical property and held daily conferences with Manager Dooin on means of strengthening the team. Then his health failed, and on July 15, 1913, the man who was expected to lead the Phillies out of the wilderness to the land of milk and honey was dead.

The death of Locke so soon after acquiring the club was to have repercussions on the Phillies for three decades. For the man who succeeded Locke to the presidency was his New York cousin, William F. Baker, the former head of New York's "finest." It was some time before Baker became a Philadelphian, and for years he commuted from his New York home to his Phillie baseball office. Under his long leadership the Phillies were to have several brilliant years, and then plunge to the depths.

Under the first year of the Locke-Baker ownership, the Phillies ran a good second to the three-time champion Giants. During a greater part of Locke's remaining lifetime, Will had the satisfaction of seeing his club in first place, as the Phillies led during most of April, and continuously from May 4th to June 30th. From then on, they held the runner-up position. The Phillies played interesting, hustling baseball, and even though the new management jacked up admission prices and almost eliminated the old two-bit bleachers, the club had one of its most successful financial seasons.

Much of the success of the club was due to the emergence of Tom Seaton into one of the ace pitchers of the game. There was no "second-year jinx" for Tom, as he hung up a magnificent record of 27 victories against 12 defeats. And, better still, all season long he knocked over the Giants. As Alexander followed with a 22-8 third-year showing, it was quite a season for old Nebraska, as the two Cornhuskers fetched in 49 of the club's 88 victories. Lefty Ad Brennan became the third ranking pitcher, and a young Jewish hurler from Atlanta, Erskine Mayer, plucked in a lucky draft from the Portsmouth, Virginia club, showed big league stuff from the start and broke even in 18 games. Long Rixey also chipped in with nine wins, and the loss of the pennant was blamed on the failure of Pitchers Moore and Chalmers. Big Earl flopped entirely, and Chalmers, still suffering from his wrenched shoulder, could do no better than three wins against ten defeats.

What's more, the Phillies blossomed out as the home run boys of the two major leagues. Home runs still were a novelty, and Dooin's men made history by pounding out 73 of them. That was an awe-inspiring total 40 years ago. The world's Champion Athletics, with their home run specialist, Frank Baker, led the American League with a more modest 33. Cravath, Luderus and Magee were responsible for this fabulous figure. Gavvy led the National League with 19, one more than young Luderus' total. Magee followed with 11. Five of the big league clubs had fewer homers than Cravath, and a sixth, Washington, matched Gavvy's mighty 19. Cravath did more than star in the home run department, as he was batting runner-up to Jake Daubert with .341, and also knocked out 34 doubles and 14 triples. "I guess that was another one of my blunders, buying old thirty-one-year-old Cravath," said Horace Fogel with bitter irony.

Hans Lobert came back nicely from his 1912 battle wounds, played 150 games, hit an even .300, and his legs were sufficiently nimble for him to steal 41 bases. A useful outfielder, Beals Becker, was acquired from Cincinnati, though Beals had played most of his ball for McGraw in New York.

Writers with other clubs constantly were poking fun at the

Philadelphia home run crop, and blaming it on the small Philadelphia ball park. This especially was true of the New Yorkers. Sid Mercer of the New York *Globe,* later of the *Journal,* never came to Philadelphia without belittling what he termed "the Philadelphia cigar box." "It's not surprising that the Phillies hit 73 home runs," he wrote. "The wonder is that they don't hit 100."

"Go get yourself a tape measure, Sid, and measure the distance at the Polo Grounds to the right field fence," shot back Billy Weart. "The Giants should be ashamed of their scant 31 homers in their own cigar box."

Nevertheless, the Philadelphia National park, once the show place of the National League, had become antiquated and suffered much when contrasted with the newer parks built from 1909 to 1913; Shibe Park; Forbes Field, Pittsburgh; the Polo Grounds, New York; Comiskey Park, Chicago; Ebbets Field, Brooklyn; and League Park, Cleveland.

The field eventually came to be known as Baker Bowl, a term used at first more or less in derision. In the era before the cork-centered ball became standard in 1911, the field was fairly adequate and outfielders had some opportunity for maneuverability. Following the 1903 accident, the balconies around the field were removed. New wooden bleachers were built in left field, and a towering 50-foot tin plate was erected where the right field galleries used to be. The left field bleachers were a respectable 341 feet from the home plate, but the distance from home plate to the right field fence at the foul line was only 280 feet. Magee and Paskert had some chance to roam in left and center fields, but Silent John Titus, Cravath and the right fielders who followed, played with their backs to the right field fence. Time after time, Phillie pitchers would see pop flies bounce off the fence for cheap hits, while the right fielder would try to play the bounce so as to hold the hit to a single. By using a shoehorn, some 18,000 could be squeezed into the park.

In a late season Saturday afternoon game with the Giants, the New Yorkers claimed some of the center fielder field bleacherites flashed mirrors into their faces when they were at bat. After Umpire Brennan requested Dooin to do something about it, he walked out to the bleachers and asked the boys to behave. But when the Giants again came up to bat, the mirrors reappeared, and Brennan, an umpire with a supposed Giant bias, forfeited the game to New York, 9 to 0. As there was a capacity crowd on hand, it raised quite a commotion. President Lynch supported his umpire, but Baker appealed to the board of directors and won a reversal. The game was ordered completed from the point where Brennan declared his forfeit the next time New York visited Philadelphia. This was done, but the Giants won the interrupted game. The Phillies' losing their New York series, 8 to 14, had much to do with the loss of the 1913 pennant.

2

In both 1889 and 1900, when the Phillies had built up strong pennant contenders, their splendid teams were broken up by baseball wars, first the Brotherhood strife and then the American League invasion. History repeated itself in 1914, when Federal League raids changed the hustling 1913 runner-up into a spiritless sixth place aggregation. The Federals got away with the Phillies' crack second base pair of Shortstop Mickey Doolan and Second sacker Otto Knabe; two of the team's crack pitchers, Tom Seaton and Ad Brennan; and Runt Walsh, the infield-outfield handy man. Knabe, Doolan, Seaton and Walsh jumped to the Baltimore Feds, and Brennan to the Chicago Whales. Knabe later managed the Baltimore outfit.

William Baker's parsimony in dealing with ball players, which later was to become notorious, first showed itself in his failure to make more of a fight to retain these valuable players. After Seaton led the National League in 1913 victories with 27, two more than the total of the great Mathewson, Tom naturally expected a substantial raise. Baker granted a modest one, and when the Feds doubled Baker's offer, Tom snatched it, and the Phillies lost a great young hurler. Doolan was on the

McGraw-Comiskey 'Round the World trip of the winter of 1913-14. When the players landed in New York, Federal League agents were at the dock with great rolls of bills in their hands, but they landed only two of the tourists, Doolan and Outfielder Steve Evans of the Cardinals. By matching the Federal offers, which in many cases meant double the 1913 salaries, other club owners held such stars among the tourists as Tris Speaker, Sam Crawford, Larry Doyle, Buck Weaver and Fred Merkle. In justice to Baker, he did manage to go high enough to save Hans Lobert, third baseman for McGraw's globe trotters, for his team.

The effects of losing such valuable infield workers as Knabe and Doolan may well be appreciated. It left a hole through the middle of the Phillie infield as wide as Broad Street. Tom, Dick and Harry, and most everyone else, took a fling at the positions. Even Sherwood Magee took a shot at shortstop, playing 39 games at Doolan's old spot. A kid from Atlanta, Milt Reed, played 22, and Jack Martin, a pick-up from the Braves, 83. Bobbie Byrne, the former Pirate third baseman, took care of 101 games at second, and a rookie with the strange name of Hal "Grump" Irelan, played in another 44. Even so, the Phillies retained the home run leadership of the two majors with a reduced total of 62, while Gavvy Cravath again was high man on the totem pole with 19. A pleasant feature of a poor season was the hitting of the Giant cast-off, Beals Becker, who was runner-up to the Brooklyn batting champ, Jake Daubert. Another was the development of Bill Killefer into one of the ace catchers of the league.

In 1913, Seaton and Brennan accounted for 41 victories. That was an awful lot of games for someone to try to make up. Alexander and young Mayer did nobly in their efforts to keep the club's head above water. Aleck won 27 games and lost 15 and Mayer won 21 and lost 19. But the rest of the staff was terrible, as Eppa Rixey, a third holdover, won only two and lost 11. A whole raft of young pitchers were brought in by the club's diligent scout, "Cap" Neale, to make up for the loss of Seaton and Brennan, and that's where Stan Baumgartner came on the scene. He had been a winning southpaw hurler with the University of Chicago and "Cap" grabbed him right after his June graduation. Stan's fellow pitching rookies were Ben Tincup, a Cherokee Indian; Joe Oeschger, also a collegian from California's St. Mary's; Henry Matteson and Roy Marshall. The latter had the best record of the newcomers, 6-7, and jumped to the Federal League in 1915. Oeschger later was to win pitching immortality when as a member of the Boston Braves he pitched the full 26 innings against Leon Cadore in the historic 1920 1-1 tie game with Brooklyn, the longest major league game.

3

It was on a hot day in June that Stan Baumgartner first walked into the old clubhouse at Broad and Lehigh, wearing a blazer and a straw hat. It was above the old center field bleachers at the extreme north east corner of the field. There was a pool table in the outer room, a few old balls and a couple of cracked cues. The boys played pool occasionally, but the table was used mostly for poker and crap games. On the floor below was a dry swimming pool, a carryover from the glorious days when the Phillie park was the showplace of baseball. Delahanty, Sam Thompson and Lajoie all had dunked themselves in it. So far as is known, the old Phillies were the only ball club ever to have their private swimming pool.

Baumgartner was given a locker in the outer room, where most of the new pitchers and infielders changed their clothes. The place was crowded with players getting out of their street attire into their uniforms. There were cuspidors in front of several of the lockers, and though the kid from Chicago U. attracted little attention, he had to step lively to keep from being sprayed with tobacco juice. A strong smell of liniment from the rubbing table permeated the atmosphere. Stan dressed as casually as he could, noting how the older players rolled their stockings and fixed their trousers.

He heard one big fellow call out from a corner of the room:

"Somebody give me a chaw of tobacco!" He recognized him as the great home run hitter, Gavvy Cravath. He made out another freckle-faced guy to be Grover Alexander, and recognized other faces because as a boy he had seem them on cigarette cards.

As Baumgartner headed for the field, another young player caught up with him and asked: "Got a place to live?"

"No, just got in, and reported right to the club," was the rejoinder.

"Well, come over with Rix [Rixey] and I," the good Samaritan said. "We've got lodgins on 17th Street, just a few blocks away, and we'll be glad to have you throw in your lot with us. It's a clean place, and they give us good food, and it's only six bucks a week."

The offer was quickly snatched up. The solicitous young player was Joe Oeschger. The players called him Bareback Joe, because he never wore an undershirt. Oeschger, Rixey and Baumgartner palled around for the rest of the season, and the other players dubbed them—not with too much respect—"those college boys."

Red Dooin didn't let the Chicago "college boy" twiddle his thumbs. "Hey you; pitch batting practice," he told Stan as soon as he reached the field. And he meant pitch. Stan figures Dooin kept him in there for an hour, and that he lost ten pounds during the operation. He was so tired that when he returned to the field after changing his shirt, he fell asleep in the outfield.

Baumgartner appeared in 15 games in 1914, and his record was two victories and two defeats. He still recalls his first complete game—a shutout over the Giants—as one of the outstanding gems of his playing career. But he gives major credit for it to his talented catcher, Bill Killefer. The young Chicago collegian walked seven men, and Killefer threw out each of the seven trying to steal.

While sports writers called Killefer "Reindeer," his fellow ball players called him "Paw Paw Bill," or just "Paw Paw." He came from Paw Paw, Michigan. In Baumgartner's book Killefer still is baseball's greatest receiver. He is the only catcher he ever knew who invariably, and by instinct, thought opposite to the batter. If the batter expected a curve, Killefer's signal to his pitcher called for a fast ball and vice versa. He still says with much gusto that pitching to Killefer was like "rolling out of bed on a foam mattress."

The flop from second to sixth in one season was bad for the club's morale and for Dooin's nerves. Dooin was put out of the game every other day because of his constant arguments and bickerings with the umpires. And Stan quickly learned that the Phillies were not one happy family. There were constant arguments and no end of fights. We've told before of how Sherry Magee liked to bully the young players. He tried it on a wrong customer in Milt Reed, the quick-tempered young Georgian who tried for a spell to make the fans forget Mickey Doolan. Reed challenged the star one day, and was so quick with his hand and foot work that he draped the great Magee over the clubhouse pool table.

Even worse was the feud between Magee and Dode Paskert. The story frequently has been printed that Johnny Evers and Joe Tinker, member of the great Cub infield, once didn't speak off the field for two years. Well, a somewhat similar affection existed between the Phillie left and center fielders. And, to make it worse, the wives and families got into the battles. One afternoon Dode Paskert hit a home run into the left field bleachers, and as he rounded third base Magee's two boys booed so loud you could hear it on the bench. And as soon as Dode reached the bench, he and Magee began throwing fists at each other.

Rixey, the boy from Culpeper, Virginia, was the butt of much ribbing. With his southern drawl, he made a perfect foil for anything that had to do with the Civil War. Bill Killefer and Eddie Burns, another young catcher, always were singing "Marching through Georgia" when they were in Rix's vicinity. On one occasion they got a drum, dressed up a few of the younger players in tattered suits, gave them broomsticks, and paraded them around the clubhouse and onto the field, all of them singing or humming the Sherman marching song. Eppa always answered in true rebel fashion, tossing gloves, buckets, anything he could lay his hands on, and he was really angry. His face flushed, the cords stuck out on his neck, and he would cuss 'em out in southern style. "Dam Yankees" was the mildest of his uncomplimentary references to northerners in general. Dooin, however, seemed to sense that he was through as manager and no one made any attempt to enforce discipline.

In Cincinnati one afternoon the "Three Collegians," all of them camera hounds, gathered several of the players in front of the old Metropole Hotel for a picture. Rixey was in front taking the snap when Sherry Magee stepped out on the fire escape on the sixth floor and dropped a paper laundry bag filled with water. The bag hit Eppa Jeptha squarely on the head, drove the brim of his hat over his shoulder, and doused him from head to foot. Rixey again was furious. He dropped his camera as though it were a hot potato, ran into the hotel and jumped into an elevator. He ordered the operator: "Don't you be waiting for no one else. You take me right up to the sixth floor, and as fast as this damn thing can go."

But, by the time he arrived at the sixth floor, Magee was nowhere to be found. Had the powerful six-foot, five-inch Rixey caught up with Magee in that frame of mind, he would have dropped him from the sixth floor. It may be that this constant baiting of the tall Virginian had much to do with his 2-11 1914 showing.

In the fall of that year, Baker gave a dinner. Even in the lean years that came later, Baker always was giving dinners to make his announcements. All the sports writers and players living in the Philadelphia vicinity were invited. It was hinted the former New York Police Commissioner would have something important to say. He did.

"We're going to have a change in manager," Baker said. "I don't blame Charley Dooin for everything that happened last season. Losing Doolan, Knabe, Seaton and Brennan were stunning blows. But Charley lost control of the team, and I think a change is advisable—and necessary. We didn't go very far in looking for a successor. I found him right in the ball club in Coach Pat Moran. I've watched Pat and like the way he goes about his work. He knows a lot of baseball, and gentlemen, I think he'll make us a fine manager."

That proved to be quite an understatement.

CHAPTER 12

Phillies Finally Make It

⚾ 1 ⚾

PAT MORAN was not only a fine manager; the Fitchburg Irishman was a great one. The next three years, under Moran's management, were to prove the best in the history of the Phillies. Pat liked his nip, was red faced, and rival players called him "Whiskey Face." But he proved a genius at running a ball club, both in directing strategy and getting the most out of his players. He was wise, sagacious, with just enough of the Irish psychic in him to give him good hunches and enable him to look through people. No phony ever got anywhere with Pat Moran.

Baker and Pat put their heads together shortly after Moran's appointment, to consider trades that might help the club; and they came up with two dandies, which meant as much to the club as Fogel's "Four for four" deal with Cincinnati four years before. Baker defied a strong contingent of Sherwood Magee fans by trading their pride to Boston for George "Possum" Whitted, center fielder of the 1914 Brave World's Champions, and Oscar Dugey, the Boston utility infielder.

Oddly enough, Whitted, assigned to left field, outhit Magee in 1915 by one point— .281 to .280. Possum, a funmaker and prankster, was one of Stan Baumgartner's favorites. He did not have the natural ability of some of the other stars on the club, but he was fast and how he hustled! In his own way, he was a National League version of Ty Cobb. George would kill you for a run, or dive into a stone wall to make a catch. He hustled from the moment he got on the ball field until he left.

An even more valuable deal than the Magee-Whitted-Dugey swap was made with McGraw of the Giants. For a long time McGraw had his eye on Hans Lobert, and Baker let him have the crack third baseman in exchange for Milton Stock, young third baseman of the Giants, Pitcher Al "Steamer" Demaree, and a young catcher, Jack Adams. This deal exploded in McGraw's face before the 1915 season got under way, as Lobert again cracked open his knee in an exhibition game in West Point, an injury which practically ended John's playing career.

Bobbie Byrne, the ex-Pirate, played two-thirds of the 1915 season at third base, but Moran shifted to young Stock in August and young Milt came along rapidly in the closing weeks of the race. He was a fine fielder, fast as a flash and a superb base runner. The Phillies called him "Handle Hit" because so many Stock hits rippled off the handle of his bat. Stock, now coach for the Pirates, is the father-in-law of the Philadelphia-born Eddie Stanky, manager of the Cardinals. As for Al Demaree, he won 14 games and lost 11 that season, but six of his victories were at the expense of his late Giant comrades. Demaree was a sports cartoonist when not busy as a pitcher.

A third deal was dictated by necessity on both sides, and it also worked all to the advantage of the Phillies. After Moran's elevation to the management, it was felt it would be embarrassing for Red Dooin to serve under his former coach as a private. Cincinnati, at the same time, had a disgruntled third baseman in Bert Niehoff. He didn't click with his manager, Buck Herzog, and threatened to jump to the Federal League. So, Dooin was returned to his former home town team, Cincinnati, in exchange for Niehoff, who became the Phillies' regular second baseman. Bert was a phlegmatic Dutchman who didn't hit too much in the averages, but was a great hit and run man with an uncanny ability to hit the right field wall on hit and run plays that gave the Phillies many scoring chances and victories.

Old "Cap" Neale did another superb job in digging up a re-

Robin Roberts, the Phillies' pitching sensation who won 28 games in 1952.

The Sporting News.

Alfred J. Reach, first president of the Phillies.

The Sporting News.

Ed Delahanty, one of the great sluggers of baseball.

The Sporting News.

Sherry Magee.

The great Napoleon "Nap" Lajoie.

The Sporting News.

Charles "Red" Dooin.

The Sporting News.

Otto Knabe.

The Sporting News.

The great Phillies team of 1899. Top row—McFarland, Abbotichio, Lajoie, Orth, Donahue, Cooley, Lauder. Middle row—Cross, Tifield, Delahanty, Manager Billy Shettsline, Pratt, Douglass, Murphy. Bottom row—Douggleby, Flick, Murphy, Con.

Baker Field as it appeared to an artist in 1887.

Pat Moran.

The Sporting News.

A snapshot of the great Grover Cleveland Alexander taken by Author Baumgartner in 1914.

Training camp hi jinks. In the usual order, Mattison, Bancroft, Niehoff, Rixey and Stan Baumgartner.

More of the same with Mattison, Bancroft, Niehoff with Stan Baumgartner astride Oeschger.

Three great Phillies stars—Casey Stengel, Gavvy Cravath and Fred Luderus.

The Sporting News.

Erskine Mayer.

The Sporting News.

Dave Bancroft.

The Sporting News.

Bill Killefer.

The Sporting News.

Dode Paskert.

The Sporting News.

John Rawlings.

The Sporting News.

Owner William F. Baker.

The Sporting News.

Irish Meusel.

The Sporting News.

Chuck Klein.

The Sporting News.

Lefty O'Doul.

The Sporting News.

Art Fletcher.

The Sporting News.

Kirby Higbe.

The Sporting News.

Claude Passeau.

The Sporting News.

Dolph Camilli.

The Sporting News.

1950 Champions (left to right). Front row—Jimmy Bloodworth, Blix Donnelly, Richie Ashburn, Ralph Caballero, Bennie Bengough, coach; Eddie Sawyer, manager; Cy Perkins, coach; Dusty Cooke, coach; Del Ennis, Dick Sisler, Willie Jones. Middle row—Frank Wiechec, trainer; Bubba Church, Bob Miller, Ken Heintzelman, Ken Silvestri, Stan Lopata, Stan Hollmig, Robin Roberts, Dick Whitman, Russ Meyer, Granville Hamner, Jocko Thompson, Frank Powell, traveling secretary. Back row—Bill Nicholson, Ken Johnson, Steve Ridzik, Eddie Waitkus, Milo Candine, Jack Mayo, Jim Konstanty, Andy Seminick, Mike Goliat, Jack Brittin, Paul Stuffel, Maje McDonnell, batting practice pitcher; Curt Simmons. Batboy Kenny Bush in front.

The Sporting News.

Del Ennis.

Curt Simmons.

Richie Ashburn.

Owner Bob Carpenter.

Eddie Sawyer.

Steve O'Neill.

placement for Mickey Doolan, the 1914 shortstop jumper. "Cap" journeyed out to the Pacific Coast League and got stuck on a young shortstop, Dave Bencroft, playing for the Portland club. Others tried to tell Neale that Bancroft wouldn't hit big league pitching, and tried to get him to take Roy Corhan, the San Francisco shortstop who had been up with the White Sox and was a much superior Coast League batsman. But after following both men, Neale recommended to Baker that he buy Bancroft. It was a happy choice, as Bancroft, nicknamed "Beauty" Bancroft because of his beautiful infielding, was a star almost from the day he joined the Phillies and became one of the all-time great shortstops of the National League. "Banny" was full of fire—snappy, vitriolic, a needler, who kept the entire club on its toes. He had a fine pair of hands, a great arm and despite his mediocre minor league batting averages he developed into one of the best switch hitters in the game. He could go behind second to field balls or into what ball players call "the hole" with equal facility.

2

During the winter, author Baumgartner went back to the University of Chicago to finish and enter law school. He didn't expect to report back to the Phillies until June, but the baseball bug bit him and he was at St. Petersburg, Florida, when the club reported in the middle of March. From the first day in training it was evident that Moran was going to run things differently. He was boss every minute of the day and night, a stickler for detail. And Baumgartner adds: "I also can say that Pat was the smartest manager I ever played for—or observed in action—in my 39 years in baseball."

The Phillies were only the second team to train in St. Petersburg, when the town was little more than an overgrown fishing village. The Browns had trained there in 1914, but Al Lang, the town's mayor and a native Pennsylvanian, induced Baker to bring his team there in 1915. Al did not permit the dignity of his office to prevent his serving with Billy Shettsline, Phillie business manager, as the official foul ball retrievers. Frequently they would wrestle kids for baseballs fouled over the stands. Ball clubs in 1915 were not million-dollar businesses.

The team practiced at what was the old Coffee Pot Park, well removed from the downtown business section and some three miles from the official headquarters, the Fifth Avenue hotel. It now is an exclusive residential district. It was a picturesque spot—different from the settings at present-day training fields. It was on a bayou, surrounded by orange groves and tall pines. The wooden grandstand didn't hold more than 500 and the dressing accommodations consisted of one cold water shower. Some of the boys brought along their fishing poles and fished in the bayou between practices.

Moran ordered the players to walk the two to three miles each way—to and from the park. Joe Oeschger and Baumgartner thought they'd do it an easier way. They hired bicycles, rode them into the woods and then walked the rest of the way to the park. That went well for about a week, when Moran found out about it and added an extra mile to the daily hikes of the two culprits.

Pat held morning and afternoon practices, and the hotel sent out the lunch. And what lunches! Fried fish with the heads still on. If the players wanted oranges, they went into the adjoining groves and helped themselves. To put it mildly, the meals were terrible, even for that period. Occasionally the diet changed, and one day it changed to roast beef. Alexander took the roast beef out of his sandwich and nailed it to his shoe as a sole. For the most part the fish in Coffee Pot Bayou got the food. Quite a change from the specially prepared sandwiches, bottles of milk, etc., which the Phillies send out to their present-day training field at Clearwater, Florida!

The first thing Moran did at the camp was to give the pitchers and catchers combination signs. In those days sign stealing was a big part of baseball, and teams would go to any lengths to get a man to second base so that the base runner could watch the rival catcher's sign and tip off the batter. Frequently managers didn't use much imagination. Usually one finger meant a fast ball, two a curve and the thumb a change of pace.

Moran determined to end all this and worked out a system of three sets of signs. The catcher then would indicate which sign the pitcher was to take. Moran had the signs so rigged up that the catcher could change from the first to the second or third without going to the box to talk it over with the pitcher. The team practiced this business hour after hour with the catcher sitting on the fence giving the sign and the pitcher translating it. Once learned, these signs never were forgotten.

Pat also was the most thorough man then in baseball in drilling his team in all the plays that make up the average game—cutoffs, pickoffs, breaking up the double steal, throwing men out at second and third on bunts, pitchers covering first and backing up bases. From the first practice game the entire club also was schooled in picking signs of the opposing club, studying pitchers to detect their mannerisms or individual manner of holding a ball which would indicate whether it was going to be a curve or a fast ball. During spring training, and also later in the season, he would assign one or two men who were not playing, to study the pitcher. At the end of the third or fourth inning he would ask questions, whether the pitcher threw his curve with his fingers closed or open, how he held his fast ball, etc. And if you didn't know or didn't have an answer, it was just too bad.

He assigned Eppa Rixey to watch the opposing pitcher one afternoon. Eppa began cutting up on the bench. Moran apparently paid no heed until about the fourth inning. Then he walked over, picked up a fungo stick and hit Rixey sharply across the toes. There was a job for everyone in Moran's thorough system of doing things. Young pitchers as well as old were expected to be able to pick opposing batters' hit and run signs. Extra catchers were told to study the signs put on by enemy coaches.

Moran's greatest success, however. was in his teaching and handling of pitchers. It was responsible for his outstanding success in Philadelphia and later in Cincinnati. He had a black book in which he kept a record not only of his own pitchers, but of all opposing pitchers. He had down not only how they pitched to his own men, but any weakness they might have in fielding, and how they reacted under heat, under riding, under patting on the back.

In batting practice he always stood behind the pitcher, wearing his big catcher's mitt and tending to the ball bag. With the youngsters, he would go through every pitch. He'd say: "Now, what are you going to pitch? The count is one-one, and a runner is on first base."

The pitcher who did not have the answer ready would get a sharp dressing down. He expected the young hurler to say: "It is a good spot for a hit and run, so I'd better pitch inside."

Again he might remark: "Man on second now; two strikes and none out. Make him hit into the dirt toward third base. What are you going to throw now?"

In 30 minutes on the mound the youngster, with Moran giving advice, asking questions and directing defensive strategy, would pitch a full game. He also kept after the older men, even Alexander, talking over hitters as Alex worked in batting practice. Even the No. 1 star had to be kept sharp.

Despite all the seriousness, there was a lot of fun, relaxation and comedy at that first Phillie camp in St. Petersburg. Two of the players became involved in romantic episodes that forced them to take to the woods for a week and it needed all the diplomatic maneuvers of Mayor Al Lang to square things. However, a few years later, when the Yankees trained in St. Petersburg, one of the ladies in question—a sturdy Irish waitress—hung a beautiful shiner on the late Izzy Kaplan, New York *Mirror* photographer. So, she either could protect herself in the clinches, or learned from her Philadelphia experience.

Rixey, Bareback Joe Oeschger, Ben Tincup and Baumgartner took a boat ride one day from St. Petersburg to Pass-a-Grille, now connected to the mainland by a causeway. The boat got stuck on a sand bar, and the four pitchers did not reach the Fifth Avenue Hotel until eight o'clock the next morning. Moran was furious and socked fines on all of the quartet, until the police and the local newspapers verified their story. On another

Sunday, Alexander, Chalmers, Mayer and a few other players were out in Tampa Bay on a fishing trip, when a terrific storm came up. The players were all green with seasickness. Several small craft were upset, and Moran gave a prayer of thanks when a skilled skipper brought his pitchers safely into port. Those 1915 Phillies were a wild crew, full of fun, and the devil, too, but they were quite a ball club.

There weren't many clubs training in Florida at that time, but Miami had given the Boston Braves a good inducement to go there following their spectacular World's Championship of 1914. The Phillies met the World's Champs in seven games, and slapped them down six times. It was a fine augury of what was to come.

3

From the start of the training season Moran reiterated that "this is not a sixth place ball club." His favorite speech at meetings which were held before games was: "This is your bread and butter as well as mine." And the boys took the advice to heart. But Moran never talked pennant. "Win this one today," was all that he ever said.

Traveling, of course, was not as comfortable as it is today. The Phillies journeyed around the country in one Pullman that the players called the "Shettsline Special"—after the traveling secretary, former manager and ex-president. The substitutes, men who weren't playing, the young pitchers, and the regular hurler who was not scheduled to go to the mound for two days slept in the upper berths, and the rest—the more important persons—occupied the lowers. The players either signed checks at the hotel or received meal money from Shettsline, $2.50 and $3.00 a day. And the players took streetcars, not taxicabs, to the ball parks.

On the first 1915 trip quite a crap game was started in the car which lasted until four in the morning and Alexander even lost his diamond ring. Players then wore diamond rings; they were a sign of affluence. Moran, who had a compartment on the train, learned about it the next morning in the way managers always find out about such things. He was in a mighty dither, called a quick halt to such skylarking, and for the rest of the season crap games were out and poker games were limited to ten-cent antes.

Even then Pat seemed to sense he had a potential pennant winner, and he didn't want the loose discipline of the year before to ruin the team at the very outset. The Phillies began rolling from the first day, and when that first pennant came, in the fortieth year of the National League and thirty-third for the Phillies, it came almost as easy as falling off a log.

The club led four-fifths of the season, and never fell below second. It naturally expected most trouble from the Braves, the 1914 champions who were managed by George Stallings, the Georgia slave driver against whom the 1898 Phillies rebelled. However, the Braves suffered a stunning loss when Bill James, their 26-7 pitcher of 1914, contracted a winter illness and was useless. While Boston eventually finished second, what little opposition the Phillies encountered came from the Cubs, managed that season by the old fire-eater, Roger Bresnahan. Philadelphia and Chicago, the clubs of the old Fogel-Murphy alliance, were the only one to hold first place.

After being tied for the lead for two days, the Phillies took undisputed possession on April 16th, and held it to May 21st. For the next three weeks they bobbed in and out of first place with the Cubs, but Chicago led for nearly a month, from June 17th to July 12th. About this time, Alexander shaded the Cubs, 1 to 0, and the next day the Phillies walloped them, 13-0. That cooled off Bresnahan's team—and for good! The Phillies snatched the lead, July 13th, which proved anything but unlucky, and held it for the remainder of the season as the Cubs fell back to fourth. The Quakers clinched their first flag on September 29th, and eventually won by a seven-game margin over the Braves.

Despite the fact that the club never was pressed after mid-July, it won with a percentage of .592 (90 Won—62 Lost), the lowest to win the National League flag up to that time. National teams were remarkably matched that year, and the Giants' eighth place team had the highest percentage ever held by a tailender—.454. Philadelphia got almost as big a boot out of McGraw being last as from Moran finishing first.

Alexander was the beacon of the club, winning thirty-one games and losing only ten. Twelve of his victories were shutouts, and he had the fabulous earned run record of 1.22. He led the National League in both earned runs and winning percentage (.756), in innings pitched, 376, and hung a record into the book which may never be duplicated, pitching four one-hit games in one season. And still more amazing, three came within a month: June 5th, against the Cardinals; June 26th, against Brooklyn; July 5th, against New York. The fourth came in the fall, September 19th, against the Braves. In addition to these four one-hitters, Aleck had three two-hitters.

Whenever the team started to slip a bit, Grover would step in, win a shutout or low-hit game and start the Phillies off again. The players admitted they wouldn't have come close without "old Pete." It was a term of affection first given Aleck in the Phillie clubhouse, and later taken up by the sports writers. With Stan Baumgartner, "old Pete" is the greatest of them all—a pitcher as well as a thrower. Cy Young, Walter Johnson, Amos Rusie, Rube Waddell, Lefty Grove, were throwers, he opines, with so much natural ability that they had to do little thinking. Alexander had great natural ability and sharpened it with smartness, as did Mathewson.

Furthermore, he never was too busy to help a young pitcher. When Baumgartner reported from college the previous season, it was Aleck who showed him how to snap a curve ball and taught him a change of pace. He was humble, friendly, helpful. He had one big superstition. He wore the same pair of pitching shoes throughout the season. When they split, he sewed them and he patched the worn-out places with tape. He would have considered it unlucky to change them. His peculiar sidearm pitching motion came from skipping stones across the river near his home when he was a boy.

Alexander was one of the fastest working hurlers we ever have had in big league baseball. He and Bill Killefer, who became his regular catcher, both liked to get games over with, and Aleck's games rarely lasted longer than an hour and a half. When Pat Moran, who had a cottage on the Jersey shore, wanted to make an early train for the resort, he always planned to do so on a day that Aleck was scheduled to pitch. And Grover rarely failed him.

Next to Alexander, the championship club's leading winner was Erskine Mayer, who won 21 games and lost 15. Erskine was married on July 4th, and after that he had trouble finishing games. Demaree helped considerably with his fourteen victories. But although Chalmers and Rixey both had flashes of brilliance, both fell a little under .500—8-9 for Dut and 11-12 for Eppa Jeptha. George McQuillan, the bad boy of the Fogel regime, was regained from Pittsburgh late in the season.

Next to Aleck, the big guy on the club was old Gavvy Cravath, by this time thirty-three. He exploded the then amazing total of 24 home runs, high for this century until Ruth knocked out all existing records some years later. A fellow hitting two dozen homers in 1915 created more excitement than a man hitting four dozen today. In the same year, Bobbie Roth led the American with a meager seven. Of course, Cravath's big production again gave the Phillies the homer leadership with 58. Only four clubs in the two majors, the Cubs and Brooklyns in the National and the Yankees and White Sox in the American, hit more home runs than Cravath. He had fully recovered from his sore wing of 1914, and his arm again was strong and true. Playing with his back against the short right field fence, he even made batters hustle on singles to right. And despite bad caroms off the high fence, he shot runners down regularly at second when they were bold enough to try for doubles.

Cravath's batting average had slipped to .285, and high man among the Phillie batters was Fred Luderus, the big Milwaukee Dutchman who was captain of the team. Fred tried to give the Phillies a batting championship to match their first pennant, but lost out to Larry Doyle of the Giants, .320 to .315, in the last few days of the race. Fred still had his fielding lapses, and when ground balls would go through his feet. Moran would yell from the bench: "Drop that board! You big Dutchman, drop that board!" At a time when most ball players had no children, or one or two at the most, the Phillie captain sired five little Luderuses. He and Gavvy carried the brunt of the club's offense, as the Champion Phillies stood only fifth in batting with a humble .247. However, only one club outscored them and then by only one run. The sixth place Cardinals, leading the league in batting, tallied 590 runs to the Phillies 589.

It was a great gang! It was a rough and ready team which put dead birds in Killefer's catching mitt, and disgruntled Dode Paskert would unload his tobacco juice in the electric fan and give everyone a shower. Beals Becker stole third a couple of times with a Phillie already on the bases, and even Aleck stole third with the bases full. But as he won the game, it took the curse off him and became an amusing incident. There were times when an angry Rixey, incensed at the loss of a tough game, ripped the shirt off his back, and a disgusted Cravath hurled his unoffending bat out of the clubhouse window. But the Phillie champions were a happy contented family, one for all and all for one.

Opposing teams still complained of the reflecting mirrors in the center field bleachers, which resulted in Brennan's forfeiting the game back in Dooin's day. They also accused the Phillies of using binoculars and flashing signs from the clubhouse window in deep center field. But Pat Moran never missed a trick. Al Demaree, the right-handed pitcher procured from the Giants, was an overhand thrower who was particularly effective at Baker Bowl on Saturdays and double headers when white-shirted fans filled the center field bleachers. Demaree almost invariably pitched the first games of double headers, and whether the weather was warm or cold, a group of shirt-sleeved boys would be in the bleachers. The story was that Pat supplied them with passes for just that purpose.

Stallings and the Boston Braves were Moran's pet victims. He would do anything to rile Stallings. The Boston manager had many superstitions, but nothing irked him more than to have bits of paper thrown in front of his bench. That supposedly brought the worst of bad luck. On days that the Phillies played the Braves, Oscar Dugey, the former Boston infielder, took the day off and sat in his street clothes in a box near the Boston dugout. At regular intervals Oscar would tear up papers and let the breezes waft them in front of Stallings. It almost drove the Miracle Man mad. At times, he would get down on his hands and knees and pick up the scraps. He flew into violent rages, and became more interested in denouncing Dugey and in clearing the ground of the torn papers than in planning the day's strategy against the Phillies.

Despite this baiting of Stallings, Moran's psychology was not to rile up the other fellow, especially the second division teams. "You can catch more flies with sugar than with vinegar," he often said.

Buck Herzog, then playing manager of the Reds, was a player Moran never wanted to stir up. "Let him sleep," Pat would say. "He won't hurt you."

One afternoon, when the Phillies had the Reds apparently beaten, 4 to 1, a player who had a standing grudge against Herzog needled him. Buck got angry, played like a demon and finally doubled in the clutch to win for the Reds. That night Moran fined the needler $25.

But at times Moran encouraged the riding of the umpires. One afternoon, after Bill Klem had given several tough decisions against the club, Pat whispered to Baumgartner, "Get on Klem. Call him Catfish." That was the worst word anyone could call Klem. Carefully screening his voice, and hiding in a corner of the bench, Stan began calling: "Catfish! Catfish! Catfish Klem!" Klem got redder and redder under his collar, halted the game, and strode over to the Phillie bench his eyes afire with indignation. He looked over the bench, and indicating first one and then another player, he bawled at the top of his voice, "Get out! Out of here! And quick!" Baumgartner moved along with the rest. "Never mind, young fellow," said Bill. "I know you didn't have anything to do with this. You can remain."

While Moran's fundamental policy was to let sleeping dogs lie, and he opposed arousing a Herzog, Larry Doyle or Heinie

Zimmerman, he enjoyed thrusting barbs into the thin skins of what he called the "Rabbit-eared players." On such occasions, nothing was too stinging, too personal, to be said. Pat never did the riding. Oh no! He was the gracious, sociable manager. The job of needling went to someone like a substitute player, or a second string pitcher such as Baumgartner, who seldom got into the game and whose voice could not be recognized. Stan was schooled what to say, and when to say it, when the player was not looking and when the baiter was walking to the water cooler or moving on to the bench.

Old Rabbit Ears would hear it, get angry and upset. Feigning indignation, Moran would soothe the fellow and say: "I'll stop that! I don't want any of that kind of baseball." But he didn't stop it and would chuckle behind his masked red face. Before three innings were played, Rabbit Ear's mind would be more on the Phillie bench, trying to find out who was riding him, than it was on the game.

But if Stan was wont to ride unsuspecting Klem and rabbit-eared players, he still was the club's rookie and victim of much horseplay. Even with Sherry Magee gone, others took up his pranks. There was a rainy day in Chicago, and Stan wanted to spend the afternoon with his parents before the team departed for Cincinnati. He asked the clubhouse man whether he would pack his stuff. Players then packed their personal things in trays just as they do today. When he unpacked his tray in Cincinnati the next afternoon, he found all of his clothes, shirts, coats and extra trousers tied in knots. Someone had dipped them in water and tied them up. Needless to say, Stan missed the entire practice.

Despite all the pranks, there was a great feeling of friendship and camaraderie in the club. The men hung together, and there were no cliques. After the games in New York the entire club would go to the Kaiserkeller for beers and dinner. After the contests in Cincinnati, the men went in a group to the saloon on the corner, had a few beers, then ate dinner. The 1915 Phillies weren't saints and they weren't sinners. They lived normal, relaxed lives and if there was anyone who broke the midnight curfew, no one ever heard of it.

Several times during the 1915 season the Phillies took up collections to buy opposing pitchers suits of clothes. This was a practice quite common at the time, but later stamped out by Judge Landis. Moran made it a point to go to the best pitcher of opposing clubs, especially of the second division teams, and say, "You go to Chicago [or Boston or Brooklyn] next, don't you? Well, there is a suit of clothes in it for you if you knock them off." Many pitchers kept themselves well dressed in that manner. Other managers also were promising them suits of clothes for beating the Phillies.

4

The 1915 World Series, played between the Phillies and Bill Carrigan's Red Sox, proved a distinct disappointment to the Phillies—and all Philadelphia. It's been a long time now since Philadelphia has flown any World's Championship banners, but at this period the Quaker City expected nothing but the best. The Athletics had won the Series of 1910, 1911 and 1913, before they fell before the Braves in 1914. Now Philadelphia fondly expected the popular Phillies to regain baseball's blue ribbon for the Quaker City.

The fans were quite sure the 1915 "blanket" was coming Philadelphia's way, when sturdy Alexander got away with the first game, a 3-1 success played at Baker Bowl. They expected old Pete to be a three-time victor as was Christy Mathewson in 1905. But it proved to be the only Phillie victory. The Phillies battled every inch of the way; Moran cajoled and coaxed, but the best the Quaker could do was to make them all close. They lost three straight games by the same score—2 to 1—and then dropped the final, 5 to 4.

Baker was roundly scored for his supposedly "penny wise-pounds foolish" policy in building some extra box seats in front of his left and center field bleachers. It reduced the already cramped playing space in the Philadelphia park and resulted in three cheap Red Sox homers in the final game. Yet, in the retrospect of thirty-eight years, perhaps the 1915 critics were too severe on Baker. His park already was antiquated, and he was concerned mostly with taking care of as many fans as was possible. Considering how the World Series money is divided—and the small percentage which goes to a club owner—Baker's share from the additional seats scarcely paid for the lumber.

In Boston, the Red Sox played in the new park of the Boston Nationals, Braves Field, with its 42,000 capacity. The Boston park then had an extensive outfield, and Duffy Lewis, the Red Sox left fielder, robbed Cravath of several extra-base hits by spectacular running catches. Lewis, now the popular road secretary of the Boston Braves, was the particular hero of the Series, as he augmented his brilliant defensive play with a .444 batting average. After the Series, Lewis made a vaudeville tour of the Pacific coast. His best line was: "If my friend and fellow Californian, Gavvy Cravath, had hit those long balls in the Philadelphia park—instead of at Braves Field—Gavvy, rather than me, would be standing before you now."

The Phillies were handicapped by the incapacity of Bill Killefer, ace catcher, who was sidelined with a lame arm. Paw Paw appeared only briefly in the Series as a pinch-hitter. However, Eddie Burns, the little second-string catcher, jumped nobly into the breach and caught a fine Series. But the loss of a key man, especially a star catcher, was bound to have an effect on the team's morale.

The first game was played at Baker Bowl, October 8th, before 19,343. Aleck's pitching opponent was the tall North Carolina righthander, Ernie Shore, who gave up only five hits, against eight Boston blows off Alexander. It had rained the previous night, which made the field soft and soggy. This proved a good break for the Phillies, as four of their hits were of the infield variety and the fifth a Texas Leaguer.

Dode Paskert started Philadelphia's scoring in the fourth, when he dumped a short fly at Harry Hooper's feet in right field for a single, advanced to second on Cravath's sacrifice and third on

Luderus' infield out, and scored when Whitted beat out his slow grounder to second base.

The Red Sox had been averaging a hit an inning against Aleck, but they couldn't tie the score until the eighth, when Tris Speaker drew one of Alexander's two walks, reached second on an infield out, and scored on the second of Lewis' singles. Dode Paskert prevented further trouble with a great running catch on Larry Gardner in front of the center field boxes, one of the top Phillie plays of the Series.

Moran's boys promptly snapped back with two runs in their half to salt away the game. They were made without a ball being hit out of the soft infield. After Alexander was tossed out by Second baseman Jack Barry, the former Athletic, "Handle Hit" Stock drew a walk. Bancroft rapped a ball over second for an apparent safe hit, but Barry made a brilliant one-handed stop behind the bag. However, to the distress of Boston rooters, Shortstop Scott was late in covering second base, and Stock beat the play to that sack. A walk to Paskert filled the bases. The soggy field then proved a blessing to the Phillies. It slowed down Cravath's roller sufficiently to deter Scott from trying for a force play at the plate. He threw out Gavvy at first, and Milt Stock scored. "Banny" came in a few minutes later when Luderus' infield tap hit a soft spot and squirted away from Shore.

In the Phillies' ninth, a fumble by Luderus gave a lift to Olaf Henriksen, a Boston pinch-hitter. Carrigan then sent a second pinch-hitter, a young left-handed pitcher, to bat for Shore. His name was George Herman "Babe" Ruth. Ruth expired on a hot grounder to "Ludey" for the second out. Little did any of the crowd then suspect that it was seeing the start of a fabulous World Series career which would see Ruth in ten World Series, in which he was to have 129 official times at bat and collect 42 hits, 15 of them home runs.

Phillie fans were so happy over the first game outcome that they rushed on the field immediately after the final putout, surrounded such players as they could reach, and happily paraded the athletes around the field on their shoulders. Alas, there were to be no more victory parades!

The next day at Baker Bowl, October 9th—a Saturday—the Phillies had the distinction of playing before the first President of the United States ever to attend a World Series game while in office. Woodrow Wilson, and his fiancée, Mrs. Edith Galt—later the second Mrs. Wilson—journeyed up from Washington to take in the clambake. Wilson threw out the first ball, which Umpire Rigler, the chap who scouted Eppa Rixey, recovered and handed to the President. By stretching the seams of the park a bit farther, and putting in a few more of those criticized field boxes, Baker upped his attendance by nearly a thousand—to 20,306. The fans saw the first of the three 2 to 1 reverses.

For his second game, Moran pitched Erskine Mayer, who still hadn't regained his early season effectiveness. But the Atlantan had a lot of heart and gamely fought off George Foster, stocky little Oklahoma rancher, who pitched a three-hitter, walked none, faced only 30 Phillies, and matched the three Phillie hits with three of his own. Mayer, on the other hand, was stung for ten hits, was constantly in trouble, but was toughest in the pinches and remained on even terms with Foster until the ninth.

The Red Sox tallied their first run in the opening inning. Hooper led off with a walk and Speaker singled him to third. The pair tried a double steal, and when Eddie Burns dropped Bancroft's return throw to the plate, Hooper scored. It was, however, Eddie's only Series error as Killefer's understudy. The Phillies concentrated practically all of their fire in the fifth inning, when Cravath and Luderus bunched doubles with none out, Gavvy scoring. Phillie fans sensed a rally, but Foster clamped down on the next three. In fact, the Phillies got only one other runner on base—Bancroft's two-out single in the sixth. After Foster's mates repeatedly had blown scoring chances, George took a hand and broke up the 1-1 tie with his third single in the ninth, driving in Larry Gardner, who had reached second on his own slashing single and Janvrin's infield out.

After the Sunday off day, the third game was played in Boston, October 11th, before a crowd of 42,300, which established a new World Series attendance record, topping a 1911 Polo Grounds standing-room crowd by nearly 4,000. The Sunday had given Alexander two full days of rest, and Moran and the Phillies were sanguine that Pete again "would do it." On his second time out Aleck yielded only six hits, but half of them went to the dreadful Duffy Lewis. Duffy was finding the Phillie pitching prince something of a "cousin" with five hits in eight times at bat in Aleck's two games. In many respects, this game followed the same pattern as the second contest in Philadelphia; again the Phillies were held to three hits, this time by a stocky lefthander, Hub "Dutch" Leonard, and again Boston snapped a 1-1 tie in the ninth to win by its magic formula, 2 to 1.

The Phillies were the first to score, pushing over one run in the third for what should had been a big inning. Burns led off with a single to right center, and Alexander was safe at first when Hoblitzel muffed Third baseman Gardner's throw. Stock shoved the pair along a notch with a sacrifice, and "Banny's" single to center scored Burns. Moran held Alexander at third, as Bancroft made second. Two great defensive plays then chopped down the Phillies. Jack Barry, the old Mackman, leaped into short right for a brilliant catch on Paskert, and Lewis raced far out to the distant left field bleachers for Cravath's tremendous smash.

Boston tied in the fourth on Speaker's triple down the right field foul line, and Dick Hoblitzel's old-fashioned sacrifice fly. Aleck then held the fort until he succumbed to that debbil man, Lewis, in the ninth. Hooper opened with a single, and Aleck got two strikes on Scott. "Scottie" then had a lot of nerve, sacrificing on the next pitch, and almost beat his bunt to Niehoff. Moran then ordered an intentional pass to Tris Speaker. Hoblitzel almost upset Pat's strategy then and there by slashing a drive toward right field, but Niehoff cut it down with a great stop. It put Hooper on third and "Spoke" on second. The general feeling in the press box was that Moran also would walk Lewis. But as Duffy already had two hits, Pat figured the law of average was against him. But Lewis prodded the first pitch to center for a solid single, and Hooper crossed with the winning run.

For the third straight time it was Red Sox, 2; Phillies, 1, at the fourth game played in Braves Field on Columbus Day, before a slightly smaller crowd of 41,196. Carrigan came back with his first game pitcher, Ernie Shore, and Moran placed his dependence on Dut Chalmers. This time the hitting was more even, seven for the Phillies and eight for the Red Sox. The Red Sox scored first, in a squabbling third inning in which even the umpires battled each other. Barry walked and Catcher Forrest got a scratch hit when his bunt eluded Chalmers. Both Luderus and Niehoff scrambled after the ball, and no one covered first. Billy Evans, the plate umpire, called a balk on Chalmers, moving up Barry and Cady. National League umpire Cy Rigler said he didn't see a balk, and after some jawing among the arbiters, Evans was reversed and the two Red Sox base runners were moved back. But they were pushed forward again on Shore's sacrifice and Barry scored on Hooper's infield single, which jumped over Dut's head. Niehoff knocked it down, but couldn't field it.

It again was Lewis in the sixth when Boston scored what proved to be the winning run. Hoblitzel singled to center, and scored on Lewis' long smash to the left field fence which only fast fielding by Whitted held down to a double. The Phillies averted a shutout and scored their daily run in the seventh when, with a two-three count, Cravath hit a hard smash to center. It hit in front of Speaker, hopped over his head, and rolled to the fence for a triple. Luderus fetched him in with a line single to center.

Back to Philadelphia for the fifth game, October 13th, the Phillies succumbed in the tragedy of the field boxes before another 20,306 crowd, 5 to 4. As the Series was fading into history, the dormant Phillie bats finally came to life; they prodded nine hits off George Foster in his second appearance, and went into the eighth leading 4 to 2. Captain Luderus drove in three runs with a double and homer. But victory again was to elude the Quakers.

Even though Alexander had had only one day of rest, it was felt that Moran would pitch his ace in an effort to keep the Series alive. But the great Aleck came up with a sore arm, one of the rare occasions in Grover's long career when he complained of an ailing flipper. So Moran tried to get by with Mayer, hoping to pitch Aleck the next day if there was a sixth game. But Erskine was knocked out in the third inning, and big Eppa Rixey couldn't keep those balls from bouncing into the stands in the late innings.

The Phillies should have broken the game wide open in the first inning. They did get two runs, despite a double play which has been discussed in World Series fanning bees through the years. It became evident early that Foster was not the same pitcher who threw the three-hitter in the second game. The Phillies filled the bases in a jiffy, and all with none out. Milt Stock was hit; Bancroft stabbed a single to left and Paskert beat out a bunt, bringing up Cravath, the 24-home-run man.

With the count two strikes and three balls on the slugger, Moran startled the crowd, especially the press gallery, by putting on the squeeze play. When Cravath bunted directly at Foster, the pitcher's toss to Catcher Chet Thomas forced Stock at the plate and Thomas' relay to Hoblitzel doubled old Gavvy at first. Having your clean-up man and the nation's home run king bunt under such conditions seemed incredible. Eddie Collins, the former Athletic immortal, almost jumped out of his box, and Hughie Fullerton, the old Chicago writer and seer, ran starry-eyed through the press box, yelling: "Now, I've seen everything! Now I've seen it all!"

Yet, Stan Baumgartner reports the Phillies weren't particularly disturbed by the play. Said other plays during the season brought more heated discussion. They had too much faith in the red-faced Irishman's judgment to second-guess a play which went wrong. After all, Cravath had made only two hits in the Series. Larry Gardner, the Boston third baseman, was playing far back for Cravath, and if the play had succeeded, it would have been smart inside baseball. Gavvy gummed it up so badly by bunting smack at the pitcher.

Anyway, Fred Luderus, who closed the Series in a blaze of glory, helped take Pat off the griddle by doubling to left field, scoring Bancroft and Paskert.

The Red Sox tied it up with single runs in the second and

third innings, and chased Mayer. In the second, Larry Gardner bounced a triple off the center field stands, the ball barely escaping a bounce into the bleachers. Larry scored on Barry's single. In the next inning, Harry Hooper's ground hit to center bounced into the bleachers for the first homer of the Series.

Luderus regained the lead for the Phillies in the fourth by driving a ball over the right field fence into Broad Street for a home run. It came right after Cravath had fanned. The Phillies then added a fourth run on singles by Niehoff and Burns and a wild throw by Hooper.

Rixey did well after relieving Mayer, until the stands caved in on the Phillies' hopes in the last two innings. In the eighth, Del Gainer, who had replaced Hoblitzel at first, scratched a single through Stock and scored ahead of Duffy Lewis when he reached the stands in right center for a homer. That tied the score at 4-4, but Hooper promptly untied it in the ninth when he bounced his second homer into the center field stands. That Harry was no home run man was evident from the fact that he had hit only two in 149 American League games.

The Series ended with a terrific panning for Phillie president, Bill Baker, in the nation's press. He was voted the Phillies' goat of the Series, and it was freely pointed out that the trick homers of the fifth game beat him out of his share of a $73,000 sixth game gate in Boston, and a possible seventh game. But that was all water over the dam. The Phillies lost because of their .182 team batting average against Shore, Foster and Leonard. Only Fred Luderus came through for the Phillies, hitting .438, just under the .444 of Lewis, the Red Sox hero. Bancroft also did well with .294, but the averages of the other Phillies told the story of the Quaker City defeat more graphically than Baker's boxes: Cravath, .125; Paskert, .158; Stock, .117; Burns, .187; Whitted, .066; Niehoff, .061.

When the Series was over, there were some wild scenes in the Phillie clubhouse at Broad and Lehigh. The players got pretty high on beer, some of them guzzling it until it came out of their ears. Some of them fell into trunks, and Bill Killefer didn't come to until he reached Altoona. It was a combination of joy and frustration; joy over winning the Phillies' first pennant and frustration over those anemic averages in the World Series. And the letdown after a season's concentration and rigorous training. Later, a losing player's share of $2,520.17 from the old National Commission helped appease the dissappointment of the World Series defeat.

CHAPTER 13

Nosed Out In 1916

1

THE Phillies were a happy bunch when they again visited St. Petersburg in the spring of 1916 for their second visit to the shores of Tampa Bay. They took all the necessary bows as new National League champions, and Al Lang, St. Petersburg mayor, took all the other bows. He felt the 1915 pennant was a direct effect of the club training in St. Pete's sunshine, and took an honest pride in the fact that the first Philadelphia National club to win a pennant conditioned in his city.

He had the club transferred from the Fifth Avenue Hotel to the Edgewater Inn, a mile closer to the ball park. It still is standing, a block in from the bay and near the present swank Vinoy Park Hotel. It was one of those paper-thin-walled hotels. If someone whispered at the end of the hall, you could hear it clearly in the other end. It was no place to put the rap on another player.

For the first time in Baumgartner's baseball career, he became acquainted with the term, "Baseball steaks." When one of the Phillies ordered a steak the waiter would go into the kitchen and shout: "One baseball steak." Because of the thin partitions, everyone in the dining room could hear him. Because of the reduced rates given to baseball clubs, the "baseball steaks" came from the poorest cuts of meat in the larder.

The food was pretty bad; the players griped daily but no one took any action until one night at dinner Alexander didn't like the steak served on his plate. He grabbed the tablecloth and with one swoop sent dishes, silverware and food clattering over the floor. Then he and Bill Killefer marched downtown to the Detroit, then St. Pete's best, and took new quarters.

Having won in 1915, and tasted World Series money, the Phillies naturally expected to do it again. From the start, Pat Moran warned against overconfidence. "We won last year, but that's now in the book," he would say. "We've got to go out again and try to win every game. If we win enough of them, we'll be back in the World's Series in the fall."

They won one more game than in 1915, and had a percentage of .598 against 1915's .595, but this year it wasn't quite enough. Members of that 1916 Phillie club still think they should have made it, but with a combination of some bad breaks, and a questionable fall Dodger-Giant series in Brooklyn, the Phillies had to be satisfied with second place, three games behind Uncle Wilbert Robinson's Brooklyn Dodgers.

It was an odd race, with all the strength massed in the East, as the first division was made up of Brooklyn, Philadelphia, Boston and New York. Even though the fourth place Giants had a spring winning streak of 17 straight and another of 26 in the fall, they never really figured and the race was a three-cornered affair between Brooklyn; the Phillies, 1915 champions; and the Braves, 1914 titleholders. As an indication of how closely the three top clubs were matched, the Phillies broke even in their 22 seasonal games with both the Dodgers and the Braves. The club led in April and for a spell in mid-September, but most of the time it ran second, breathing down Uncle Robbie's neck.

One of the pities of 1916 is that Alexander couldn't have capped his greatest season with another shot at the Red Sox, again the American League champions, in the World Series. For 1916 was the peak of Grover's eminent career. He won 33 games and lost 12, and turned in the brilliant mark of 16 shutouts, a record which is more durable than Babe Ruth's 60 home runs. He pitched 389 innings in his effort to spark the team to a second pennant, and had an earned run record of 1.55.

After previous flashes of latent talent, Rixey finally found himself under Moran's able coaching, and had his first big season, a 22 Won—10 Lost—1.85 earned-run affair. Demaree, the former Giant, again helped admirably, winning 19 and losing 14. It meant the big three—Aleck, Rix and Steamer Al—won 74 of the club's 91 games.

It was to the discredit of the remainder of the pitching staff that it couldn't bring in the 21 additional games necessary to assure a pennant. Mayer was the biggest flop, and many blamed him for the loss of the pennant. After winning 21 games in both 1914 and 1915, he subsided to a 7-7 showing. But Chalmers folded even worse, winning only one and losing four, and Moran kept fooling with McQuillan, the once budding star, until George could show only one victory against seven defeats. The Federal League had blown up the previous winter, and Baker grabbed Chief Bender, the former Athletic great, from the Baltimore Feds. The Chief, still in Connie Mack's doghouse at the time, retained some of his old cunning and matched Mayer's 7-7 performance. Early in the season, Moran sent his University of Chicago lefthander, Baumgartner, to the Providence club.

The secondary pitching wasn't all that retrogressed. Neither Cravath nor Luderus had years comparable with 1915. Gavvy's home run crop shrank from 24 to 11, and Ludey's average came down from .315 to .281. For the first time in years, the club lost the season's home run derby to the Cubs. The Chicagoans hit 46 round-trippers; the Phillies were tied with the Giants with 42.

The Giants struck the Phillies some cruel blows in September and early October. Moran's brave lads had taken the lead, September 5th, but the Giants knocked them off the top perch three days later, while they were in the midst of a four straight clean-up of the Quakers. They were the second, third, fourth and fifth victories of the Giants' famous 26-game winning streak. Even the Phillie aces, Alexander and Rixey, couldn't tame the red-hot New York bats, as Aleck went down, 9 to 3, and Rix, 9 to 4.

Despite these setbacks to New York, the Phillies clung to

Brooklyn's heels, and could have regained the lead had they won their two games with the Dodgers in Brooklyn on Saturday, September 30th. As it had rained on Friday, the thrifty Charley Ebbets, Brooklyn Squire, decreed morning and afternoon games on the Saturday. Rixey was in fine fettle in the afterbreakfast session and easily upset the Brooklyn ace, Jeff Pfeffer, by 7 to 2. Luderus had a few extra wheat cakes for breakfast, and lashed out a homer and two doubles. It gave the Phillies a lead of a few points for some five hours.

Alexander, however, disappointed in the afternoon tilt, losing to Rube Marquard, 6 to 1, as Grover was pounded for 11 hits in seven innings. The Phillies ended the day two points in arrears. On the same day, the Boston Braves snapped the Giants' 26-game winning streak, officially eliminating New York from the race. That was to prove a bad break for the Phillies.

In the meantime, the Phillies suffered a grievous injury when Shortstop Dave Bancroft, the key man of the infield, snapped an ankle. With "Banny" on the shelf, the Phillies' goose was cooked in a series of double headers, Phillies vs Braves at Baker Bowl and Dodgers vs Giants at Ebbets Field, Brooklyn, on October 2nd and 3rd. Alexander, with only the Sunday to rest, came back brilliantly on Monday, pitching his thirty-third victory, a three-hit 2 to 0 job against Pat Ragan. But Ed Reulbach, one of Moran's favorites on the old Cubs, beat Demaree in the second game, and disaster overwhelmed the Phillies on the 3rd, when the Braves swept a double header, 6-3 and 8-1, as Rixey and Mayer were layed low.

The club still was smarting from the ugly news which had come out of Brooklyn the day before. The Giants, who so recently had swept all before them, dropped two games to the Dodgers. But worse still, John McGraw, Giant manager, walked out on the proceedings, first calling up to the press stand, "I want you fellows to know that I am not a party to this."

Pressed later for more details, he told reporters: "I couldn't sit there and see what was going on without making a protest. That's all I've got to say. I just saw some things out there I didn't like and that I couldn't stand for."

Among the things he didn't like was "Poll" Perritt, his pitcher, taking a long wind-up with a runner on first and some balls going through the infield that McGraw thought should have been fielded.

Three valuable members of the Giant champions of 1911-12-13, Pitcher Rube Marquard; the Indian catcher, Chief Meyers; and First baseman Fred Merkle, were members of that Brooklyn club, going there in 1915 and 1916 deals. It was freely hinted the Giants, with their pennant chance gone, preferred to see their old buddies get the World Series dough. There then were no shares for the other first division clubs.

The Phillies were furious, and Moran bellowed his resentment to the high heavens. "It's one of the rawest things I've ever seen, or heard of, in my long career in baseball," said Pat. "The Giants play their heads off against us, and then when they play the Dodgers, they just don't give a damn. When McGraw walks out on his own ball game, you know something stinks."

Moran called on league president John K. Tener, the former Pennsylvania Governor and Chicago pitcher of the 80's, for an investigation. Tener did make an investigation of sorts after the 1916 Series, but McGraw had cooled off after the interval and his comments before Tener were more guarded and temperate. Some apologists for the Giants said there had been a natural reaction after their 26-game streak was broken. Nothing came of the investigation, but Moran and most of his players seethed through the winter and felt they had been victims of a shabby deal.

2

The Phillies had another second-placer in 1917, our first year in World War I, but instead of being a hot pursuer as in 1916, the Quakers trailed the champion Giants by ten games. The Quakers ran first for a good part of April, May and June, but after surrendering first place to the Giants on June 24th, the Phillies never again had the thrill of riding in the front seat. For some weeks thereafter they kept the race fairly close, but a midseason Phillie pitching collapse widened the gulf between first and second to the width of Delaware Bay at Cape May. Still, their 87 victories were only three less than the total of the 1915 champs.

Alexander turned in 30 victories or more for the third successive season. This time it was 30 victories and 13 defeats and an earned run mark of 1.85, as usual tops for the league. In his three top seasons with the Phillies Alexander won 94 games and lost 35 for a percentage of .728. Rixey again did a lot of pitching but was unlucky, and his 16 victories were offset by 21 defeats. Joe Oeschger, old Bareback Joe of Stan Baumgartner's rookie days, who had been optioned out in several seasons, finally started to pay off and won 15 games while losing 14. Mayer made a partial comeback with 11-6, and Chief Bender, with an 8-2 record, had days when he looked like the old Bender. He was especially effective against the champion Giants. Pitcher Jimmy Lavender was procured from the Cubs after the 1916 season, and in midseason of 1917, Steamer Al Demaree was disposed of to the Chicagoans.

The club still had to win too many games by close scores, as the leading hitters were Cravath and Whitted, tied at .280. Luderus dropped 20 points more—to .261. Cravath had a dozen homers, which put him in a tie with the Giant right fielder, Davey Robertson, for the home run crown. The Phillies, playing in their "cigar box," could hit only 38 homers, one less than the Giants, league leaders, could hit in their Polo Grounds "home run range." All in all, most persons agreed Pat Moran did another fine job in finishing a comfortable second, five games ahead of the third place Cardinals.

Nobody then knew it, but the Phillies had just passed through five years which were to prove the golden era of their history, netting a pennant and three runners-up. In the first thirty-five years of the club, twenty-five had been spent in the first division, a respectable record. Ahead were many pitfalls, a wide chasm and a deep abyss. Were any soothsayer rash enough to predict what was in store for the club, and its loyal fans, in the next three decades, they probably would have hung him from the old "Chinese Wall" on Market Street.

CHAPTER 14

War-scared Baker Sells Star Battery

1

On December 11, 1917, during the National League meetings in New York, came the dark deed which was to turn the Phillies from a strong contender and a fairly regular occupant of the first division, into one of the door-mat teams of baseball.

Following the close of the 1917 season, word came from Nebraska that Grover Alexander had been drafted for military service and that the famous pitcher had been instructed to hold himself in readiness for his Army call. Baker, sensing the possible loss of such an investment on the battlefields of France, preferred that someone with more money should take the wartime gamble on Aleck's safe return. He sold his famous battery of Grover Alexander and Bill Killefer to William Weeghman, the former Federal Leaguer who now owned the Cubs, for $60,000 and a young Cub battery: Pitcher Mike Pendergast and Catcher William "Pickles" Dilhoefer.

The battery tossed in by Weeghman was not exactly junk. Pendergast was a promising pitcher who had a 13-14 Philadelphia record in 1918. Dilhoefer was regarded by baseball men as a potentially great catcher. He, too, was drafted after playing only nine games with the Phillies. Traded to the Cardinals, he died an early death in 1922.

Alexander pitched only three 1918 games for the Cubs before exchanging his baseball flannels for Army khaki. Yet the sale of Alexander, who won 180 games in eight seasons with the Phillies, and his great catcher, Killefer, left Philadelphia aghast. "How could Baker have done such a thing?" the fans kept asking themselves.

Some years later, when Cullen Cain of the *Public Ledger* sports staff and later National League publicity man, first met Baker, he had a prejudice against the man for having sold Aleck and Paw Paw Bill. He asked him point-blank, "Why did you sell Alexander, Mr. Baker?"

Baker looked him straight in the eye, and replied: "Because I needed the money."

Yet, after four of Baker's clubs had run one-two in five years, bringing good patronage at home and on the road, that is hard to believe. Furthermore, Baker never ran his club on spendthrift lines. Pat Moran didn't even have a coach to assist him.

The Alexander-Killefer sale did not immediately wreck the club, but it was the start of a vicious circle which continued for years. Sell stars and meet the bills. With rundown teams, the patronage fell and fell. The remedy, of course: sell more desirable players. If you developed any players, sell them to the highest bidder. For some thirty years there was no thought of winning, but of keeping one's head above water and staying one jump ahead of the sheriff.

With a little more business perspicacity, Baker might have had plenty of money to work with. In the spring of 1918, the Phillies trained in St. Petersburg for the fourth and last time. It was in our second war year, and everybody was playing it close to the belt. Mayor Lang offered to sell Baker the training field, with some adjoining lots, a pump and equipment, the small stands, etc., for the bargain price of $25,000. Baker told Sunshine Al: "I can think up better ways of throwing away $25,000." Six years later, during the Florida boom, the real estate was worth $500,-000; today the value of that property is $2,000,000.

One can't directly blame the flop of the 1918 team, from second to sixth in one year, on the loss of Alexander. He couldn't have helped the Phillies carrying his rifle around France. Rixey also went into service. That put a heavy crimp on the pitching staff. Bradley Hogg, a Georgian with a slow drawl, took up some of the slack, breaking even in 26 games. Niehoff was traded to the Cardinals for Milt "Mule" Watson, a Texas-born pitcher. That left a gap at second, and Pearce, McGaffigan and Hemingway vainly tried to fill it. Dode Paskert, the boy who could make the acrobatic catches, was traded to the Cubs for Outfielder Fred "Cy" Williams, whose home run bat soon would take some of the curse from Phillie defeats. Cy, a Hoosier, was a long-legged six foot, two inch bean-pole. He hit six home runs that year, as Cravath led the National League with a humble eight. Babe Ruth and Clarence Walker were tied in the American League with eleven. While the Army was doing its drafting, the Phillies put in a lucky baseball draft and gained Emil "Irish" Meusel, of the slugging Meusel brothers, from the Los Angeles club. "Irish" furnished the team with a new sock, but it all added up to sixth place.

That wasn't good enough for Bill Baker. The manager must have been at fault, so at the season's close, faithful Pat Moran was sent on his way. Besides, Baker's ears had singed when he heard some of the forthright Patrick's comments on the Alexander deal. Pat made out all right. At first, he caught on with John McGraw as a coach. But when Captain Christy Mathewson, manager of the Reds, was late in returning from his military duties in France, Garry Herrmann appointed Moran to the leadership of the Reds. There Pat repeated his Philadelphia feat of 1915. In his first season in charge, he led the Reds to their first National League pennant.

"I've let Pat Moran go," Baker told a press dinner, "but I know you will all commend me on my choice as Pat's successor. He is Jack Coombs, the former Athletic great. All of you fellows repeatedly have said Jack is a managerial natural. I think so, too. So, we'll give Jack a chance to prove it."

Combs, a Colby graduate, was one of Connie Mack's great pitching trio of Coombs, Bender and Plank. In 1910, Jack had a real Alexandrian year with the Athletics, 31 victories, 13 of them shutouts, and 9 defeats, and 3 World Series scalps. After Mack broke up his great team, Jack pitched three seasons for

Brooklyn and was a member of the 1916 team that nosed out the Phillies. Everyone agreed with Baker that he had great managerial possibilities. At seventy, he recently retired as the beloved baseball coach of Duke University.

2

The boys came marching back in 1919, and Alexander marched back to the Cubs. Had he marched back to the Phillies, he might have been the old bellwether and helped Coombs pick up the team from its sixth place position of 1918. Instead, there was no one to rally around, and the Phillies plunged two positions lower —to the very bottom of the class. It was the first tailender since 1904, and only the third in the team's history. But it was the forerunner of a hideous series of eighth place finishes which were to follow. Poor Jack Coombs! Disillusioned and disgusted, he had his last showdown with Baker around July 4th. Jack quit, or was fired—it doesn't matter—and Gavvy Cravath was named his successor without benefit of a party or fireworks. Old Cactus was now thirty-seven, but managing apparently agreed with him. Though he played in only 83 games, he upped his batting average from .232 in 1918 to .341. His 12 home runs gave him his last home run crown, and his old legs still were fast enough to steal eight bases.

In justice to Baker, he didn't go around sitting on his hands, but tried his best to get new cards. Baker matched wits with Branch Rickey, the then youthful Mr. Brains of the Cardinals, and Bill didn't come off so badly. In a pre-season swap with St. Louis, the Phillies gave up Third baseman Milt Stock; Catcher "Pickles" Dilhoefer, who came in the Alexander deal; and Pitcher Dixie Davis for Infielders Doug Baird and Stuffy Stewart and Pitcher Gene Packard. After the season got under way, Baker sent Pitchers Jacobs and Woodward to St. Louis for Pitcher Lee "Specs" Meadows, who developed into a top-ranking pitcher. In a late season deal, the Phillies landed First baseman Gene Paulette from the Redbirds to replace the slowing Fred

Luderus. This one might have turned out all right but for Gene's unsavory background. One of the first moves by Judge Landis after he took over a year and a half later was to throw Paulette out of baseball for too close association with gamblers during his St. Louis days.

Infielder Russell "Lena" Blackburne, from Philadelphia's New Jersey suburbs, and Catcher Tragessor were obtained from the Braves, and in September Baker wished the fun-loving, happy-go-lucky Casey Stengel, now nimble-witted Yankee manager, on Cravath. He was acquired from Pittsburgh in a deal for "Possum" Whitted. That didn't work so good, as Casey had a flat tire and refused to report until the following spring.

In an August game in Chicago, heavy money was bet on the tailend Phillies to beat the Cubs. It was the turn of Claude Hendrix, a pretty good spitballer, to pitch for Chicago. There was a lot of loose talk around Chicago about a fix, and two Chicago baseball writers received telephone calls that the game was "in the bag" for the Phillies. Bill Veeck, Cub president and father of the present Brown owner, requested his manager, Fred Mitchell, to switch from Hendrix to Alexander. But Aleck met no soft touch that day in Lee Meadows, the new pitcher from the Cardinals. Specs won, 3 to 0.

When the club returned east and was in New York, the "fix" talk still made the headlines. Genial Bill Brandt, baseball writer for the *Evening Bulletin*, telephoned Manager Cravath at his hotel to get his reactions.

"Sure, I heard something about it," said Gavvy sleepily, "but I certainly don't know anything about it. Jeez, I don't know why they gotta bring a thing like this up just because we win one. Gee, we're likely to win a game most any time."

The Phillie victory had many repercussions. For one, it blew Hendrix right out of Organized Baseball, and it was the investigation of this Philadelphia-Chicago game by a Chicago grand jury in September, 1920, which exploded into the Black Sox World Series scandal. In looking into a molehill for irregularities, they came up with a mountain in the way of skulduggery.

3

Gavvy Cravath didn't think he was so badly off when he brought his team back to Philadelphia for the 1920 spring series with the Athletics. Shifting his chaw from one side of his face to the other, he remarked: "We're not a last place club. That's one thing I know. I'll have a lot of power in my outfield with Cy Williams, Casey Stengel and "Irish" Meusel. That fellow Meusel really can rap the ball. Should make a great hitter. Paulette's going to do all right at first, and I've still got the best shortstop in baseball in 'Banny.' "

Gavvy had Dave Bancroft then, but he didn't have him two months later. Baker again needed the money, and this time perhaps more than when he sold Alexander and Killefer in December, 1917. Anyway, he made what he thought was a very smart deal with the Giants for his brilliant shortstop. New York guessed that the purchase price was $100,000, plus Arthur Fletcher, the fiery Giant shortstop, and a fair right-handed pitching prospect, Wilbur Hubbell, no relation to the Giants' left-handed pitching immortal, Carl Hubbell.

Lieb met Baker on a New York-Philadelphia train shortly after the transaction, and Will grew surprisingly confidential in discussing the trade. He admitted the $100,000 wasn't exaggerated. It actually was $95,000, but the extra $5,000 was in settlement for some second-rate player. "I didn't want to sell Bancroft," Baker said. "But Stoneham just wouldn't take no. McGraw wanted Bancroft so badly that they finally offered a price that I couldn't turn down. I think I made a splendid deal for the Philadelphia ball club. After all, Fletcher is no slouch at shortstop. We'll do just as well with him in the line-up. And we've picked up a pitcher in Hubbell who should be a real help to Gavvy."

However, the point Baker missed—or ignored—was that Bancroft was twenty-eight, in his sixth year in the league, while Fletcher was thirty-five and in his twelfth National League season. But the worst part of the deal for Philadelphia fans was that Baker was learning he could get by with substantial checks from more opulent contending clubs. It stifled the incentive to try to build up another contender of his own, and to get it back at the gate.

When Cravath said, "We're not a last place team," his statement wasn't disproved until the final day of the season. The Boston Braves nosed them out for seventh place by a half game and two points—.409 to .407. Cy Williams, the man who came for Paskert, had a fine season, batted .325 and led the National League with 15 homers. But that was the year Babe Ruth hit his 54 for the Yankees, a feat which soon revolutionized the style of baseball in both leagues. "Irish" Meusel hit .309, and trailed Williams in homers by only one. Stengel hit .292 and collected 9 homers, but his legs gave him trouble, and he didn't hide the fact that he didn't find it funny playing for Bill Baker.

Irish Meusel in left field had a weak throwing arm, and Stengel in right had back trouble, though Baker termed Casey "just plain plumb lazy." Whenever a fly ball went up, both Stengel and Meusel would yell to Center fielder Williams, "Come on, Cy; you take it."

"Come on, Cy," became the battle cry of the club.

Casey, however, was full of pranks. One day the team played an exhibition game at Fort Wayne. Stengel failed to appear at the hotel to dress, and was not in the Philadelphia line-up when the game started.

In the second inning one of the farmers started to heckle the Phillies, shouting: "I can do as good as you can. You can't hit, you city loafers!" The crowd took up the cry. One of the Phillies moved over to the stand and said to the farmer, "Well, you try it, if you think you're so smart." The farmer was Stengel and the Phillies went along with the gag. They loaned him a pair of baseball shoes, and he hit a home run over the right field fence. But the fans who watched the game kept wondering weeks afterwards whatever had happened to the farmer boy who had showed up the big leaguers. They never heard of him again.

A better known prank was Casey's famous hat trick, which he already had worked in Brooklyn. On a quiet afternoon at Baker Bowl, with not more than 500 in the stands, Stengel found a bird in the outfield as he was going to his position. He swooped his cap down, caught the bird and placed the cap back on his head. A moment later a fly ball went up in his direction. He lifted his cap and the bird flew out. He also often sent the fans into hysterics by catching fly balls behind his back, a trick not appreciated by Baker or Cravath.

Doug Baird was traded back to the Cardinals during this 1920 season, and Second baseman Johnny Rawlings was acquired from the Braves on waivers. The club also hired two newcomers who could hit—Russell Wrightstone, a Pennsylvania Dutchman from Bowmansdale, Pennsylvania, and a California Frenchman with the fancy handle of DeWitt Wiley LeBourveau. Naturally DeWitt preferred being called Bevo. Wrightstone, a left-handed hitter, could pound a ball, even home runs, into the left field bleachers. But no Phillie manager in nine seasons ever discovered a position he could play adequately. The players dubbed him "Folding Legs." Bevo also never won any medals with his outfielding.

At the end of the often hilarious '20 season, it was "So long, Gavvy. Wish you all the luck in the world!" Everyone knew Cravath's Phillie managerial and outfielding career had reached its end. He played a few more seasons of minor league ball—with Salt Lake City and Minneapolis—and then entered politics in California. He now is a Justice of the Peace.

CHAPTER 15

More Stars on the Auction Block

1

BY THE winter of 1920-21, Baker threw another party for the press. Object: Announcement of a new manager. The former New York Police Commissioner again appealed to Philadelphia sentiment; he picked a real Philadelphia boy in Wild Bill Donovan. Though Bill was born in Lawrence, Massachusetts, Donovan's parents brought him to Philly when he was a child, and he reached big league baseball by way of the famous Fairmount Park "park sparrows." He was called Wild Bill because of his early wildness in Brooklyn, and Smiling Bill because of his chronic good nature. He jumped to Detroit during the American League war, and though he beat the Athletics out of several pennants, Philadelphia loved him. His sister kept a rooming-house on Arch Street, and Bill knew every sports-minded person around town. He wasn't a newcomer in the managerial ranks, having managed the Yankees in 1915-16-17, and several minor league clubs.

Bill's popularity was of little avail in getting the Phillies off the ground. He lost two regular infielders before opening day. Judge Landis threw out his first baseman, Gene Paulette; and Art Fletcher, still a fighting shortstop, stayed out for the season after losing his father and brother within a few weeks. The lumbering first base veteran, Ed Konetchy, near the end of his career, was picked up from Brooklyn on waivers, and a Trenton boy, Frankie Parkinson, a fair fielder but light hitter, was dug up for the shortstop hole. Baker didn't help by trading his big southpaw, Eppa Rixey, for right-handed pitcher Jimmy Ring, a former Brooklyn semi-pro, and Outfielder Greasy Neale, the present football coach. Jimmy had an indifferent 10-19 season, and after Greasy hit only .211, he was shunted back to the Reds.

The 1921 season got off to a strange start. On the team's first night at Gainesville, Fla., their new training spot, the Klu Klux Klan paraded past their hotel. Two years before, the Giants, with such sturdy hombres as Heinie Zimmerman, Fred Toney, Benny Kauff and Rube Benton, had trained in Gainesville and hadn't left too good an impression. The parade supposedly was a warning for the boys to be good.

They didn't take their warning too seriously. The Phillies stopped at a hotel called The White House, the scene of much fun and laughter. The two pitchers, Lee Meadows and Jimmy Ring, were the leading pranksters. Meadows would sit in the shadows of the porch, and imitating the puncture of an automobile tire with a sharp slap of a newspaper and a whistle, he stopped car after car.

The Washington Senators played the Phillies several exhibition games at Gainesville, bringing along their coaching clowns, Nick Altrock and Al Schacht. They made a tremendous comedy team —also getting into scrapes—and once landed in the Gainesville jail for heckling a barker at one of the country carnivals.

That spring the Phillies played on the University of Florida football field. Before the team reported, it had been dug up and was a mess to practice on. "How can I be expected to get a team into condition on anything like this?" demanded Bill Donovan.

Wild Bill had several good pitchers in Lee Meadows, Jimmy Ring and Cecil Causey, but no one ever wanted to pitch. Meadows complained continually of a sore arm and Doc Van Ronk, famous Philadelphia osteopath, a friend of Meadows, sat on the bench and manipulated his arm between innings. Ring had an even better excuse for dodging mound assignments. Whenever it was his turn to pitch, he would show up with iodine over two or three fingers, explaining he had sprained them. "Get in there and pitch, anyway," stormed Donovan. Causey just couldn't get himself into the proper mood to pitch.

Bill Hubbell, a big righthander procured from the Giants in the Bancroft deal, was another of the hurlers, a good pitcher, too, but it was impossible to make any record in Baker Bowl with an infield that was a sieve and that short right field fence. One afternoon a line drive from Rogers Hornsby's bat hit Hubbell in the forehead, knocking him down as the ball bounded into Wrightstone's hands for the putout. Hubbell staggered to his feet and exclaimed, "Well, that's one way of getting Hornsby out."

No wonder the 1921 Phillies got off to a sickening start, hit the cellar early and never got out. This time it wasn't close, and the sorry finish was: Games Won, 51; Games Lost, 103. Percentage .338. Philadelphians were asking: "How long is this going on?" and "What have we done to deserve this?"

John McGraw, Giant manager, was in a hot pennant scramble that season with the Pirates. He needed players, and Baker again needed money. It wasn't that the Phillies were player rich, but they had some men that McGraw needed. Judge Landis nixed a deal whereby McGraw had expected to get Heinie Groh, the Reds' holdout third baseman. So McGraw reached into Philadelphia for Johnny Rawlings, played him at second and moved Frisch to third. Then he grabbed Casey Stengel and wound up by taking "Irish" Meusel and Pitcher Cecil Causey, who already had been with the Giants.

Stengel was absolutely dee-lighted with the deal which sent him to the Giants. He had complained continually of his sore back. One afternoon, midway during the season, rain postponed the game and the men were playing cards in the clubhouse to pass away the time.

Jimmy Hagen, traveling secretary, came to the clubhouse. This was bad news. It always meant that someone was on his way. Hagen called Casey and handed him a slip.

Stengel tore open the envelope, jumped up with joy, ran to his locker and dressed in his baseball clothes (although it was pouring outside). The startled trainer cautioned, "Be careful of your back, Case, be careful!"

"My back, hell," shouted Stengel as he ran out on the field, dashed to home plate, ran around the bases, sliding in the mud at every base. The bewildered players watched him return to the clubhouse, thinking he had gone completely screwy.

"I've just been traded to the Giants," he roared with glee, and laying aside the muddy suit, said, "Tell Baker to —— have it cleaned." He then dashed to the North Philadelphia station for a train to New York.

Meusel, however, was the boy who "made" the 1921 Giants. They were seven games behind Pittsburgh when he joined the club. Shortly afterwards the Giants, with a red-hot Meusel, knocked off the Pirates five straight in a late August series and went on to win the pennant.

In the four deals with the Giants, Baker acquired Third baseman Joe "Goldie" Rapp, Outfielders Lance Richbourg, Curt Walker and Lee King, Catcher Butch Henline and Pitcher Jesse Winters, plus another $100,000. Rapp was disabled by appendicitis shortly after he joined the club, and Henline, who took over as regular catcher, and King brought the only worthwhile help.

The Meusel deal left quite a stench. Judge Landis later told Lieb that if he had known all the inside details of the transaction, he never would have sanctioned it. Before the deal, Baker had charged Meusel with indifference; "Irish" was benched for several days; and when the deal was made for $30,000, Henline, Walker and Winters, Baker gave out that the trade was made "for the team's good." There is no doubt that Meusel was anxious to join Bancroft and Stengel on the Giants, a team with World Series money in sight. But Jimmy Isaminger wrote in *Sporting News:* "Of course, nobody believes Mr. Baker when he said he got rid of Meusel for the team's good. If that really was the case, he would be subject to severe censure for thus rewarding a bad actor."

Around the time that Meusel was traded, Baker also fired

Donovan as manager. And his statement of dismissal irked both Landis and Bill's legion of friends: "Donovan's activities with the Philadelphia National League club for the balance of the season will be limited to the endorsement of his pay check every two weeks—provided, however, that he does not break the rules of Organized Baseball."

At the time of Bill's dismissal he had been called to testify in the Black Sox trial in Chicago. He admitted knowing Philadelphia gamblers, as he knew most everyone around the Quaker City connected with sports—promoters, ball players, pro golfers, fighters and racing men. Landis sent Leslie O'Connor, his secretary, to Philadelphia to get Donovan's version of both his dismissal and the Meusel business. Bill said he never suspended Meusel, nor charged him with indifference, nor reported him to Baker. Landis ordered that Donovan's salary be paid in full, without any strings, and in off-the-record discourses with sports writers he scorched the hide of the Philadelphia club owner.

Donovan's successor was Irving Key "Kaiser" Wilhelm, who was an economy manager. He started, himself, with an economical salary. He had been a run-of-the-mine pitcher with the Pirates, Braves, Dodgers and Baltimore Federals. During his playing career he acquired his nickname, "Kaiser," which Philadelphia sports writers shortened to "Kize." He was a likable chap, knew a lot of practical baseball, but was licked before he started. As he finished the season at the helm, the tailend Phillies regained their loop's home run laurels with 88, the most for any National League club up to that time. Cy Williams poled 18, but he trailed George Kelly of New York and Hornsby of the Cardinals. In the rival league, Babe Ruth boosted his total to 59. The home run picnic was on.

After a season with Providence, and several years of independent ball, Stan Baumgartner had a second two season fling with the Phillies. After having ridden with Moran at the head of the procession, he now explored the National League's cellar and subcellar under Donovan and Wilhelm.

⚾ 2 ⚾

The Phillies moved to Leesburg, Florida, the following spring —1922. Leesburg is an inland town and then was so filled with mosquitoes the Phillies had to paint their faces with a preparation to discourage the bugs, which they named the "Canadian Royal Mounted"—because they always got their man.

Leesburg was famous for the 2 o'clock infield—a group of four including Russ Wrightstone and Jimmy Smith, later father-in-law of Billy Conn, the heavyweight fighter. Jimmy was a good shortstop, a light hitter, but a live wire in every respect. He was a dapper dresser, full of fire, fight and pep—who would use his fists at the drop of a hat. And he was in more than one fight that spring.

The 2 o'clock infield was so named because it would take the field after the regular workout and give a dazzling exhibition —and then go to sleep for the rest of the day.

Florida roads weren't as well paved as they are today and travel was much more difficult. One Sunday, then an off day for Florida training ball players, several Phillies decided to take a trip to Ocala and Silver Springs. Some of the travel was over roads made by dropping palmetto leaves in the sand. Two of the automobiles got off the leaves, buried in the sand, and eight players did not get back to the Leesburg training base until the following Tuesday morning.

The season of 1922, Wilhelm's complete season in command, always will be remembered as the year of the 26-23 defeat in Chicago on August 25th. Forty-nine runs by two clubs still is the all-time record. To the credit of the Phillies it must be said they waged an admirable fight, almost pulling out the game after trailing 25 to 6 at the end of the fourth. They had Manager Fred Mitchell of the Cubs berserk as they came up with 8 runs in the eighth and 6 in the ninth. The Phillies used only two pitchers, Jimmy Ring and Phil Weinert, against five for the Cubs. Wilhelm could have been accused of cruelty and inhumanity to pitchers by refusing to lift Ring in the second, when the Cubs scored 10 runs. Jimmy retired the side runless in the fourth, but the

Chicago thumpers teed off again on Ring in the fourth. This time Kize called on Weinert to give a hand and by the time Phil put out the fire, the Cubs had belted over 14 more runs. Marty Callaghan, Chicago right fielder, batted three times in that inning, smashing out two hits and striking out.

The Phillies actually outhit the Cubs, 26 to 23, as Wrightstone and Curt Walker each bagged four. On the Cubs side, Cliff Heathcote had five runs and five hits in five official times at bat, while big Hack Miller and Marty Krug each collected four hits. Even though the 1922 Phillies soared to a new National League high of 116 homers, oddly enough they poled none during this carnage. The game's three homers went to the Cubs, two for Hack Miller and a third for Bob O'Farrell.

The lively ball and home run era now was on in earnest. The Phillies batted .282 as a team, which won them only seventh place in club batting. A few years before, such an average would easily have led the league. Even though Rogers Hornsby led the league with a new home run high of 42, the Phillies were labeled: "Kize Wilhelm's Home Run Congress." Williams was second to the St. Louis Rajah with 26; Butch Henline, the new catcher, slammed 14; Curt Walker hit 12, and the kid from Trenton, Parkinson, amazed by hitting 15. As Walker and Henline, two players acquired in the Meusel deal, hit .337 and .316 respectively, Baker said ironically: "Where are all the people who said I was such a fool in disposing of Meusel?" "Irish" hit .330 that year for the World's Champion Giants.

As the ball of the 1920's became pepped up with more and more dynamite, Baker Bowl became tougher and tougher for the pitchers. The Phillies hadn't too many, but the best games pitched by Meadows, Ring, Hubbell or Weinert could be knocked from under them by some silly pop fly which would hit the right field metal fence or the screen above it, and plop back into the playing field. If the Philadelphia "cigar box" helped the Phillies, good or bad, gain the annual National League home run crown, it also helped rival hitters to many so-called "Chinese" homers at the expense of Philadelphia pitchers.

Phillie ball players of this period had to take a lot of ribbing about their pay checks. Other players taunted them by saying: "Baker's payroll is only $250 a month, and Cy Williams gets $200 of it." Unfortunately Williams, one of the game's real stars, never got the kind of money he deserved. His salary was peanuts compared to the dough Babe Ruth was making in the American League. Now a successful architect in Three Lakes, Wisconsin, tall Cy was one of the game's outstanding home run hitters. While Cy had a soft touch in that right field fence, the height of the fence cut off as many homers as Williams got over it. He hit a fierce low line drive which would have gained him many homers at the Polo Grounds and Yankee Stadium. The ball would bounce back sharply, and frequently be held to a single. Cy was one of the most confirmed pull-hitters in the history of the game, as much so as the latter-day Ted Williams of the Red Sox. Long before Lou Boudreau used his famous right field shift for Ted Williams, McGraw, Wilbert Robinson and other National League managers played the same shift for Cy Williams.

Wilhelm finished seventh—ahead of the Braves—but his number was up, and in 1923, Arthur Fletcher, the scrappy shortstop who returned after his one year's absence, began four stormy years in the managerial driver's seat.

3

Art Fletcher was a paradoxical character. Off the field he was a soft-spoken gentlemanly fellow, a regular church attendant and high up in Masonry. On the ball field he could be a fiend. Not only was he a hard aggressive player, but there was nothing he wouldn't say to a rival player or umpire. He never forgot his McGravian education. When he was the Giants' shortstop-captain, he'd chirp "Whiskey face" at Pat Moran in a monotonous repetition.

It was natural that Fletcher should have fighting teams. Certainly he injected something of his own drive into lackadaisical players, and though he couldn't lift the Phillies above the lower recesses of the second division, no manager who ever worked for

Baker gave him greater service or tried harder to do something with the team. Art battled umpires so furiously and relentlessly that league president Heydler once told Lieb: "Fletcher today is my No. 1 problem. He has become far worse than McGraw. I cannot understand how a man can come into my office and speak so politely and sincerely, and then act as he does on the ball field. At first I found it difficult to believe my umpires, or felt they exaggerated. But so many tell me the same story about Fletcher's abuse that I know they speak the truth."

Fletcher quit playing when he took over the reins of the club in 1923. He started off badly, losing 104 games, one more than the miserable tailender of 1921. That, of course, spelled a poor last. By 1924, Art won five more games and finished seventh, and he seemed definitely on his way in 1925 when his club won 68 games and lost 85 to tie Brooklyn for sixth. After the bad ball of the previous six years, a .444 percentage was half respectable. But that was to remain the high for quite a spell. Not only Philadelphians but other baseball men felt Fletcher was headed for the first division and a possible contender. But by 1926, he was back where he started—in the cellar.

Yet there were plenty of interesting developments during the hectic Fletcher regime. Stan Baumgartner has good reason to remember one. In 1923, he was sent to New Haven in part payment for a black-haired catcher, a native Philadelphian, Jimmy Wilson. He was the best player developed by the Phillies under the Baker ownership. Wilson was the son of English-born parents, and in his youth he was one of the best soccer players in Philadelphia. For a time, Jimmy was undecided which was his first love, baseball or soccer, but baseball won out. He became one of the National League's foremost catchers, caught brilliantly in four World Series and two early All-Star games.

Cy Williams continued to belt home runs, and in 1923 he had the distinction of tying Babe Ruth with 41 for the high in both major leagues. Then there was the "trading" of Lee Meadows. For some time it was rumored that "Specs" wanted to get away from the Phillies and land on one of the "big dough" teams. Lieb questioned owner Baker about the report. "I've heard reports that Meadows isn't overly happy here," Baker replied, "but he'll pitch for the Phillies until his whiskers grow down to his knees." Lee didn't really have to wait that long. He hardly had time to grow chin whiskers before Baker swapped him to the Pirates on May 23, 1923, for Infielder "Cotton" Tierney and Pitcher "Whitey" Glazner. Rawlings, who had been regained by the Phillies, also went to Pittsburgh. And, of course, Dreyfuss salted the deal with a $50,000 check. Meadows proved worth it, as he won 19 games for each of the Pirate champions of 1925 and 1927.

In 1924, the Phillies traded Curt Walker to Cincinnati for another outfielder, George Harper, who hammered the Baker Bowl fences for a spell. Another outfielder, Johnny Mokan, was a lucky pick-up from Pittsburgh. He had several fine seasons, and hit .325 in 1925, a year in which the club batted .295. The Phillies got several fair years out of Walter Holke, the former Giant and Brave first baseman. Outfielder Fred Leach, a Springfield, Missouri, boy, came in 1923 and developed into a consistent .300 hitter.

A silly attempt was made by some persons on the Giants to bribe Heinie Sand, the Phillies' rookie shortstop from Salt Lake City, in the final week of the 1924 season. What made the attempt so foolhardy is that the Giants led Brooklyn by a game and a half, as they had only three games left with the Phillies while the Dodgers had two with the Braves. Anyway, as Sand moved out to his position for the Saturday game of September 27th at the Polo Grounds, Jimmy O'Connell, McGraw's $75,000 Coast League rookie, approached him and said under his breath, "It'll be worth $500 to you, if you don't bear down too hard against us today." Sand and O'Connell had played together in the Coast League but not on the same team.

Sand promptly repeated the remark to his manager, Fletcher, who slept on it and then telephoned league president Heydler at his Long Island home the following Sunday morning. Heydler immediately telephoned Commissioner Judge Landis in Chicago. Landis promptly hopped a train and arrived in New York on the Monday. Calling in O'Connell and Sand, the former naïvely admitted to the bribe attempt, saying, "I merely followed instructions from Cozy Dolan, our coach."

On further questioning, O'Connell named three top Giant stars, Frank Frisch, Ross Youngs and George Kelly, as players who "knew what was going on." Landis immediately expelled O'Connell and Dolan from Organized Baseball, but after a winter hearing he exonerated Frisch, Youngs and Kelly. The Giants eventually won the 1924 pennant by a game and a half, but the incident left a bad taste in everyone's mouth. Philadelphians especially resented this effort to "buy" this last series from the humble Phillies. It also left strained relations between Fletcher and his former boss, McGraw. The latter felt Art should have told him about it before reporting the matter to John Heydler.

4

In 1925, the club acquired Barney Friberg, who could play second, third and the outfield, from the Cubs on waivers, and bought Lew Fonseca, the present promotion man of the two big leagues, from the Cincinnati Reds. The Fonseca business still doesn't make sense. After Lew hit .319 as the Phillies' regular 1925 second baseman, he was sold to the Newark Internationals, perhaps as a cover-up for Newark's parent club, the Yankees. A year later, Cleveland bought Fonseca back for $50,000, and in 1929, he was the American League batting champion. Baker apparently rooked himself on that one.

Pitchers came and went. Some didn't stay long enough for the other players and the Philadelphia sports writers to learn their names. Every so often Fletcher would get a well-pitched game out of Walter Betts, the Millsborough, Delaware, peach; Claude Willoughby, Frank Ullrich or Clarence Mitchell, the left-handed spitballer. Baker put his fingers in the autumn draft grab bag in 1923 and came up with Hal Carlson of Wichita Falls, who had seven Pirate years behind him. Hal quickly became the most valuable pitcher on the staff—so valuable, in fact, that Baker disposed of him at a profit of several thousand per cent on his draft investment. Bareback Oeschger regained his old locker at Broad and Lehigh in 1924, after stretches in Boston and New York.

Russ Wrightstone played every infield position in 1925. Finally, in 1926, Fletcher stuck him in the outfield. He was assigned to left field one day when the Phillies put on one of their typical exhibitions against the Cubs in Chicago. In the ninth, the Phillies had a one-run advantage and Elmer "Jack" Knight, a big country boy who always got up at five in the morning for a cup of black coffee, was pitching. Knight loaded the bases with two out and Charlie Grimm, the present-day Brave manager, at bat. Charlie lifted a tame fly to left and it looked as though the Phillies were in. Wrightstone measured it, gazed at it hungrily and reached for it. The ball plopped into his glove and right out again and onto the ground. Two surprised, but willing, Cubs dashed across the plate.

It was such a horrible muff that none of the newspaper boys said much about it. Wrightstone had been going badly enough. As for Fletcher, he almost blew a gasket. Wrightstone felt worse about it than anyone else. The players knew he couldn't get it out of his mind, because he wouldn't say a word. But late that night, over a cup of coffee, he broke his silence, saying, "You know what was the matter? I'll tell you. It was just too goddam *high!*"

In September, 1926, came the famous "Catfish" scoreboard incident at Baker Bowl. It happened as the St. Louis Cardinals practically clinched their first pennant by drubbing the Phillies by such outlandish scores as 9-2, 23-3, 10-2, 10-1 and 7-2 before the Quakers got away with the last game. Such scores were enough to drive any manager into a frenzy. As the Phillies were losing the first game of a double header, September 16th, Jimmy Wilson was tossed out of the game by Umpire Bill Klem. Fletcher took up the argument on behalf of his catcher until Klem bawled, "You say another word, Mr. Fletcher, and you can join Wilson in the clubhouse."

Arthur returned to the bench, but about ten minutes later something occurred to him that he hadn't said before, so he rushed to the plate with his latest observations. Klem listened for a few moments, and roared: "Now you can follow Wilson."

Fletcher didn't go immediately, and continued the discussion until Klem threatened to forfeit the game. Eventually Art sauntered slowly across the field, stopping to talk to some center field bleacherites. Shortly after he disappeared the double header crowd was in titters. At first Klem didn't know what the laugh was about, but he sensed that he was the object for all this mirth. Then he happened to look up at the center field scoreboard and turned crimson. It was hung outside of the Phillie clubhouse. Thrifty Bill Baker still was using blackboards on which the scoreboard boy printed the names of the batteries. But, instead of the name of a battery, a large catfish was drawn on the board, with the explanatory caption: CATFISH KLEM.

Klem was furious, and so was his New York chief, John Heydler, when Bill reported the incident. Heydler suspended Fletcher indefinitely.

Klem and Heydler punished an innocent man. It was a case of finding a man guilty by circumstantial evidence. After Fletcher came to the Yankees as coach, he told Lieb: "I was as innocent of this thing as you are. I wasn't even in the clubhouse when they hung out the sign, as I stopped under the center field bleachers and looked at the game from a gap in the bleachers. The idea of the Catfish sign was entirely Wilson's. He drew it, and hung it on the scoreboard. Jimmy wanted to confess and declare my innocence. But I knew I was through in Philadelphia, and thought if Wilson told his part in it, it might affect his 1927 contract. So, I took the rap."

During Fletcher's indefinite suspension, which lasted to the end of the season, Baker also fired him as manager. Fletcher's four years as manager of the Phillies took such a terrific toll on him that he lost all hankering to manage a big league club again. After accepting a coaching job on the Yankees, he was offered managerial posts by the Cleveland Indians, Detroit Tigers, Cincinnati Reds and St. Louis Browns, but refused them all. After the Yankee manager, Miller Huggins, died in 1929, Fletcher was the first man Col. Ruppert considered as "Hug's" successor.

"I thank you, Colonel, for offering me the job," said Fletcher, "but I'd rather stay with you as coach."

"But why, Fletcher?" insisted Ruppert. "Just because you had that trouble with Baker, and he sold your players? Well, we've got lots of players—and money—in this organization."

"Just the same, Colonel, I'd rather you'd give the managerial job to someone else and that I could stay with the team as coach."

5

For the third time in eight years Baker made an appeal to Philadelphia's baseball sentiment in naming Fletcher's successor. In 1919, it was the old Athletic pitching favorite, Jack Coombs, and a year later the old Fairmount Park Sparrow, Bill Donovan. In 1927, it was Jack "Stuffy" McInnis, the first base member of the Athletics' immortal "Hundred Thousand Dollar Infield" of Baker, Barry, Collins and McInnis. Today that quartet would be worth a million. After a meritorious American League career with the Athletics and Red Sox, McInnis, a Gloucester, Massachusetts, boy, had closed his career in the National and contributed handsomely to Pittsburgh's World's Championship in 1925.

President Baker, who still was lavish with the press even if he remained parsimonious as he dealt out meal money to his players, put on a large spread when Stuffy was hired. Jimmy Isaminger, the late talented sports writer for the Philadelphia *Inquirer* whose heart belonged to the Athletics, hemmed and hawed his way through a brief talk and concluded: "The Phillies have turned the corner." Quipped Gordon McKay of the *Record,* the next speaker, "The Phillies may have turned the corner but only God knows where they're going."

Yet, the only corner the McInnis Phillies turned was deeper into the coal pit. This club won 51 games and dropped 103. Baker made more deals. Harper went to the Giants in a three-cornered swap with New York and Brooklyn, whereby the Phillies came up with the personable second baseman, Fresco Thompson, now a Dodger vice-president, and the pitching veteran, Jack Scott. Just to help Stuffy, in the early season Baker traded Hal Carlson, who had a 17-12 record with the 1926 tailender, to the Cubs for Pitcher Tony Kaufman, Infielder Jim Cooney, and a little matter said to be $50,000.

The .331-percentage club was fourth in team batting with .280, but its homer production dropped to 57, far behind the 109 of the leading Giants. Even so, Cy Williams figured in his last homer championship, tying the chubby Cub, Hack Wilson, product of the Philadelphia suburbs, with 30. A pitcher with the sugary name of Lester Sweetland, a St. Ignace, Michigan, cookie who came from the Spartansburg, South Carolina, club, joined Claude Willoughby on the fancy-named pitching staff. Lester was no "sweetie" as a pitcher, winning only two while losing ten. And Stan Baumgartner, after having seen the acrobatics of the Phillies from the playing field, now saw them look just as bad from the press coop.

CHAPTER 16

Chuck Klein Makes the Welkin Ring

1

IN 1928, under the leadership of Burt Shotton, successful Brooklyn manager of recent years, the Phillies plunged to the absolute depths of their post-World War I years of frustration. This club had the ignoble record of 43 victories, 109 defeats, and a percentage of .283, one of the most abject tailenders of this century. Yet Shotton was a manager of considerable ability who was to make substantial progress in his sixth-year tenure as head man at Baker Bowl.

Originally a fast-running outfielder on the St. Louis Browns, Shotton became Branch Rickey's fill-in Sunday manager on both the Browns and Cardinals. Burt also had done well as manager of the Syracuse Internationals before Baker induced him to come to Philadelphia. An off-season barber during his playing career, Barney Shotton was a friendly soul with a lot of baseball savvy, who had picked up some good ideas from his mentor and hero, Rickey.

The 1928 Phillies got off to their usual dismal start, and by early May, Baker again was in need of money. This time, he found Sam Breadon and Branch Rickey of the Cardinals willing to part with some of it. After winning the 1926 World Series and losing the 1927 flag by a game and a half, the Cardinals were handicapped by Catcher Bob O'Farrell's lame arm. So Rickey cast avid eyes in the direction of Jimmy Wilson, whose catching had stood out even on Phillie tailenders. And Baker was willing, even though Wilson had been one of his favorites. Other players teased Jimmy by calling him "Baker's boy." The deal enabled the Cardinals to regain the N. L. pennant in 1928, but it wasn't a bad deal for Baker or the Phillies. Bill got the hefty St. Louis catcher, Virgil "Spud" Davis, a fair outfielder in Homer Peel and something like $30,000 in the green stuff. Spud Davis soon was to join other biffing Phillies in hammering down the fences.

Making matters even worse for the pathetic 1928 tailender was the resurgence of the Athletics at Shibe Park. Connie Mack was starting on his great comeback, and his new Athletics, built around Al Simmons, Mickey Cochrane, Lefty Grove, George Earnshaw, Jimmy Foxx and Jimmy Dykes, fought the great Yankee team down to the wire before losing the flag by two games. As the crowds swarmed back to Shibe Park, the Phillie park frequently was all but deserted. Among the few regulars was a coterie of gamblers who would make daily book on the extent of the Phillie defeats. The park needed paint and repairs; the seats were grimy with the accumulated dust and soot from the Reading Railroad tracks across the street, and when a foul landed on the roof, the customers under the spot—if any—threw their hands over their heads to ward off scales of rust that showered down.

It was at this time that a big awkward Indianapolis German, a rookie from the Fort Wayne club of the Central League, sauntered into the Phillie clubhouse. It was at the end of July. The big boy carried a suitcase in each hand, and announced "I'm Klein. They call me Chuck Klein."

"All right, Klein; get in uniform," snapped Shotton. "They tell me you can hit. Goodness knows we need hitters." And then, as a sad afterthought, "We need everything."

Charles Herbert "Chuck" Klein, a six foot, 195-pounder, had been purchased from Fort Wayne for $5,000. The Yankees had an option on him but neglected to exercise it. Chuck was too crude. He never became a finished outfielder, but he was to hang slugging records into the book which were to bring back memories of Sam Thompson and Ed Delahanty. In his first six-year sojourn with the club he set new National League slugging and scoring records; passed or exceeded some marks of the great Hans Wagner; even inserted a record for outfield assists; was named his league's most valuable player; played in the early All-Star games; and showered home runs into Broad Street in such profusion that he became a menace to traffic. As another homer boomed off Chuck's big bat, kids in the upper stand galloped to the corner where the stands abutted the fence to peer over and see whose windshield was going to get it. Yes, Baker had to pay for broken windshields, but the brawny-armed Chuck more than paid for it. He gave the club a fillip at a time when it was needed most.

The first day he reported, Shotton told him, "Grab a bat, and hit for my pitcher." Chuck popped out, but the next day Barney had him in his regular line-up and Klein prodded a homer and a double, and he was off on a batting spree which gave him a .360 batting average for 64 games in which he hit 14 doubles, 4 triples and 11 home runs.

2

Connie Mack won his seventh pennant in 1929, with a lead of nineteen games over the second place Yankees. But that wasn't more of a wonder work than Shotton wrought at Baker Bowl the same year. As a result of Klein's continued bombardment of the fences and some advantageous trades, the Phillies changed almost overnight from a door-mat to a club which made trouble for the best in the league. It won 28 more games than the year before, and enjoyed its best finish since the second-placer of 1917. The fifth place club had a 71-82, .464 record. And how that club could clout! Eddie Pollock, Bill Brandt and Baumgartner wore down their pencils recording Phillie bingles. The 1929 Phillies hit .309 as a team against the .296 of the new Athletic World's Champions.

The club was far ahead in homers with 153, with Chuck Klein (43), Lefty O'Doul (32), and Don Hurst, a new first baseman from Syracuse (31), getting 106 between them. In his first full season with the club, Klein batted .356; he smacked out 219 hits, scored 126 runs and drove in 145. His 43 homers gave him the league leadership and proved the high for Chuck's major league career. It would have been even higher but for a strange procedure by Baker. Klein was propelling homers over the right field fence with such frequency that Baker tacked an additional 15 feet of screen to the old screen above the right field fence. As Klein was a pronounced left-handed pull hitter, the great majority of his drives went to right field—over or against the barrier. Baker explained his action by saying, "Home runs have become too cheap at the Philadelphia ball park." Some of his detractors said he put on the new screen to hold down Klein's homers before they reached Ruthian dimensions. The fear was that if Klein got into the 50 home run class, he would want a Ruthian salary, and the whole club would want to be paid salaries in proportion. It is certain, however, that the new screen prevented Klein from hitting 50 home runs.

Good as Klein was that season, he almost played second fiddle to Frank "Lefty" O'Doul, the man in the green suit, now the successful manager of the San Diego club. In his early years in the majors O'Doul, a happy-go-lucky San Franciscan, had been a promising left-handed pitcher with the Yankees and Red Sox. He had arm trouble, turned outfielder in the Coast League, and was brought back by the Giants in 1928, where Lefty had a fair season, hitting .319 in 114 games. His acquisition by Baker was one of the old Commissioner's smartest deals. By turning Outfielder Fred Leach over to McGraw, he received a $20,000 check and O'Doul.

All O'Doul did that season was to bang out 254 hits for a new National League record (it was tied by Bill Terry a year later); and lead the league with a brilliant average of .398. He was the first Phillie batting champion since Sherry Magee in 1910. The loquacious O'Doul also carried in 154 runs.

There were other clouters. Spud Davis, the new catcher, hit .342; Art Whitney, a new third baseman drafted the year before from New Orleans, was a .327 man; Fresco Thompson was no slouch at .324 and Don Hurst hit .304 in his second N. L. season.

They tied a record by having four players drive in better than 100 runs—Klein, 145; Hurst, 125; O'Doul, 122; Whitney, 115. Shortstop Tommy Thevenow, the former Cardinal star, was acquired from St. Louis for Heinie Sand and a little cash. He was expected to be a lot of help, and the club's position would have been even better if Tommy hadn't run into a nasty accident during the training season.

One night when Thevenow was returning from Tampa to Winter Haven, the 1929 training camp, the automobile he was driving went off the road. Tommy was seriously injured and taken to a hospital. A handsome lad, his face was so disfigured he never really got over the effects of the smashup. He was able to play only 90 games that season, and hit .227.

The accident had its counterpart in another attempted shift of position. Barney Friberg, the former Chicago infielder and outfielder, was learning to be a pitcher that year, again because of the shortage of first-class hurlers. He made excellent progress at Winter Haven and seemed destined to become an acceptable pitcher. Thevenow's accident cut this all short. Barney had to jump in and fill the gap at shortstop.

Claude Willoughby led the pitchers that year with 15 victories against 14 defeats, and Baker made another lucky draft on the New Orleans club and came up with another winning pitcher, Fidgety Phil Collins. Phil was quite a character, and a butcher when he wasn't a pitcher. He helped his brothers in their Chicago retail meat markets. But Phil, despite his fidgetyness on the mound, butchered few games. He won 9 and lost 7 that season, which he advanced to 16-11 in 1930.

Fresco Thompson felt his .324 batting average was worthy of a tidy raise. When he broached the subject to Baker, the Philadelphia president showed him several clippings intimating that Fresco was not so hot as a second baseman. Thompson was back next day with two large scrapbooks, heaped full of clippings extolling Thompson and his play. "Mr. Baker, if you are going to pay off on clippings, I wish you'd read some of mine," said the spunky infielder.

3

These Phillies of the latter Baker regime just couldn't stand prosperity. Once they moved up in the standing a bit, the exhilaration went to their heads. Everybody expected the club to show further improvement in 1930; the first division was the goal, but the new slugging Phillies flopped ignobly, and to the chagrin of Baker, and the Philadelphia fans, plunged back into the cellar. If the 1929 club won 28 more games than the miserable 1928 team, this 1930 edition suffered 20 more defeats than the previous year's fifth-placer.

What's more, it didn't seem to make any sense, especially after John Heydler issued his annual figures. This undoubtedly was the most unusual tailender of all baseball history. The club hit .315, being second to the .319 of the Giants, the highest club batting average of this century. The club smacked 126 home runs. Chuck Klein had his most gorgeous season. He reached his batting peak of .386, which was topped only by Bill Terry and Babe Herman. His 158 runs scored still is a modern National League record. He cracked out 250 hits, only four under the O'Doul-Terry record. He led the league in doubles with 59, and was runner-up to Hack Wilson of the Cubs in homers with 40. Twice during the season he had slugging binges in which he knocked out 5 homers in three successive games. His 170 runs batted in and 445 total bases are Phillie highs for this century. Chuck also set his record for outfield assists with 44.

O'Doul wasn't quite as potent as the year before, but finished fourth in batting with .383. He missed 16 games because of a leg injury, but still poked out 27 doubles, 7 triples and 22 home runs. Pinky Whitney, Friberg and Hurst all batted better than .325.

"How can you finish last with such a hitting club?" someone asked Barney Shotton.

"Have you looked at my pitching by any chance," replied the manager with a wry smile.

Outside of Collins' credible performance and a fair 11-15 job by Ray Benge, the rest was terrible: Willoughby, 4-17; Sweetland, 7-15; Earl Collard, 6-12; Hal Elliott, 6-11. The staff yielded a grand total of 1,199 runs—a record that may last forever.

As the 1911 Phillies saw the sensational debut of Grover Cleveland Alexander, the 1930 team saw Aleck's exit from the big leagues. The great pitcher had ended the 1929 season under indefinite suspension by the Cardinals, but Baker regained him in a trade, Pitcher Bob McGraw and Outfielder Homer Peel for Alexander and Harry McCurdy, a catcher. But Aleck was forty-three, and the years hadn't changed his habits. During the training season in Leesburg, Florida, Grover, while in a drinking mood, annoyed one of the natives. He prepared to crown Alexander with a bottle, when Cy Williams, acting quickly, floored Grover's antagonist with a hard left to the jaw. Williams, a clean fellow who rarely frequented drinking places, just happened to be there to deliver this telling punch.

However, it saved Grover for only a few weeks. When he returned to the Phillies he had 373 National League victories, and needed only one more to break the tie with Christy Mathewson for most N. L. scalps. He never broke it. After he had appeared in nine games and was charged with three defeats he was released unconditionally, and sang his swan song later in the season with the Dallas Texas League club.

This was William F. Baker's last tailender. The man who had run the Phillies since Will Locke's unfortunate death in 1913 died unexpectedly at the Ritz-Carlton Hotel in Montreal, December 4, 1930, while attending the annual minor league meeting. Baker was sixty-four years old, and a true New Yorker despite his activities in Philadelphia. Funeral services were held in New York, and he was buried in Brooklyn's Greenwood Cemetery.

Baker was a controversial figure to the end. Many Philadelphians regarded him in the same way as Bostonians regarded Harry Frazee, New York theatrical man, who after an early 1918 pennant wrecked the Red Sox by selling their top players to the Yankees. Baker's Phillies never were the same after the sale of Alexander. He wasn't a rich man, but well to do. After his original investment, he put little of his own money into the club.

He tried to make the club carry itself, pay his president's salary and pay off notes on the Locke and other stock. And if he needed money, he always knew a club which would part with it.

Baker was succeeded as president by another New Yorker, genial Charley Ruch, a minority stockholder who had been one of Baker's early New York business associates. But Baker left a surprising will. He willed his Phillie stock to Mrs. Baker and Mrs. May Mallon Nugent, formerly his secretary and by this time the club secretary. Mrs. Nugent's share was greater than that of the widow. When Mrs. Baker died a few years later, she also willed her Phillie stock, securities and jewels to Mrs. Nugent and her son, Gerald, Jr. Not long before Baker's death, he cast off the club's faithful servant, Billy Shettsline, and handed his job of business manager over to Gerald Nugent, Sr., May Mallon's husband. Phillie sports writers liked Gerry Nugent, but they considered the ditching of old "Shetts" unforgivable. Billy, the man who held every post on the Phillies, died in his native city, February 22, 1933.

4

A month before Bill Baker's death, he made his last big deals. Despite the fact that Lefty O'Doul had hit .398 and .383 in his two seasons in Philadelphia, he had become too expensive to carry. The O'Doodle, as he was known to some of his pals, had had a few flairs of temperament and let it be known he didn't rate Baker high as a paymaster. So Baker traded O'Doul and Fresco Thompson to Brooklyn for Pitchers Jim "Jumbo" Elliott and Elzie Clise Dudley, Outfielder Hal Lee and that fellow named Cash. Baker really put something over on Barney Dreyfuss when he acquired Pittsburgh's fine young shortstop, Dick Bartell, for Shortstop Tommy Thevenow and Pitcher Claude Willoughby. Rowdy Dick, a fine aggressive player and consistent .300 hitter, advanced rapidly in Philadelphia until he, too, became too valuable to carry.

Baker's excuse for trading O'Doul was that the O'Doodle had

a "punk arm" and he could sacrifice a hitter to bolster the bad pitching staff. That proved true—to a degree—for in 1931, Jim Elliott, a 235-pound, six-foot, three-inch mastodon from St. Louis, won 19 games and lost 14. Clise Dudley, the other pitcher who came from Brooklyn, won his first 5 games as a Phillie, and then acted more naturally; he won 3 of his last 17. Phil Collins and Ray Benge had good seasons, the former winning considerable acclaim with a one-hitter against McGraw's power Giant hitters. Improved pitching saw the 1931 club snap back to sixth with 66 victories, 88 defeats and a percentage of .429.

Klein continued to blister the ball. Some of the dynamite had been taken out of the official 1931 sphere. Chick Hafey, Bill Terry and Jim Bottomley were in a practical tie for the batting lead with .348, and Chuck came next with .337. He whacked out an even 200 hits and tied Terry for the lead in runs scored with 121. Oddly enough, he also hammered in 121, tops for the league. He also was boss man in homers with 31 and total bases, 347. He was still quite a boy in Baker Bowl!

CHAPTER 17

Fourth Place, by Gosh

BACK in the nineties, Col. John Rogers spoke disdainfully of the Phillies' fourth place rut. Later, in the first decade of this century, the club traveled in the so-called "fourth place groove." But when the 1932 club lifted itself into fourth place, it was like a gift from heaven for the Philadelphia fans. After all, that was first division, and the Phillies surprisingly divided $9,095, their share of fourth place money from the Cub-Yankee World Series. Since the second place club of 1917, the Phillies had one fifth, three sixths, two sevenths and eight eighths. So, this was Burt Shotton's shining hour as Phillie chieftain.

Fourth place wasn't won until the last day of the season, when the Phillies nosed out the Braves, .506 to .500. The 1932 Phillies won two more games than they lost, 78 to 76, and that was something. As usual, they were far more effective in their Broad and Huntington "Cigar Box" than on the road. For instance, they did fairly well with the championship Cubs at home, winning five and losing six. But in Chicago, it was a sad and different story; there they got away with only one game in eleven.

But it was a biff-bang club and beaming Charley Ruch well could ask the New York writers, "How do you fellows like our hitters?" The Phillies had plenty of them, and Shotton could let loose bundles of TNT against opposition pitchers. With the de-emphasized ball, they led the sixteen major league clubs with a club batting average of .292. They led the National League in most everything but winning percentage. They scored 844 runs, 124 more than were tallied by the champion Cubs, and also led in doubles, 330, and homers, 122. They established a new major league record by having the top three men in runs batted in—Hurst, 143; Klein, 137; Whitney, 124.

O'Doul, the ex-Phillie, led the league while playing for Brooklyn, but the belting Klein was third with .346, Don Hurst sixth with .339, and Spud Davis eighth with .335. The rest of the line-up, with the exception of Second baseman Les Mallon, was over .300 or in that vicinity: George "Kiddo" Davis, .309; Dick Bartell, .308; Hal Lee, .302; and Art Whitney, .298. Kiddo Davis, a one-year center fielder, was a New York University graduate and former Yankee farm hand. He was purchased from New York's St. Paul Club.

Sports writers were comparing the Klein-Hurst two-man destruction team with the better publicized Babe Ruth-Lou Gehrig "One-Two punch" of the 1932 Yankee World's Champions. And the comparison was by no means odious. That year the Phillie pair hit for 737 total bases (420 for Chuck and 317 for Don) against 672 for the two great Yanks (370 for Gehrig and 302 for Babe).

Klein again was utterly devastating. He scored 152 runs, six below his earlier National League record; drove in 137 runs; and his 226 hits included 50 doubles, 17 triples and 38 homers. A young New Yorker, Mel Ott, playing in the Polo Grounds "home run orchard," managed to tie Klein's 38 round-trippers. Chuck won the *Sporting News'* Most Valuable Player prize for the National League in both 1931 and 1932. Hurst scored 109 runs and knocked in 147. How could the Phillies lose?

Again, the fault rested with the pitchers. If the Phillies scored the most runs in the league, they also had the most runs scored against them: 796. Only three pitchers—Benge; Flint Rhem, picked up from the Cardinals, June 4th; and Edgar Holley, purchased from Kansas City, appeared in the list of pitchers who took part in ten complete games.

Collins and Benge had almost the same won and lost records, 14-12 and 13-12; Jim Elliott slumped to 11-10; and Hal Elliott and

Clise Dudley flopped dismally. Rhem did well after joining the club. He was an almost unbelievable character and cut up plenty of capers in Baker Bowl, including a game he wouldn't pitch until the groundkeeper built him a new pitcher's mound. A stocky South Carolinian, with a slow drawl and a big thirst, he had figured in numerous bizarre happenings as a St. Louis Cardinal. Once, for the good of the team, he drank Alexander's liquor so that Grover would be in condition to pitch next day. Again, when he was slated to pitch a vital Cardinal-Brooklyn game in 1930, Rhem allegedly was kidnapped and taken to a mysterious place in New Jersey, where his abductors, with a pistol at his midriff, poured cups of raw whiskey down his gullet.

CHAPTER 18

Chuting the Chutes with Gerry Nugent

1

BY 1933, Gerald P. Nugent had taken the driver's seat as the Philadelphia president. It started another unhappy period, in which the trend was down, down and further down. Even the occasional fifth and sixth place clubs were to be denied to Philadelphia fans. It wasn't even all sixes and sevens, but all sevens and eights.

Gerry Nugent had been a shoe salesman before joining the Phillies. Yet, unlike the New Yorker Baker, he was a born Philadelphian, and a Phillie fan from 'way back. He had played baseball for Northeast High, and with other Philadelphia amateur teams. He actually suffered when the Phillies lost, and in his silent hours he dreamed of being the president of a championship Phillie club. But he and his wife soon were caught in a financial trap, and the only exits seemed to be the old Baker recipe—sell players.

Throughout the Nugent regime there was an endless parade of ball players through the Phillies' clubhouse. The depression was on, and everybody in baseball was suffering. Whenever a player became of any real value to the Phillies, he usually was sold for a price that would keep the team in business for another year. Poor attendance and poor teams kept Nugent in a rut from which he never could escape. There even was talk of shifting this valuable National League franchise. Yet how Gerry built up players who had been tossed into his cash deals as a little something extra, and then sold them for fat prices, became an outstanding bit of baseball legerdemain.

For a while there was hope the club would capitalize on the fourth-placer of 1932, and build up from there. That hope quickly was dissipated. It started at the December, 1932, National League annual meeting with the trading of Ray Benge, one of the few dependable pitchers, to Brooklyn for two mediocre infielders, Mickey Finn and Jack Warner; Pitcher Cy Moore; and $15,000. And the Phillies needed pitchers more than anything else! A three-cornered deal with the Giants and Pittsburgh made at the same time didn't turn out so badly. The Phillies acquired Chick Fullis, a center fielder, and Gus Dugas, outfielder-first baseman who quickly flopped, while the Giants landed Kiddo Davis and Pitcher Glenn Spencer. Pittsburgh won the former Giant star, Freddy Lindstrom. Fullis made Nugent look good on that one in 1933, hitting .309 to Davis' 258, though Kiddo helped Bill Terry win the 1933 World's Championship.

However, when the club started poorly in the spring, and Nugent needed more money, Gerry dealt the fans a hard blow. He sacrificed Pinky Whitney, then one of the league's top third basemen, and Outfielder Hal Lee to Boston for two mediocrities, Outfielder Wes Schulmerich, Infielder Fritz Knothe and cash. Schulmerich actually hit like a fool when he first came to Baker Bowl, but lost the trick the next year and was shunted to the Reds.

The 1933 club slipped to seventh with a 60-92, .395 finish, and ended the six-year reign of Burt Shotton. It had the distinction of having the league's No. 1 and 2 batsmen, Chuck Klein and Spud Davis; it had two players, Chuck Klein and Shortstop Dick Bartell, in McGraw's starting line-up in the first All-Star game; but had only one pitcher, Edgar Holley, listed among National League regulars—men who pitched in at least ten complete games.

Klein won the league's triple crown, batting champion with .368, runs batted in leader with 120 and home run king with a reduced 28. But the league had taken a few more springs out of the Jackrabbit ball. It still was live enough for Chuck to crack out 223 hits for a total of 365 bases. That enabled him to tie an old mark of Hans Wagner: most consecutive years to lead the N. L. in total bases.

Chuck's continued bombardment of the Phillie and other National League fences made quite an impression on Bill Veeck, president of the rich Chicago Cubs, and father of the present baseball impresario in St. Louis. The elder Veeck entertained a strong yen to see the broad-shouldered Hoosier in Cub regalia, and Nugent could see no objection provided Veeck could deliver a sufficiently large check with the Wrigley autograph. Unfortunately for Veeck, he died before the deal could be consummated, but his successors carried on, and on November 21, 1933, Philadelphia was shocked to hear that its greatest slugger since Delahanty had been sold to the Cubs. In exchange for the man who had won the National League's three top honors of 1933, Nugent received $65,000, Pitcher Ted Kleinhans, Infielder Mark Koenig and Outfielder Harvey Henrick. Koenig, former Yankee shortstop great, was near the end of his career and was sold to the Reds; the other two throw-ins helped little.

The sale of Klein didn't raise as much indignation as that of Alexander to Chicago fifteen years before. Philadelphia fans were becoming used to these sales. But many fans who had remained loyal through thick and thin threw up their hands, and asked: "What's the use?" Yet Klein soon was to prove a disappointment in Chicago, return to Philadelphia two and a half years later, and Nugent's two Klein deals were to become masterpieces in baseball acumen.

2

The man selected by the Nugents to replace Shotton was the home town boy, Catcher Jimmy Wilson, sold to the Cardinals in 1928. Wilson still was one of the game's top catchers, but Branch Rickey had come up with a great youngster, Bill Delancy, and was willing to let Jimmy return to Philadelphia and realize a managerial ambition. Oddly enough, Spud Davis, who came to

Philadelphia in the original Wilson deal, and Ed Delker, another ex-Cardinal, were traded back to St. Louis for Wilson.

The Nugents had the same regard for Wilson as did Baker, their benefactor. Relations between Wilson and Gerry Nugent always were close. It didn't prevent the president from selling the manager's top players, but Jimmy understood, rarely complained and did his best with the material put at his disposal. His managerial tenure was to last four years, two less than Shotton's.

Jim's 1934 club finished seventh, with four less victories and one more defeat than Shotton's last club. Some wisecrackers quipped, "Well, Chuck Klein's going has cost us just one game." The 1934 team had two successive months which were enough to drive any manager into the lock ward. In July, Wilson's boys enjoyed their best month, winning 18 and losing 13. They paid for it in August, when they won 4 and lost 21. "How can a ball club be so inconsistent?" asked Nugent. "You tell me," shot back Wilson. Just before the end of the season, they helped knock the Giants out of the pennant, and handed it to Frisch's Cardinals by beating Terry's New Yorkers at the Polo Grounds, 4-0 and 5-4. Those defeats hurt New York as much as Coveleskie's victories of 1908.

The Nugents got some kind of a break when Sunday ball was legalized in Pennsylvania in 1934. The Phillies played the first Sunday National League game ever played in Philadelphia, April 29th, and the fans got a real run for their money. The home team lost, but they battled to the last putout before losing to Brooklyn, 8 to 7. By this time some of the writers tried to take some of the curse off the team by calling them the Phils, rather than the Phillies.

The club came up with one of its lucky drafts, snaring Pitcher Curt Davis from the San Francisco club. Curt, a long, lanky Missourian, paid quick dividends; he appeared in 51 games, most for a National League pitcher that year, and won 19 games while losing 17, a remarkable showing with a seventh-placer. Soon he was to bring high value on the N. L. Player Exchange.

Nugent continued to operate on the old Baker system. On June 11th, he sold the second part of the Klein-Hurst "One-Two" punch, Don Hurst, to the Cubs for $30,000. Chicago graciously tossed in a young first baseman from the Coast, Dolph Camilli, who proved a jewel in the rough. If Klein disappointed in Chicago, Hurst proved a complete flop. It led to the expression "Philadelphia hitters"—men who could lash hits against the right field screen at Baker Bowl but were of little use elsewhere.

At the end of the season Gerry disposed of his All-Star shortstop, Rowdy Dick Bartell, to the Giants for cash and a raft of secondary players: Third baseman Johnny Vergez, Shortstop Blondie Ryan, Outfielder George Watkins and Pitcher John "Pretzels" Pezzulo. Ryan and Vergez had been regulars on the Giant World's Champions of 1933, but they had been hot for just that season and were of little help to the Phils.

A pretty good May deal was arranged with the Reds—Outfielders Wes Schulmerich and Bill Ruble and Pitcher Kleinhans for Outfielder Johnny Moore and the pitching veteran, Sylvester Johnson. Moore hit .330 against Schulmerich's .260, which made Nugent chuckle, "I don't look so bad on that one; do I?"

Another outfielder, Ethan Allen, a fleet runner from the University of Cincinnati, matched Moore's .330. Wilson turned much of his catching over to Al Todd, a Troy, New Yorker who had been drafted a few years before from Dallas. Big Al hit .318 in 91 games. Bartell hit .310 in his last year in Phillie, and Lou Chiozza, second base draftee from Memphis, poked the ball for .305. Yes, the Phillies were seventh, but they still could bombard that tired old tin wall in right field. And, of course, the opposition did likewise. Baker Bowl still was no place for pitchers, young or old, good or bad. During a six-game stretch in July, while the Dodgers and Braves were in town, the Phillies scored 63 runs to 55 for the visitors.

Some of these slugfests with Brooklyn lasted for hours and wore out a dozen pitchers. In one typical Dodger-Phillies affair, Casey Stengel, then boss man of the Brooks, had a big right-hander in the box named Walter "Boom-Boom" Beck, who was later to find his way into the uniform of the Phils. Casey wore a path from the dugout to the mound as Beck teetered on the brink of disaster, inning after inning.

During one interlude Hack Wilson, playing right field for Brooklyn and tired from chasing line drives, relaxed against the fence. In a moment, he was dozing away in the hot afternoon sun. Meanwhile, Beck had been told he was through for the afternoon, and in a fit of anger he took the ball and heaved it with all his might against the right field fence. It struck with a clang a few feet above Wilson's head. Hack jumped, stared about him wildly, then chased after the ball, grabbed it and heaved it on a line to second base. To the genial and playful Hack, life had become just one base hit after another.

3

During the 1934 season the Phillies picked up a strong-throwing third baseman, William "Bucky" Walters, on inter-league waivers from the Red Sox. Walters was a fine-looking Philadelphia boy, hailing from the Germantown section, and an old friend of Wilson's. He had been with both Boston clubs as an infielder and had played with half a dozen minor league clubs. In his first year in pro ball, 1929, he had pitched for High Point in the Piedmont League, but a season later he switched to the infield. Bucky was a fair third baseman and hit .260 for the 1934 Phillies in 83 games, but as the season drew to a close, Wilson asked him: "How'd you like to try pitching, Bucky? Your ball is fairly alive when you throw it, and if you can control it, I believe you'd have one of the best fast balls in the league. Besides, we're getting Vergez from the Giants to play third base, and this may keep you in the league."

Bucky agreed, and pitched seven innings in two September games. At the 1935 training camp at Leesburg, Wilson continued the experiment. In an early exhibition game with Cincinnati, Walters was so wild that he almost killed his opponents. He had them dropping to the ground to avoid his "live" delivery. He hit two and gave up a mess of bases on balls. Wilson had to pull him out. Bucky was completely disgusted with himself, and though he always has been a clean-living athlete, that night he tried to drown his sorrows and bad control in illicit concoctions of that part of dry Florida. But when his head cleared the next morning, it was with a fresh resolve to make good as a pitcher. As for Wilson, he never lost his confidence, and patience, with the tall, handsome fellow Philadelphian. "From now on, you're one of my regular pitchers," he told the Germantown boy, "and before I'm through with you, you'll be one of the best in the game." What's more, Jimmy offered Bucky a case of champagne if he'd stick to it, and follow Wilson's coaching.

In 1935, as the Phillies had their third straight seventh-placer (64-89), Pitcher Bucky won nine games and lost nine. He improved steadily from then on, until all of Wilson's fine hopes were realized.

As Curt Davis had a 16-14 record in his second year with the club, and old Sylvester Johnson stood at 10-8, the futility of the rest of the staff may well be realized. Fidgety Phil Collins was sold to the Cardinals, and Nugent got his money out of the Fidgeter just in time, as Collins faded into the minors in 1936. The Phillies did come up with a promising pitching youngster, a broad-shouldered New Englander, Hugh Noyes Mulcahy, who toiled faithfully for the Philadelphia rear guard until Uncle Sam took priority on the stocky righthander.

Catcher Todd caught 107 games this season and hit .287. His fine work was recognized in the other corner of the state, and in November, Bill Benswanger, new Pirate president, gave Nugent $20,000 for Todd and threw in a battery: Pitcher Claude Passeau, then a Pirate farm hand, and Catcher Bob Grace. That was another deal which was to bring Gerry many chuckles.

CHAPTER 19

Deeper and Deeper into the Cellar

1

NUGENT's team hit bottom again in 1936, the first absolute tail-ender since 1930, but Gerry won baseball's highest award for artistic juggling when he regained Chuck Klein from the Cubs on May 21st. The Cubs were so anxious to get Curt Davis, the Phillies $7,500 draft pitcher, that they turned back Klein and threw in $50,000 and Pitcher Kowalik, whose main claim to distinction was breaking Hank Greenberg's wrist in the 1935 Cub-Tiger World Series, putting Hank out of the Series and the 1936 season. The Phillies also sent Center fielder Ethan Allen to the Cubs in the same deal.

Getting $65,000 for Chuck in 1934 and then getting another $50,000 to take him back in '36 was really something in high baseball finance. It put Gerry in a class with the big Wall Street boys, who know just when to sell and when to buy.

After Klein hit .301 and .293 for the Cubs in 1934 and 1935, Chuck batted .306 in 1936 and smote in 104 runs, his last year to drive in 100 or more tallies. But he performed another feat which writes his name indelibly into the baseball records. On July 10th, a month and a half after rejoining the team, he became the fourth big leaguer, and second since Delahanty, to hit four homers in one game. Chuck put on his show at Forbes Field, Pittsburgh, and it won for the Phils, 9 to 6.

Oddly enough, Philadelphia was intimately associated with three of the first four of these feats. After Bobbie Lowe of Boston was the first four-homer-a-game man in 1894, Ed Delahanty was the second in 1896. It wasn't until 1932 that a third man, Lou Gehrig of the Yankees, turned the trick and he selected Shibe Park for the locale. Then Chuck was No. 4 in 1936.

However, unlike the others, Klein made his four homers in a ten-inning game. The score was 6-6 at the end of the ninth, when Chuck hit his fourth, and longest of the day, off Bill Swift's first tenth inning pitch. Chuck almost made it five that day, when in the second inning he backed Paul Waner to the fence in deepest right for his smoking drive.

Klein's clubbing couldn't prevent the club receding to the old 100 defeat class. The Phils lost an even 100 and won 54. They didn't go completely to pot until August 1st. On that day, the National League's Sixtieth Anniversary Day in Philadelphia, they defeated the Cardinals, 11 to 4. After that, they dropped 14 straight, Passeau snapping the slump, August 18th, with a shutout against the Braves. But by that time the club was hopelessly in the cellar.

Still, the club had some strong performing players. Dolph Camilli, the first baseman the Cubs tossed into the Hurst sale, came fast that season, jacking his batting average from .261 in 1935 to .315. And the California Italian hit the long ball, 29 doubles, 13 triples, 28 homers, and 102 runs batted in. Passeau, the young pitcher picked up in the Todd deal, won 11 games and lost 15. Other clubs already were looking at them with avid eyes. Third baseman Pinkey Whitney was regained from Boston in an early season trade for Mickey Haslin, a smart piece of business for Nugent and Wilson.

At the close of the season Nugent peddled little Lou Chiozza, who had built up quite a following among Philadelphia's Italian citizenry, to the Giants for George Scharein and $20,000. Scharein played shortstop for the Phillies for the next three years. Terry converted Chiozza into a part-time center fielder, and the little fellow was a valuable member of the 1937 Giant N. L. Champions.

2

There was a little improvement in the 1937 Phillies. Wilson got the club back to seventh and within a point of .400 (61-92, .399). Alas, that was to be the highest for a long time! Whitney was so glad to be back at Baker Bowl that he hit .353, which had him up with the league's leading five. Camilli advanced to .337, and socked 27 homers. Klein hit .325 (his last .300 average), but injuries limited him to 115 games. Johnny Moore was well up the list with .322. Yes, the club still had power. Even with the limping Klein down to 15 homers, the club ranked high in that department, getting 103 to 111 for the league leader, the pennant-winning Giants.

The pitching wasn't too bad, and four pitchers were closely bunched: Passeau, 14-18; Walters, 14-15; Wayne LaMaster, 15-19; Max Butcher, 11-15. They looked worse in the National League's earned run department. Among the first pitching group, Passeau was fourth from the bottom, while Walters and LaMaster stood at the bottom of the class. Mulcahy wasn't in this group, having pitched only 9 complete games, but people were beginning to say nice things about him. Farmed to Hazleton in 1936, he was a sensation, winning 25 games and losing 14. Back with the Phillies, he won 8 and lost 18, but suffered some of the club's most heartbreaking defeats.

Things again might have looked better for the Phillies if it hadn't been for tempters among National League club owners and Gerry Nugent's itching palm. He got rid of two of the club's most valuable assets. First baseman Dolph Camilli of the big home run bat, and the fast-coming converted pitcher, Bucky Walters.

Camilli went first, on March 6th, at the very start of the 1938 training season. The high-powered Larry McPhail had moved from Cincinnati to Brooklyn, and one of his first strengthening moves was to entice the slugging Californian away from the Phillies. His bait was a $45,000 check, signed by the Brooklyn Trust Co., and a .188-hitting outfielder, Ed Morgan. Dolph immediately was adopted by the Ebbets Field fans, and in 1941 he helped win the flag for the Dodgers with 34 home runs and 120 runs batted in. Quite properly, he was named the league's Most Valuable Player.

Walters stuck with the Phillies until June 13th, when he went to Cincinnati for $55,000, the return of old Spud Davis, and left-handed Pitcher Al Hollingsworth. Warren Giles, MacPhail's Cincinnati successor, and Bill McKechnie were building a pennant contender in Cincinnati and Bucky put them over. Some Phillie fans turned green with envy as the Germantown boy helped the Reds to pennants in 1939 and 1940 with magnificent records of 27-11 and 22-10, respectively. He beat Camilli to the league's player award by two years.

The departure of Camilli and Walters dealt the Phils more of a knockout blow than the sale of the stars who preceded them—Alexander, Killefer, Bancroft, Meusel, Meadows, Klein, Bartell and the rest. This time the Phils plunged right through the standing to the abysmal pit. They finished such a bad last (45-105, .300) that they came home 27½ games behind the seventh place Dodgers.

Perhaps it was Nugent's need for money in June, after two harrowing months, which dictated the sale of Walters. But the earlier sale of Camilli had put a gaping hole at first base. Two mediocrities, Gene Corbett and Jim Browne, puttered around at the position until Phil Weintraub, a former Giant and Red, was purchased from Baltimore. The Jewish lad had a pretty good punch but never won any medals with his fielding. He hit .310 in an even 100 games, and was the club's only .300 hitter, though Outfielder Herschel Martin, a product of the Cardinal farm system, was close with .298 and showed much promise.

In the past the Phillies had had some respectable tailenders, like the old home run leaders of the Cravath-Wilhelm-Fletcher period and the 1930 club, which hit .315 and was stocked with .300 hitters. But this '38 tailender couldn't even hit. It was seventh in team batting with a poorly .254 and last in homers with a paltry 40. Camilli hit 24 that season for Brooklyn.

The drop in home run production was partly due to the move to Shibe Park in the middle of the season, when the Nugents became tenants of Connie Mack and the Shibe heirs. The move had been discussed for years, was advocated by the league, but never acted upon. The Phillies had a 99-year lease on the Broad and Huntington property, and this supposedly was one of the club's biggest assets. At one time several industrial concerns wanted the property, but after the Phillies vacated it, it was used for midget racing, circuses, carnivals, wrestling, as an ice skating rink, even for miniature golf; and now is a P. T. C. parking lot.

No tears were shed at the closing of the rusty old bandbox, though in the nineties it had been the pride of Reach and Rogers and the showplace of the National League. Later it was responsible for some of the funniest, goofiest and wildest incidents in the long history of Philadelphia baseball. Moreover, the park had become a firetrap and it was almost as hazardous for the fans as for the pitchers.

Jimmy Wilson wasn't there at the finish. He resigned in late September, commenting: "Even Connie Mack finishes last, when he has no ball players." The faithful Phillie coach, old Hans Lobert, the flash of 1911, was at the helm when the curtain was rung down on the dismal season. Jimmy Wilson wasn't the best manager in baseball, as attested by his later work in Chicago, but he deserved better tools to work with than the Nugents put at his disposal. He retired to the bench in 1938, catching only three games. Nugent felt the pitching might have been better had Jimmy personally caught some of the young twirlers.

Wilson moved on to Cincinnati as coach and bullpen catcher, rejoining his protégé, Bucky Walters. All Philadelphia got a big kick out of the 1940 World Series, when, with the Red catching staff disabled, Jimmy donned his old armor, caught brilliantly, hit .353, stole the only base of the Series, and helped Bucky Walters and Paul Derringer win a spirited seven-game Series from the Detroit Tigers. Walters and Wilson were welcomed back to the Quaker City as conquering heroes. But a few groaners commented, "If only they could have done that for the Phillies!"

CHAPTER 20

A Few More Startling Transactions

1

IN LOOKING for a successor to Jimmy Wilson, Nugent reached into the Southern Association and pulled out a dentist, Doc James Thompson Prothro. Prothro, a native of Memphis, had won pennants for both his native Memphis and Little Rock, and was considered a bit of a genius south of the Mason and Dixon line. A baseball and football star at prep school and college, Doc had matriculated at the University of Tennessee and was a practicing dentist at Dyersburg, Tennesee, when Clark Griffith signed him for Washington in 1920. He was a third baseman-shortstop of modest ability, and for three years "Griff" shunted him back and forth between his parent club in the capital and minor league affiliates. Doc showed some success as a hitter, batting .333 in 46 games with the 1924 Senators and .313 in 119 games with the 1925 Red Sox. He bowed out of the majors as a player after a brief engagement with the 1926 Cincinnati Reds.

While in Washington, Prothro served under Bucky Harris, the boy genius of 1924, who took a club which had been 23 games off the pace in 1923 and led it to a breath-taking American League flag and World's Championship. It made young Bucky the toast of the nation. Perhaps these Washington successes of a quarter of a century ago made Doc believe in baseball miracles and encouraged him in the thought that he, too, might be another miracle worker.

"Every ball player and minor league manager has an ambition

to manage in the majors," said Doc when he took over the 1939 Phillies. "The Phillies are down, but they still are the major league." After three years in command he wasn't so sure of the Phillies' major league status. Though in later years Prothro became the owner of extensive real estate and farm properties in Tennessee and Arkansas, in his earlier years as a player and manager he practiced dentistry between seasons. But if he brought pain to others by yanking their molars, the Phillies surely settled accounts for his patients. They tortured Doc as few managers have been tortured before. In view of what had gone on before, it may seem almost libelous to say so, but the three Prothro clubs, and the 1942 team under Hans Lobert, were the worst of all Phillie ball clubs, perhaps the worst four successive tailenders in baseball history. Only one emerged with a percentage above .300. The horrible details—1939: 45-106, .298; 1940: 50-103, .327; 1941: 43-111, .279; 1942: 42-109, .278.

Philadelphia is a big town; many of its rooters are dyed-in-the-wool National League fans, oldsters from the era of Delahanty and Lajoie, those who remember Pat Moran's champions, and later converts. Bad as the Phillies were, they could attract about a quarter million fans a year at home. Night ball, which came to Shibe Park in 1939, also helped. And though Eddie Pollock, Bill Dooly, Don Donaghey, Frank Yeutter, Red Smith, Eddie Delaney and Stan Baumgartner usually left the Phillie press box with wild stares, they continued to record the doings of these Phillie misfits, their hits, runs—and many errors—for posterity. And though they suffered with the team, they had to applaud as Gerry Nugent tried vainly to keep his head above water as he swam upstream into a relentless current.

Even out-of-town writers, who panned Nugent for the type of teams he brought to their towns, couldn't help but admire the way he worked his deals. The pitching of Claude Passeau, the pitcher Benswanger tossed into the 1935 Todd transaction, stood out, even on that terrible team. Claude was a Mississippi collegian with a degree from Millsaps College. Anyone with half an eye could see that he would be a winner with a real team behind him.

So just before Decoration Day, 1939, Nugent made the Cubs a present. He let them have Claude, the Millsaps boy. All he exacted from Jimmy Gallagher, the Chicago general manager, was $50,000; Outfielder Joe Marty, a regular on the Cub champions of 1938; and two pitchers, Ray Harrell and Walter Kirby Higbe. Passeau did all right on the Cubs, and pitched a one-hitter in the 1945 World Series. But in parting with Higbe, the Cubs made the same blunder they did in 1934 when they tossed young Camilli into the Hurst deal.

Higbe, an untrammeled soul from South Carolina, had joined the Cubs as an uninhibited rookie in the spring of 1939. He had been a strike-out king in the minors with Portsmouth, Virginia, Moline and Birmingham. "Ol' Higgleby," as they later called him at Ebbets Field, was an immediate success after Doc Prothro gave him regular work. Even the tailender of 1940 couldn't conceal his talents, and "Hig" wasn't one to hide his light under a bushel. He had a fast ball that really jumped. Kirby pitched 283 innings, had a record of 14 wins and 19 defeats and was the National League's strike-out leader with 137.

Larry MacPhail, who had such a yen for Camilli in 1938, now got a terrific crush on Ol' Higgleby. The redhead had advanced the Dodgers to second in 1940, and Kirby Higbe was the man he wanted to put the Dodgers in the World Series. Again, like Barkis, Gerry Nugent was willing. Other clubs also were bidding, so Gerry exacted his price, and this time the cash reached six figures, $100,000, Catcher Mickey Livingston and Pitchers Vito Tamulis and Bill Crouch. What a profit in a year and a half on the Cub pitching throw-in of the Passeau deal!

As Passeau was a Memorial Day present for the Cubs, so Higbe was an Armistice Day baby for the Brooklyn fans. The deal was closed on November 11, 1940. McPhail never had occasion to regret it, and it paid off handsomely next season when Higbe's 22 victories and Camilli's slugging helped Brooklyn gain its first pennant in twenty-one years after a tight race with the Cardinals.

With the going of Higbe, the Phillies were worse than ever, as the 1941 club skidded to the all-time Phillie low of .279. Lesser players had been sold for lesser sums: Pitcher Al Hollingsworth was traded to the Yankee farm team in Newark for Second baseman Roy Hughes, and the battery of Max Butcher and Spud Davis was disposed of to the Pirates. In 1939, Spud had been one of the team's two .300 hitters, and he won considerable distinction by going through 85 games without an error. But Nugent was finding out the truth of one of Colonel Ruppert's apt observations, when offered money for one of his stars; "I can't play a check in left field." However, Gerry Nugent was no millionaire brewer; he was selling players to stay in business, for despite the fat checks, he and his wife were going deeper and deeper into the hole with their baseball inheritance.

2

There were a few bright spots during these dismal years. A Jewish outfielder, Morrie Arnovich, hit like blazes in 1939. While he closed the season with a satisfactory .324, at the time of the mid-season All-Star game at Yankee Stadium, Morrie was hitting .375 and was named for the National League squad. Though the National League lost, 3 to 1, Arnovich was permitted to sit on his haunches all through the game. Even though Gabby Hartnett, the National League manager, had four occasions to use a pinch-hitter, he always looked the other way from Morrie and called on the ex-Phillie Camilli, Billy Herman, Johnny Mize and Babe Phelps. Jewish fans in Philadelphia and New York never forgave Gabby and booed him as long as he remained in the National League.

Unfortunately, the magic ran out of Morrie, or his bat, the next season, and he was traded to Cincinnati for Johnny Rizzo, a hot-tempered Italian who connected for twenty of his twenty-four 1940 home runs after coming to Shibe Park. In the fall of 1938, the Phillies drafted Merrill May, a Newark Yankee farm hand; he hit .293 for the 1940 Quakers and was considered good enough to play third base for the National League stars when they won their 4-0 shutout in the St. Louis All-Star game of that year.

Late in the season of 1940, the Phillies came up with Daniel

Webster "Danny" Litwhiler, a Pennsylvania Dutchman from Ringtown, Pennsylvania, and graduate of Bloomsburg, Pennsylvania Teacher's College. From the start Danny swung an explosive bat. In 36 games he hit .345 and sent five balls over the fences for homers. In the horrible season of 1941, Danny was almost the lone ray of sunshine, hitting .305, while his bat bag contained 25 doubles, 6 triples and 18 homers.

The war also caught up with the Phillies. Uncle Sam didn't even wait for Pearl Harbor to clamp down on the team, drafting Hughie Mulcahy before the 1941 season got under way. Hughie was the losin'est pitcher in the league with 20 defeats in 1938 and 22 in 1940. In the latter season, he also had the doubtful distinction of being blasted for the most hits, 283, but that only meant he was a hard industrious worker and a workhorse. The stocky Irish lad from Brighton won 13 games in 1940, and the press box boys were speculating which rich club would get this prize, when Mulcahy received his "Greetings" letter from the President of the United States. The Army kept Hughie for four years, and by the time he rejoined the Phillies late in the 1945 season much of the pitching talent had been drilled out of him. He might have hung up a great record in the books with another club, and in another period.

The same held true of Pitchers Tommy Hughes, a Wilkes-Barre lad, and Ike Pearson, a tall lanky Mississipian, who also went into Service. Hughes had a 12-18 record with Lobert's 1942 team, and though Pearson could show no better than 4-14 in '41, Ike turned in some well-pitched games. But neither had it when they returned after years of military service. Johnny Prodgjny, a product of the Chester, Pennsylvania, sand lots, had several fair seasons before being waived to the Pirates.

Nugent got himself into Judge Landis' doghouse late in the Judge's career as Baseball Commissioner and late in Gerry's career as Phillie president. In the 1940 minor league draft Nugent, having an early crack at the minor league stars because of the low standing of his club, came up with a big six-foot five-inch North Carolina pitcher, Reuben Franklin Melton, of the Columbus, Ohio, club. Though Rube had a record of only 10-10 in Columbus, he was highly regarded in the Cardinal organization because of his great size and a smoking fast ball, and many smart baseball men considered him the best young pitching prospect in the country.

Before the draft, Larry MacPhail of Brooklyn was keenly interested in Melton, and Branch Rickey, then still head of the Cardinal farm system, quoted him a price of $30,000.

"Thirty thousand dollars nothing," stormed MacPhail. "I'll get Melton for half of that price."

The fall after Nugent drafted Melton, he sold the pitcher to Brooklyn for $15,000. It also was reported that MacPhail had advanced Nugent the old $7,500 Class AAA draft price he had put out for the pitcher. Even before Rickey demanded an investigation, Landis said he detected "something smelly." After he made a thorough investigation, he vetoed the deal and gave both MacPhail and Nugent a verbal spanking. Melton showed up at the Phils' training camp next spring with his wife, children and father, who promptly were shipped home on the first train to North Carolina after Hans Lobert discovered them.

The Melton case had an interesting aftermath. Rube did little with the 1941 Phillies, but in 1942, Hans Lobert gave him lots of work and he emerged with a record of 9 victories and 20 defeats. While he led the league in bases on balls, he also struck out 107 and began to show some of the stuff expected of him. By this time Larry MacPhail was in the Army and Branch Rickey had succeeded him as major-domo in Brooklyn. Branch never had lost his faith that Melton had the makings of another Dizzy Dean and handed Nugent $30,000, the price he originally quoted MacPhail, for the Rube. Rickey also threw in Pitcher Johnny Allen, who never reported to the Phils. However, Melton was wild in more ways than his control and never lived up to Rickey's expectations.

In 1941, the Phillies acquired First baseman Nick Etten, a Villa Nova collegian and former property of the Athletics, from the Baltimore club. Nick hit .311 in 1941 and .264 in 1942, and every now and then would clout one for the distance. On January 22, 1943, Etten figured in Nugent's last deal. In an inter-league transaction, Gerry traded Etten to the Yankees for two Yankee farm hands, Pitcher Allen Gettel and First baseman Ed Levy and a badly needed $10,000. It was the last check Nugent would cash for a player. Etten became a pretty good wartime first baseman for the Yankees, leading the American League in home runs in 1944 and runs batted in, in 1945. As for Gettel and Levy, they never reported to the Phils.

CHAPTER 21

Bill Cox Gets Quick Heave-Ho

AFTER a decade of Nugent operation, in which the club had four seventh-placers and six tailenders, the National League decided to step in. Despite the big prices that Nugent received for his players, especially the $180,000 deposited in the Passeau, Higbe and Melton deals, the club was deeply in debt to the league. Other clubs also wearied of the spiritless aggregations Nugent was bringing to their towns. After some weeks of negotiation, the National League took over the club in February, 1943, and a short time later Ford Frick, then the league executive, dug up a purchaser for the sick franchise in the person of William D. Cox, who was in the lumber business and had dabbled in professional sports, especially football. Like Bill Baker, Bill Cox was a New Yorker. He had played prep school baseball, and later was a member of the Yale diamond squad.

Most folks thought Bill Cox got a good break when earlier in the winter Clark Griffith terminated the capable Bucky Harris' second engagement in Washington. It put the personable Harris on the market. Cox jumped at the chance to engage Harris as his manager, but today Cox probably judges that as one of the worst breaks of his life. One of Harris' first moves was to advise the hiring of Elwood "Schoolboy" Rowe, former Tiger pitching ace and joint holder of the American League record of sixteen straight wins. The elongated perennial Arkansas Schoolboy was purchased from the Brooklyn farm in Montreal.

However, by the time the Phillies assembled at their 1943 war training camp at Hershey, Pennsylvania, they were indeed a sorry aggregation. The war had made heavy inroads on the tailenders, and Nugent had shaved down the roster to the bone just before he got out. Only sixteen players answered the first roll call. In the early practice periods, it really was hysterical. Old Chuck Klein, who hit .100 in twelve games that season, worked out at first base, and Rowe at shortstop. Even Boss Cox worked out as a pitcher and at shortstop, and he wasn't so bad a pitcher, either. The club practiced on a field that was not much bigger than a "Little League" field, and any well-hit ball wound up in Cocoa Creek. The club was housed in the Community House and the players ate their meals at a cafeteria.

Yet surprisingly enough, Harris did a great job, and by the time the regular season started, Bucky had the club playing pretty good ball—at least a far better brand than the last Nugent .278 tailender. Rowe made a splendid comeback, and finished that season with a 14-8 record. But Bucky also turned out some other pretty fair mound workers: Kewpie Barrett, purchased from the Cubs; and two left-handed newcomers, Jack Kraus and Al Gerheauser. The latter, a St. Louisan, did especially well against the Cardinal wartime champions of his native city.

One of the league's former ace pitchers, Bill Lee, also was picked up later in the season from the Cubs on waivers. In the spring Manuel "Gyp" Salvo, a huge Californian, was an earlier waiver acquisition from the Braves, but when he wasn't in shape to pitch, Cox raised such hell that the Boston club refunded the money. Though Cox's Phillie career was doomed to be short, he established one record by being the only club owner who ever got his dough back for a waiver player.

Jim Wasdell, a former Dodger, and Babe Dahlgren, Lou Gehrig's first successor on the Yankees, took care of Nick Etten's vacant first base post. But the deal which gave Cox most pleasure was the trading of Danny Litwhiler, the popular Pennsylvania Dutchman, and Earl Naylor, a pitcher-outfielder, to the Cardinals for Outfielders Elvin "Buster" Adams, Coaker Triplett and Dain Clay. The latter was released to the Reds. Buster Adams was Cox's pride and joy. "He'll make Philadelphia fans think Dode Paskert is back playing center field for them," he predicted. Buster was a fly-hawk, and proved to be a fair wartime hitter.

Philadelphia liked Rowe's pitching and hitting (he hit .300 in 82 games), Adams' fielding and other improvements, and gave Cox support such as no Phillie club had received in years. It was moving along in sixth place, with a percentage around .425, when on July 28th, the lid suddenly blew off the visitors' clubhouse in St. Louis.

When the players reached there, they learned that Bucky Harris no longer was manager, and that fat Freddy Fitzsimmons, Brooklyn pitcher, had been named Bucky's successor. Bucky had learned of his dismissal from St. Louis newspapermen who told him of press association dispatches from Philadelphia to that effect. Four hours before telephoning Harris, Cox had given out the Philadelphia press release that Bucky was out, and Fitz was in.

The Phillies were so indignant at what they regarded a "bum rap" for their discarded chief that they decided to strike. While no official statement ever was made, it generally was understood that Schoolboy Rowe was the moving spirit. At any rate, it was practically unanimous. When time came for the club to take the field for practice before a night game in Sportsman's Park, the Phillies remained in the clubhouse. Jimmy Hagen, the traveling secretary, tried to patch up the trouble but met with no success. Shortly before game time, Harris, though terribly burned up, entered the clubhouse and said, "Better take the field, fellows. This won't help. Do it, for my sake." The strike then was called off, and the game was played under Fitz's direction.

Just what precipitated this early Cox-Harris break-up? Cox was a 'round the clock worker; between his New York business interests and his baseball he spent 16 hours a day flying about trying to make changes to improve the ball team. Harris, on the other hand, was the type of manager who left his baseball on the field. After the day's toil was over, he wasn't available until shortly before the next game. That's how he managed under Griffith. It didn't suit Cox, who wanted a 24-hour-a-day manager, a manager he could contact any hour of the day or night. That didn't fit into Harris' schedule. It opened the breach that widened with other things.

Cox brought in a trainer, a fellow who had been his track coach at prep school and had trained the Hungarian Olympic team. What he didn't know about training a baseball team would fill Delaware Bay. But Harris, who thinks calisthenics are for birds as far as baseball is concerned, put up with his setting-up and sitting-down exercises at Hershey. The trainer's favorite dietary items were oranges cut in quarters which were spread out on the bench. The climax came when the trainer fell sound asleep on the bench, right in the midst of his sliced oranges, and Harris fired him.

All this friction worked up to a climax and Cox consulted with Branch Rickey. He had been close to the former Dodger mandarin ever since he came into the league. Rickey recommended Fred Fitzsimmons, winding up his pitching career in Brooklyn, as a manager. "Fred is smart," said Branch, "and I really think he would make quite a man for you." So fat Freddy was appointed.

The firing of Harris was to have repercussions of which Bill Cox never dreamed. Bucky still was on fire when he returned to Philadelphia a day later and called a meeting of the Philadelphia newspapermen in his suite at the Benjamin Franklin Hotel. He told his side of the case, called Cox an All-American jerk or something of that sort, and then as the men were about to leave dropped his bombshell: "He's a fine guy to fire me—when he gambles on games his club plays."

Two sports writers at the meeting jumped up. "That will finish him with Landis. His goose is cooked," they chimed in.

"If the Judge *hears* of it, it will go hard with him," said Bucky significantly.

The Judge, Commissioner of all baseball, did hear of it through a letter written by the sports editor of one of the Philadelphia newspapers. Landis started an immediate investigation. Things dragged on for a while, but everybody in baseball knew the young club owner was in Landis' doghouse. The old Commissioner was a stickler on this betting business. After he had acquitted Ty Cobb and Tris Speaker in a baseball betting case in 1927, he had the club owners enact a strict code which called for permanent banishment for anyone betting on a game, whether he be club owner, manager, player, umpire or bat boy. And it made no difference whether the offender bet for or against his team.

Landis called Cox, Harris and others to his Chicago office. Bucky testified that Cox frequently had bet on the team. Girl secretaries in Cox's office verified that they had called up betting commissioners for odds on the day's games and had telephoned the boss's betting instructions. Cox claimed ignorance of baseball's anti-gambling statute, and for a while was inclined to fight his ouster. Landis summoned him to a meeting in New York, December 4, 1943, saying he might bring counsel, but Cox resigned his presidency and wrote Landis: "I do not see that any useful purpose would be served by my attending any further meeting before you."

The Judge then tossed Cox out of the game, November 23rd, declaring him permanently ineligible to hold any office or employment with the Philadelphia National League club, or any other major or miner league club in Organized Baseball. Bucky Harris had had his revenge, and the Phillies had the sad distinction of being the only club to have two of its presidents thrown out on their ears, Fogel in 1912 and Cox in 1943.

In a "Goodbye to Baseball" radio message on the night of Landis' finding, Cox admitted he had made sentimental bets on baseball before he knew there was a rule against it. In closing, he said: "In saying goodbye to baseball forever, I want to say that I looked up to, rather than at, my fellow club presidents with a sincere hope that I could emulate the best of their individual deeds. I hope I have not offended them. I have endeavored in every way to lead an exemplary life and conduct myself with the proper viewpoint to this great sport. Good luck and goodbye to every one in baseball."

Even with the trouble in the front office, the 1943 season had some compensations. While the club's final position was seventh, the Phillies won 22 more games and had a .138 percentage gain over 1942. They won 9 games from the strong champion Cardinals, who spreadeagled the league with 105 victories. Bill Cox even tried to change the club's nickname from the time-honored

Phillies to the Blue Jays. Blue Jays made the club's stationery; some writers occasionally used the new name, but with the fans they remained the Phillies.

In the new player department, the club acquired a 190-pound Russian catcher from the Knoxville club, Andrew Wasal Seminick. Andy was a former coal miner from Pierce, West Virginia, who at that stage of his career doubled as an outfielder. He hit only .181 in 22 games, but of his 13 hits, two were homers and two were doubles. But whether his smoking drives went fair or foul, landed safely for hits or were caught deep in the outfield, there was a lot of heft behind them. As Andy developed, he was to become quite a factor in the Phillie story.

CHAPTER 22

Babe Alexander Finds Savior in Bob Carpenter

1

BILL COX's quick effacement from the Philadelphia scene was a tough break for the New York lumber man, but it was followed by one of the best breaks ever to come to the Phillies. Cox had brought into the Phillie organization a capable, pleasant, dapper young fellow, Nathan "Babe" Alexander, as his public relations director. Babe previously had served Cox in the latter's New York football and lumber interests. With Cox banned permanently from baseball by Landis, it became necessary for him to dispose of his Phillie stock at the earliest moment. Alexander dug up a buyer in Robert R. M. Carpenter, Sr., of Wilmington, Delaware, a multimillionaire partner in the great duPont organization. Carpenter, who had been a catcher at prep school, was chairman of the board of the great industrial corporation at the time he purchased Cox's stock in late 1943 for an estimated $400,000. It was a happy solution for Ford Frick, National League president, who for years had regarded the Phillies as his No. 1 problem.

Carpenter's main purpose in buying the club was to find an activity for his son, Robert R. M. Carpenter, Jr., who immediately was installed as president. Young Bob didn't care much for big industry but had a decided flair for sports. He had played baseball and football at Duke, his alma mater, and once was a member of a Duke Rose Bowl team. After graduation he interested himself in promoting sports around Wilmington—baseball, football and boxing. At the time the Carpenters bought the Phillies, they operated a Wilmington club in the Interstate League in close affiliation with the Athletics.

The coming of the Carpenters into Philadelphia baseball ushered in a new era. Gone were the poverty-stricken days when it was necessary to peddle players to meet payrolls and running expenses. The new owners knew it was necessary to spend money to make money. Furthermore, they had the money to spend. They decided if they could give Philadelphia a winning team, the pleased fans would make their investment profitable.

Carpenter's first important move was to engage Herb Pennock, then farm director for the Red Sox, as his general manager. The millionaire Yawkey readily gave his consent when Pennock showed interest in the Philadelphia proposition. Herb was the genial fox-hunter from Kennett Square, Pennsylvania. Both of the Carpenters long had been admirers of Pennock as a pitcher, and young Bob and the former great Yankee lefthander were personal friends.

When Bob Carpenter, Jr., went into the Army shortly after his family gained control of the club, most of the burden of building up the Phillies was placed on Pennock's slender shoulders. Perhaps Pennock's association with the Red Sox, as well as unsettled war conditions, turned him against the old Yawkey policy of buying established stars. He had noted that the purchase of such headliners as Lefty Grove, Jimmy Foxx, George Pipgras, Wes Ferrell, Billy Werber, Ben Chapman and Pinky Higgins had brought no pennants to the Red Sox. He and the Carpenters concurred that the way to build up a winning team was to go after the best youngsters available and rear them in a Phillie organization.

Herb's reorganization job wasn't easy. Cobwebs from the unsuccessful Nugent regime had to be swept away. There was a wartime shortage of players, but Pennock formed the nucleus of a farm system. As Pennock was a former Yankee great, it was natural that ex-Yankees should gravitate to him as lieutenants. Two of the first of what was to become a real Yankee colony were scout Johnny Nee and Eddie Sawyer, who as player and manager had spent a decade in the Barrow-Weiss farm system.

Eddie switched his base of operation from the Yankees' Binghamton farm in the Eastern League to the new Phillie Utica farm in the same organization.

However, the early Carpenter-Pennock years were uninspiring. After some progress seemingly had been made in the Cox year, it was back to the cellar in 1944 and 1945. The '44 team was a fairly respectable tailender with a 61-92, .399 finish, but '45 proved an abject year: 46-108, .299.

Philadelphia fans moaned, "Owners change, managers change, but it's the same old tailender. Nothing really changes on the Phillies."

It took no less than 19 pitchers to lose those 108 games in 1945. It was the fourth year of American participation in the war, and club presidents and managers were scraping the bottom of the barrel for players. Among the Phillie pitchers were the now forgotten names of Karl, Lucier, Kennedy, Chetkovich, Mauney, Grate, Monteagudo, Sproull, Kraus, Schantz, Judd, Coffman, Kewpie Barrett. Hugh Mulcahy returned after the Japanese surrender, but he left his fast ball in the Army. Two names will be remembered, Bill Lee, who had been a great one on the Cubs, and Lefty Ken Raffensberger, who in 1952 still was a useful pitcher on the Cincinnati Reds.

Ben Chapman, the former Yankee outfielder speed-boy, also pitched in three games in the latter part of the season. Ben could put himself in, or yank himself out, at his own discretion, for he was the new manager. Faithful Freddy Fitzsimmons was given the big bounce, June 30, 1945, after his charges had won only 17 games. Chapman, his successor, was procured in a player swap with Brooklyn for Catcher Johnny Peacock.

After stealing 61 bases for the 1931 Yankees and starring twelve seasons as an American League outfielder, Chapman had turned pitcher while managing the Richmond, Virginia, club of the Piedmont League, and during the war player shortage he had returned to the majors as a Dodger pitcher in 1944. Ben is a hot-tempered Alabaman, with a touch of Indian blood, and as a player supposedly was a difficult man to handle. As a minor league manager he was suspended for the 1943 season for punching an umpire.

With the appointment of Chappie as manager, the Yankee influence on the Phillies became even greater. Gravitating to the club was Pennock's old New York battery mate, Bennie Bengough; Ralph Cy Perkins, the old Athletic catcher who wound up his playing career as bull-pen catcher on the Yankees; and Dusty Cooke, the former outfielder who broke into the Yankee organization with Chapman. Ben and Dusty were pals all through their respective playing careers. Bengough and Perkins joined the coaching staff, and Cooke at first enlisted as a trainer. Later Dusty, too, joined the coaching staff.

The 1945 season saw two baseball celebrities, First baseman Jimmy Foxx and Catcher Gus Mancuso wind up their long and illustrious big league career as Phillies. It was the twenty-first big league season for Jimmie, the former "Beast" of the Athletics and Red Sox; the seventeenth for Mancuso. Twenty years before, Foxx had broken in with the Athletics at Shibe Park as a seventeen-year-old catcher. The broad-shouldered, big-armed Jimmie still had power in his bat in 1945, hitting .268 for 89 games. The last seven of his majestic total of 534 homers were made in a Phillie uniform. It put him second to Ruth in total home runs, and first among right-handed hitters. Gus Mancuso, catcher for five National League championship clubs in St. Louis and New York, didn't do as good, bowing out with a .199 mark for 70 games.

Philadelphia fans also were seeing the first of Granny Hamner, who was to develop into the club's best shortstop since Bancroft. At the age of seventeen, Granny played 21 games at shortstop for the 1944 Phillies, hitting .247. For the better part of the '45 season, he was sent to Eddie Sawyer in Utica for a prep course. But back with the Phillies in the fall, he hit only .171 for 14 games.

There were two of these Granville boys, Wesley Garvin and Granville Wilbur, three years younger than Garvin, and their signing made considerable wartime sports copy in Philadelphia. Both were infielders; they came from Richmond, and Wesley

Garvin got his start under Ben Chapman on the Richmond club of the Piedmont League. The Richmond club sold W. Garvin to the Giants in 1944, but Judge Bramham, the former minor league Tsar, voided the sale and made Garvin a free agent because he had been signed as a minor. Garvin then was signed by the Phillies in October, 1944.

In the same year the younger brother, Granville, made a pilgrimage to Flatbush and tried to sell himself to Branch Rickey, then head man of the Dodgers. Branch was not impressed with the brash kid, and Granny had to borrow money from Coach Jake Pitler to get back to Richmond. Later in the year Ben Chapman, by this time in Brooklyn, recommended Granny to his old Yankee associate, Pennock, and Granville was signed to a Phillie contract on September 14, 1944. The kid collected a $6,500 bonus. Wes Garvin also received a smaller bonus of undisclosed amount. In each case their mother, Mrs. Robert Hamner, signed their Phillie contract for them, since both boys were minors.

An amusing incident in the story of the Hamner boys developed a few years later. After being sent out in 1945, Granville was sent to Utica for more minor league education in 1947, but he was not draftable. However, the Browns saw the name of G. Hamner in the draft hopper and drafted him, thinking they had caught the agile Granny in their draft net. Instead, they came up with W. Garvin. The older brother never developed as did Granny, and in 1952 was back in Richmond with the team with which he started.

2

In many respects, the 1946 season was the most remarkable in the long history of the club. Prior to that year, the Phillies' attendance high was 515,365, made long before night or Sunday ball in 1916, the year Brooklyn nosed out Pat Moran's team for the pennant in the last two days of the season. Thirty years later, the Phillies practically doubled that with a splendid attendance of 1,045,247. They outdrew the Athletics, for many years top dog in Philadelphia attendance, by 423,454.

Of course, all baseball was enjoying a tremendous postwar boom, but this attendance was amazing inasmuch as it was hung up by a fifth place aggregation. The 1946 finish, 69-85, .448 was no better than some of the Fletcher and Shotton clubs, but somehow the team captured the imagination of Phillie fans as no Philadelphia National League club in a generation. Day after day the fans poured into Shibe Park to see the fightin' Phillies. Crowds from 25,000 to 35,000 were the rule, rather than the exception.

The 1946 team started as the usual Phillies and trailed for the first two months of the race. Then they caught fire, and began to knock off their betters. In a week in latter June they moved out of the cellar into sixth place and eventually wound up fifth, their best position since Shotton's 1932 fourth-placer. But what impressed the fans was that the club never was licked. Many of their victories were pulled out in eighth- and ninth-inning rallies. Chapman really had them fighting and hustling. They won eight games from the strong Cardinals, 1946 World's Champions, and ten from the third place Cubs, 1945 N. L. champions. The club was dressed in new snappy uniforms, with red and blue trimmings. Again they looked like real big leaguers.

The fans also felt the new owners were doing something constructive, and that a better deal for them was ahead. As several hundred big leaguers returned from the war, a lot of good excess players were available. Young Carpenter, himself just returned from service, and Pennock went through all the big lists with a fine comb. They came up with an entirely new infield. First baseman Frank McCormick, the National League's most valuable player in 1940, was purchased from the Reds; Second baseman Emil Verban, a fielding fool, from the Cardinals; and Third baseman Jim Tabor and Shortstop Lamar Newsome from the Red Sox. Tabor was a problem child for his managers, but every so often he could hit a terrific ball. He is one of the three players to hit two grand slam homers in the same contest.

However, the purchase of McCormick, Tabor and Lamar was

a temporary expedient, to field a presentable postwar club. The club's fixed policy still was to develop its own stars. The team's particular pride in 1946 was a home-grown outfielder, Del Ennis, a product of North Philadelphia. The Phillies had signed him right out of high school; he played for Trenton in 1943, spent 1944 and 1945 in the Army, and in 1946, he was rookie of the year with a batting average of .313, fifth among the 100-game players, and an extra-base bag of 30 doubles, 6 triples and 17 homers. He reminded some of the old-timers of Sherry Magee when he broke in four decades before. Andy Seminick, developing his full potentialities, caught 126 games, while another Slav, Outfielder Johnny Wyrostek, product of the Cardinal farm system, hit a satisfactory .281 and showed promise of being a long-ball hitter. Schoolboy Rowe, back after two years of soldiering, was the darling of the pitching staff. He had won 11 games out of 15, when sidelined for the season by an injury. Chappie would have fared even better if such returned servicemen as Pitchers Tommy Hughes, Hugh Mulcahy and Frank Hoerst had come closer to emulating their prewar chucking.

CHAPTER 23

A Gallant Third Place Finish

1

THE 1947 season was an old Philadelphia story. As happened so often in the past, the Phillies got their fans all worked up and then let them down again. After the hopes engendered by the 1946 fifth-placer, the club slipped back to a seventh place tie with the Pirates, also under new owners. Each of the Pennsylvania clubs came home with 62 victories and 92 defeats for a percentage of .403. But Philadelphia had acquired the Phillie habit; the fans retained their faith in young Carpenter and Pennock, and this new tailender drew a remarkable 907,332. "After such loyalty by our fans, we owe them a real team," Carpenter told Herb.

A new Phillie batting champion, Harry (the Hat) Walker, helped bring out the fans. Harry had one of those years that a ball player dreams about. A son of the former Washington pitcher, Ewart "Dixie" Walker, and a younger brother of the Brooklyn outfielder, Fred "Dixie" Walker, Harry had quite a World Series with the Cardinals in 1946 when he hit .412 and was a big factor in the Redbirds' victory over the favored Red Sox. However, Walker started the 1947 season in low gear, and on May 3rd, his St. Louis boss, Sam Breadon, traded Harry and a wartime Cardinal pitcher, Fred Schmidt, to the Phillies for Outfielder Ron Northey and a sizable Carpenter check. Northey, a former Duke player, had been acquired by the Phillies during the war. He was somewhat of a roley-poley, hit a long ball, but wasn't overly spry in the outfield.

The shift to Shibe Park proved an unexpected tonic for Harry Walker. He started hitting as soon as he arrived, and for weeks rival pitchers couldn't get him out. He hit over .400 at one stage, and eventually won the batting championship with a margin from here to Christmas. He wound up with .363; Frank McCormick, who started with the Phillies but finished in Boston, was second with .333 for 96 games; Bob Elliott followed with .317. Walker, who led off for the Phillies, was regarded as a "singles" hitter, though his bat bag contained 29 doubles, 16 triples and one homer. Walker's 1947 average was a one-year freak, as he never again approached his title-winning figure.

Another 1947 oddity is that though the Phillies slipped to last in team batting, they had three of the first four batting leaders: Walker, McCormick, the part-time Phillie, and Catcher Don Padgett. Like Walker, Don was a product of the Cardinal farm system, and came from Boston in a trade for Pitcher Anton Karl.

Emil Verban, the Jugo-Slav second baseman, had another grand season. He hit .285, played every one of the team's 155 games, was far ahead in second base putouts and assists with 450 and 453, respectively, and for the second successive year played for the National League in the July All-Star game.

Yet the Phillies were quietly building up for the future, and Carpenter money was bringing joy to numerous households as the Quaker management signed brilliant sandlotters and collegians with an eye on the future. Two unknowns, Third baseman Willie Edward "Puddin' Head" Jones and Catcher Stan Lopata, were little more than names at the 1947 Clearwater training camp. Lopata, a big 210-pound Polish youth from Detroit, didn't even appear on the club's roster.

Steve O'Neill, the present Phillie pilot, now can get a good laugh on how the Phillie scout, Eddie Krajnik, stole Lopata from the Tigers while he was managing the Michigan club. The hefty kid had starred for three years in Detroit amateur circles, and the Tigers, along with other clubs, showed a lively interest in him. But the Detroit club didn't act fast enough. Krajnik handed the promising kid a $19,000 check and signed Stan to a Phillie contract under the Detroit stands. Lopata was farmed to Terre

Haute in 1946, and in 1947 was sent to Eddie Sawyer in Utica for additional schooling.

Puddin' Head Jones, another well-constructed lad from Laurel Hill, North Carolina, was fetched in by Johnny Nee, the former Yankee Scout. Johnny had found Willie in a South Carolina semi-pro circuit, where the boy's extra-base hits were fantastic. He was hitting better than .500, after hitting .700 for a Navy team during the war. Willie also showed a fine pair of fielding hands, and Nee pronounced him a "natural." He signed Willie for a $16,000 bonus and that winter the Joneses ate high on the hog. As for Willie, he reported at the Clearwater camp fat as a porker. He couldn't bend and he couldn't throw, and Ben Chapman quipped, "He must have trained on corn pone and beans." Jones was farmed to Terre Haute in the Three-Eye League, where he melted down, hit .307 and drove in 107 runs in 123 games. Given a chance with the Phillies in the fall of 1947, Puddin' Head, then twenty-two, had to be satisfied with .226 for 18 games.

Another great kid in the organization was a flaxen-haired outfielder from Tilden, Nebraska, Richie Ashburn. The kid first imagined himself a catcher, and represented the West in an Esquire-sponsored East vs. West game at New York's Polo Grounds. The Phillies were lucky to get him, as Richie had signed earlier contracts with both the Cubs and Cleveland Indians. Each time, the Baseball Commissioner made the boy a free agent. Eddie Krajnik signed Ashburn to a legal Phillie contract at five o'clock in the morning and got him for a modest $4,500. Eddie Sawyer had Richie in Utica and decided to shift him to the outfield. He was destined to become a great Phillie center fielder, a modern reincarnation of the famed Dode Paskert. After a year in military service Richie took another year under Sawyer at Utica, where a 1947 batting average of .362 was his graduation mark for a steady job on the Phillies.

Two other prize acquisitions were a pair of pitchers, Righthander Robin Roberts, of Springfield, Illinois, and Southpaw Curtis Thomas Simmons of Egypt, Pennsylvania. Curt, and his family, proved to be the better business people. He got a whopping $65,000 as his bonus for signing his Phillie contract; Roberts accepted a more moderate check for $25,000. Both became pitching headliners of the first order.

Simmons, of Pennsylvania Dutch ancestry, had been a schoolboy sensation while pitching for the Whitehall High School of Egypt. Rarely striking out less than 15 batters, he pitched his school to three Lehigh Valley championships and his American Legion team to two Pennsylvania titles. But Curt's fame went out of Egypt and Bucks and Lehigh counties. He, too, made that All-American Boy East vs. West game at the Polo Grounds. Simmons pitched and played the outfield for Babe Ruth's club which beat Ty Cobb's team, 5 to 4. Curt's ninth-inning triple gave the Easterners the victory. Ty Cobb was so impressed with the Pennsylvania boy's hitting that he offered a bit of advice. "Anybody who can hit as well as you do shouldn't fool with pitching," said the great one. "Better stick to outfield, where you can play every day."

Fortunately for Curt, he disregarded Cobb's advice and stuck to pitching. Among his later feats in independent baseball were a pair of no-hitters and a 23 strike-out job. The Phillies always had the inside track to the young pitching wizard because Cy Morgan, Phillie scout, was an old friend of the Simmons family. But, friend or no friend, the Simmonses didn't sign for peanuts. Shortly before Curt was signed personally by Herb Pennock in 1947, the Phillies took advantage of an open date to play an exhibition game at Egypt. Curt struck out twelve of Ben Chapman's players, while holding the big leaguers to a 4-4 tie. That did the trick, and the boy, then eighteen, got 65,000 of the Carpenter dollars.

The Phillies sent the youth to Wilmington in the Inter-State League, where he won thirteen games and lost five. Back with the Phillies in the last week of the season, Curt assured the Quakers of a tie with Pittsburgh for seventh place by defeating the Giants by a 3 to 1 score in the season's last game. The fast balling kid lefthander gave up only five hits and struck out nine.

Unlike Simmons, Robin Roberts, with a name like one of the characters in an old Frank Merriwell novel, didn't stand out as a pitcher almost from the day that he could walk. In fact, in his early years at Michigan State, Robin was considered a better basketball player than a ball player. The rigors of Army training built up Robin and the careful coaching of Ray Fisher, the old Yankee pitcher, in a Green Mountain summer league brought out Robin's inherent talents. "Ray Fisher taught me more about pitching than anyone else," Robin once remarked. "He showed me things about pitching that up to then I hadn't even suspected." Anyway, in his last spring at Michigan State, Roberts became a bearcat on the mound and one of the most sought-after college pitchers in the country. Chuck Ward fetched him into the Phillie camp with a $25,000 bait. The first thing the youngster did with his money was to buy a new home for his mother.

In 1947, or thereabouts, the Phillies signed a batch of others. They gave $25,000 to Stan Hollmig, Texas A. and M. football and baseball star. He won fame as a great forward passer, and he got his bonus on the strength of a 455-foot homer in college. Stan was tried out both in the outfield and at first base, but made slow progress.

Bob Miller, a sandlot associate of Lopata in Detroit, was to experience one good year after two prep seasons in the Utica farm. Pitcher Hugh Radcliffe, son of a Carolina mill executive, was signed to a much publicized $40,000 bonus contract, but it provided for year to year installments. This was a period when a bonus player signed for more than $6,000 could be optioned out only one year, or the club engaging the player was in danger of losing him through the draft or on waivers. It was a rule always hotly fought by Bob Carpenter. The Phillies eventually lost Radcliffe in the draft to the Yankees, who assumed the big contract, but Hugh never lived up to his high school promise. The Phillies also paid $12,000 to Charlie Bicknell, a Plainfield, New Jersey, pitching sensation, carried him two seasons, and eventually lost him to the Braves for the $10,000 draft price. But Bicknell never had more than just a fair fast ball, and represented a loss to the Phillies of only $2,000.

2

The new Phillies suffered a sad blow in late January, 1948, Young Bob Carpenter and General Manager Pennock went to New York for the late-winter major league meetings and the annual dinner of the New York baseball writers. Herb seemed all right when he left Philadelphia, but the former pitching ace collapsed during the New York sessions and died January 30th of a cerebral hemorrhage, just a fortnight before he would have celebrated his forty-eighth birthday.

His passing was a terrific blow to the entire organization, and came at a time when Herb felt his hard work and careful planning were about to bring results. It also was a challenge to young Bob Carpenter. His father had died in the meantime, and it was up to the young club owner to demonstrate what he could do working on his own.

Pennock's death in January was a precursor to the passing of Herb's former Yankee teammate, Ben Chapman, as manager in July. Though Chappie was a sound baseball man and an aggressive leader, he lacked tact and diplomacy. A hot-tempered Alabaman, his injudicious remarks got him into disfavor with several of the racial groups that make up the Phillie clientele.

Shortly after Pennock died, Chapman expressed a vigorous thought that the Phillies should have another experienced baseball man at the helm. Ben was not hesitant in speaking his piece. The Phillies made little progress on the field in the first half of the 1948 season and the day before the All-Star game in St. Louis, Ben again voiced his sentiments on the subject to a sportswriting friend.

It just happened that later in the day the sports writer had dinner with young Bob. The writer, with no thought of being other than constructive, suggested: "I think, Bob, that what the Phillies need is a strong baseball man to head the club, somebody like Pennock, or George Weiss of the Yankees."

Carpenter knew where the advice had originated, and somehow it was the straw which broke the camel's back. He had determined on a sports executive's career and felt that he was perfectly capable of running the Phillies. Unlike some of the other wealthy men who had acquired ball clubs, Bob's idea of the Phillies was not that of a sideline—or a hobby—but his main business. Before he had left Philadelphia, Chapman had been attacked from many sides. The entire matter seethed in Carpenter's mind all night, and when morning came he had made up his mind to fire Chapman.

"It was a combination of things," said Carpenter, when announcing that Chapman would be let out. Though Ben never could make himself believe this explanation, it was exactly what had happened. A lot of little things that had been built into a mound were exploded by the remark of the sports writer on the preceding day.

Chapman's temporary successor was his old pal Dusty Cooke, former trainer and then serving as coach. After Dusty had run the club for ten days, Bob Carpenter had another surprise for Philadelphia fans. The new manager was Edwin Milby "Eddie" Sawyer, the former Yankee farm manager, who never had played any baseball higher than the Class A Eastern League. He came from Westerly, Rhode Island, not far from Woonsocket, first home town of the great Phillie of the nineties, Nap Lajoie.

Sawyer that year had shifted from the Phillies' Utica farm team to the Toronto Maple Leafs, a club with which the Phillies then had a working agreement. An erudite man, with a flow of perfect English, Sawyer was a unique type among baseball managers. A product of Ithaca College, he was a member of its faculty during the off season. While Eddie taught biology, he also was strong on psychology, and had a memory for names and faces like the famed political memory of Jim Farley. After one casual introduction to a person, Sawyer would remember him for the remainder of his days. "I guess I got that way remembering the first names of some fifteen hundred kids in my classes," he quipped, explaining his gift. But more important to Phillie fans, Sawyer was a well-grounded baseball man and sound tactician.

In the Chapman-Sawyer year, the 1948 Phillies finished sixth. They won 66 games and lost 88, as Cincinnati and Chicago trailed them in the final standing. It was a year of trades and more changes. In a February swap consummated a week after Pennock's death, the Phillies acquired the veteran shortstop, Eddie Miller, from the Reds for Outfielder Johnny Wyrostek and cash. A few days before the opening of the season, Carpenter gave Sam Breadon of the Cardinals $20,000 and a young infielder, Ralph Lapointe, for First baseman-outfielder Dick Sisler. Dick is the son of the Hall of Fame first base immortal, George Sisler. While the sturdy 210-pound Dick lacked his father's speed and grace, he could make the ball travel when he got the Sisler heft behind it.

In a midseason deal, the Pennsylvania Dutch lefthander, Ken Raffensberger, along with Catcher Hugh Poland, were swapped to the Reds for Catcher Al Lakeman. After two brilliant seasons at second base, Emil Verban tapered off in both his fielding and hitting and was waived to the Cubs, as Granny Hamner, the enthusiastic kid from Richmond, finished the season at the keystone sack. Ralph "Putsy" Caballero, New Orleans boy, with the Phillies off and on since 1944, played in 113 games at third and second.

Other bonus boys also were breaking into the line-up. Richie Ashburn, the Nebraska Jackrabbit, played 117 games in center field before breaking a finger while sliding into second base. Before that, the kid had batted .333 and led the league in stolen bases with 32. Richie also enjoyed a batting streak which ran through 23 consecutive games, highest for a National League freshman. He was named by the *Sporting News* as Rookie of the Year.

Willie Jones had the odd experience of playing for Sawyer in both Toronto and Philadelphia in 1948. His September batting average of .333 and two homers in 17 games proved he now belonged in the big time. After that, he was the Phillies' regular third baseman.

The old bonus rule handicapped the club with its high-priced pitchers. Having sent Curt Simmons to Wilmington in 1947, the Phillies now had to keep him, and the powerful southpaw from Egypt had a fair year, winning seven games and losing thirteen. He had his streaks of wildness, and in 170 innings he walked 108 batters while striking out 86. Robin Roberts had need of little minor league development. The Michigan State collegian started his professional career in 1948 with Wilmington, but after winning nine out of ten games, he promptly was promoted to the Phillies, where he won seven games and lost nine. But Robin, less than a season in Organized Baseball, already was getting rave notices. Critics commented on his terrific stuff, his varied deliveries, and coolness under fire. All this in spite of ulcers, which required Robin to be fed a milk diet every two hours.

At the suggestion of Sawyer, one of his Toronto pitchers, Casimer James Konstanty, a spectacled Syracuse University Bachelor of Science, was acquired in the fag end of the season. The erudite Pole had been little better than a third-stringer in previous National League engagements with the Reds and Braves. Konstanty soon was due for considerable more publicity.

Schoolboy Rowe broke even in 20 games; Blix Donnelly, a Cardinal pick-up, had his bright moments, but the real darling of the staff was the thirty-eight-year-old knuckleballer, Emil "Dutch" Leonard. He was the staff's hardest worker, and though he lost seventeen games against his twelve victories, he ranked second to the Cardinals' left-handed ace, Harry Brecheen, in low earned runs.

3

There was a real convulsion in the National League standing at the finish of the 1949 season. People had to look at it twice to make sure they weren't seeing things. The Phillies were in third place. That might not have been an earth-shattering event with clubs such as the Yankees, Dodgers and Cardinals, but for Phillie fans it was the beginning of a new day. It was the first time the club moved into the first four since Burt Shotton's fourth-placer of 1932, and the highest Phillie finish since Pat Moran ran second to the 1917 Giants.

The once docile Quakers had become the Fightin' Phillies, and everyone recognized them as one of baseball's coming ball clubs. Three advantageous deals with the Cubs helped lift the Phillies into the first division. Shortly after the close of the 1948 season, Bob Carpenter traded Harry Walker, his 1946 batting champion, to Chicago for the veteran outfielder, Bill "Swish" Nicholson. Bill, a brawny collegian from Chestertown, Maryland, had been an Athletic rookie in his youth, and playing with the Cubs had been the National League's wartime home run and runs-batted-in leader. Nicholson was thirty-four years old, but still had a home run swish in his big bat.

A few days after the Nicholson deal, the Phillies purchased the Cubs' obstreperous righthander, Russ Meyer, for a sum well over the waiver price. Russ is a pleasant fellow in many respects but has a fiery temper, and believes firmly that a pitcher never should lose. At least, not a pitcher named Russ Meyer. After a defeat he used to get very mad, and on occasions wrecked the joint. He also took out his wrath on inanimate objects, and once kicked a steel locker so hard that he broke a toe. Meyer didn't have to kick in many lockers in 1947; he really had it that season, winning seventeen games against eight defeats and ranking sixth in earned run efficiency.

In a third Phillie-Cub transaction two months later, young Bob gave up Pitchers Dutch Leonard and Walter Dubiel for the Chicago first baseman, Eddie Waitkus, and Pitcher Hank Borowy. Everyone hated to see conscientious Leonard go, but the club's high brass decided the team needed a spryer first baseman than Dick Sisler. Waitkus, a lean, lithe left-handed Lithuanian from Cambridge, Massachusetts, was especially adept in the field and had averaged around .300 at bat. The deal seemed to be working out nicely for the Phillies, with Eddie hitting .306 for 54 games, when Waitkus' life almost came to a tragic and untimely end in Chicago.

While the Phillies were on their second western trip, June 15th, and stopping at Chicago's Edgewater Beach Hotel, Waitkus received a note shortly after midnight from a girl in the hotel, nineteen-year-old Ruth Ann Steinhagen. It read: *It's extremely important that I see you as soon as possible.* The player's first thought was to ignore the missive, but his curiosity was aroused; he dressed and took the elevator to the girl's room.

Eddie got an entirely unexpected reception; a bullet from the girl's .22-caliber rifle drilled through his chest. The bullet penetrated a lung and stopped in the heavy muscular part of the back near the spine. The first baseman was in a critical condition, and was bedridden in a Chicago hospital for weeks. There was no thought of Waitkus' playing again in 1949; doctors wondered whether he ever would play ball again. Waitkus never had known the girl; it later developed that Miss Steinhagen had had a long-distance crush on Eddie since the time when he was a member of the Cubs. She never had spoken to the player, but decided if she couldn't have him, nobody else could. Ruth Ann was sent to an Illinois mental institution.

With Waitkus fighting for his life, Dick Sisler, who had been helping out in the outfield, moved back to first base and played the best first base of his career.

The Fightin' Phillies did not make third place the easy way. It took a real fightin' speech by Eddie Sawyer, a talk that has become an epic in Phillie lore, to get the team mad enough to pull down third money. In mid-August, the club was in fifth place and apparently in its usual second division doldrums. The club had lost a particularly discouraging game to New York, and Eddie was in anything but a sweet mood. From his suite at the Hotel Commodore he could see Andy Seminick, the big Russian catcher, eating a heavy breakfast in his room at 10 A.M. There had been no night game on the day before. Sawyer also had noted that several of his younger players were burned a lobster red, souvenirs of spending an off day at the beach. They acted like a lot of carefree kids, without a care in the world.

Sawyer sent his coaches and road secretary Frank Powell to round up the players for a meeting in his suite. He didn't mince words, but got right down to cases. Furthermore, Eddie didn't talk like a college professor. "We've come to the crossroads of our lives, yours and mine," he began. "For the past month and a half, we've been going downhill steadily. We're slipping not only in our play on the field but in our thinking, and in our conduct after we leave the ball park. There is only one result—another year in the second division. And that means less money for everybody—second division money, and less fun, for it's no fun finishing with the also rans. Now, we are going to do an about face, or you guys can guess the rest."

Somehow that lecture did it; the Phillies seemed a changed club immediately afterwards and began to tear through the league as though they were astride a General Patton tank. They won a double header from Brooklyn that very day. By Labor Day they had passed the Braves, 1948 champions, and the Giants, and moved into third place, and they held on by winning 16 of their last 26 games. On the last week end of the season they almost forced the Dodgers, 1949 National League champions, into a play-off series with the Cardinals. The Phillies set back the Dodgers in the Saturday encounter of October 1st, leaving Brooklyn one game ahead. As St. Louis won on the final Sunday, the Phils gave the Dodgers a bad scare. Though trailing 5 to 0 in the early innings, they knocked out Don Newcombe, the Brooklyn ace, and had the game deadlocked at 7-7 in the sixth. From there on the clubs battled on even terms until the tenth, when the Dodgers put over two runs on Ken Heintzelman, sixth Phillie pitcher, to win the game, 9 to 7, and the pennant. The Phillies came home with 81 victories, 73 defeats and a percentage of .526.

Granny Hamner moved back to shortstop, his natural position, in this first division year, playing the entire 154 games. Eddie Miller shifted over to second, but in the latter part of the season he was relieved by Mike Goliat, a Polish boy from Yatesboro, Pennsylvania, who was pulled in from Toronto after having spent the 1948 season in the Phillie farm in Wilmington. Usually well down in the batting lists, Mike had the happy faculty of doing his best hitting in the clutch. While Ennis and Ashburn were the regular left and center fielders and Bill Nicholson played right field against righthanders, Sawyer tried to get back some of the club's investment in Stan Hollmig, playing the Texas collegian whenever possible. Stan hit .255 in 81 games.

Among the Phillies' bonus pitchers, Robin Roberts came faster than Curt Simmons. Robin broke even in 30 games, while Lefty Curt could show only four victories against ten defeats. People were saying: "Too bad Curt can't be sent to the minors again," and Sawyer expressed it, "With that kind of talent, one needs to have all kinds of patience." Ken Heintzelman, veteran lefthander, matched Russ Meyer's seventeen victories, even though he blew that last game to Brooklyn. Jim Konstanty made himself most useful to Sawyer in relief, participating in 53 games, and was credited with nine victories against five defeats. Hank Borowy, who came with Waitkus in the Cub deal, won a dozen and lost a dozen, while the Perennial Schoolboy, Lynwood Rowe, reached the end of the line with three victories against seven defeats.

CHAPTER 24

Dick Sisler's Big Home Run

1

BY THE early spring of 1950, strange as it may seem, some persons were talking as though the Phillies might win a pennant. During the training season Ford Frick, then president of the National League, remarked, "They're the coming team of our league." Frank O'Rourke, a young enthusiastic Nebraska-born magazine writer and hero worshiper of Richie Ashburn—who had written a book in 1949 predicting the Phillies' third place finish—wrote a sequel putting them in the 1950 World Series.

During some friendly ribbing of Cardinal owner Fred Saigh at a Phillie-St. Louis exhibition game at St. Petersburg, some writers pointed to Baumgartner and said, "Look, Fred, there's a guy who thinks the Cardinals are going to finish in the second division."

"And *where* do you think the Phillies will finish?" Saigh asked Baumgartner, with no effort to hide his scorn.

"Why, I think they are going to win the pennant," said Stan unabashed.

"Don't be silly," replied Saigh.

What's more, the other writers with the Phillies, Frank Yeutter of the *Bulletin* and Lans McCurley of the *Daily News,* wearing their Fightin' Phillies shirts, shared Stan's idiocy.

Of course the Phillie delegation was a minority, and voices crying in the wilderness. A baseball writers' poll before the season put the Phillies fourth, a position below 1949. Eddie

Sawyer merely smiled at that one. He sensed the predictions of the Phillie writers were not silly, and the Fightin' Phils proceeded to make Stan, Yeutter and O'Rourke look good in a surprising and dramatic fashion. They brought home the club's second pennant, the first in thirty-five years, and though it was won only after the tightest squeak in early October, for the greater part of the way it looked as easy as Pat Moran's flag of 1915.

The team, dubbed the Whiz Kids by Philly reporters—a name that won quick favor with writers and fans—electrified the nation. The average age of the team was twenty-six, so Whiz Kids was no misnomer. People who before had no interest in the Phillies—or Philadelphia—found themselves pulling for Sawyer's fast-running Whiz Kids. In a year when major league attendances were down 16 per cent from 1949, the Phillies, erstwhile door mats in the National League's turnstile department, led their league in attendance with 1,217,035. The management even timed a snappy new red and white peppermint-striped uniform for the new champions.

Yet it didn't just happen, and the 1950 pennant was the fruition of the careful planning of Bob Carpenter and his late aide, Herb Pennock. The club had spent an estimated $2,000,000 in long-range improvements; over a half million of it had gone to promising youngsters in the way of bonuses. Joe Reardon headed an organization of some twenty-eight full-time scouts and the farm system had been expanded to eleven clubs. One had to rub his eyes, and ask: "Is it possible that these are the once penny-pinching Phillies who floundered in the cellar only a few years before?"

For a good part of the season Sawyer had so much good pitching he was like the old lady who lived in the shoe. There weren't enough opportunities to use his splendid staff. The two big bonus kids, Robin (20-11) Roberts and Curt (17-8) Simmons, both came through magnificently. They sparked the staff as Curt acquired the winning knack almost overnight. Robin was given the distinction of starting the 1950 All-Star game, the first won by the National League since 1944. Two kids, Bob

Miller (11-6) and Emory "Bubba" Church (8-6) pitched some splendid baseball. They were reared in the new Phillie farm system; Church, an Alabaman, was moved up from Toronto, where he had pitched for Sawyer in 1948. Meyer didn't have anything like his 1949 success; he had frequent occasions for tantrums, winning only nine games against eleven defeats. Ken Johnson, tall, lanky lefthander picked up from the Cardinals, lent a helping hand. Everybody could win but poor old Ken Heintzelman. He continued to pitch good ball, but it didn't get him anywhere. The boys either wouldn't hit behind him, or they would blow his games some other way. From 17-10 in 1949, Heintzie slipped to 3-9 in 1950.

In back of this pitching was the best relief pitching ever seen in the major leagues, greater than that of Wilcy Moore and Joe Page, aces on Yankee World's Championship clubs. It was contributed by the erudite, spectacled Jim Konstanty. While his official record was 16 games won and 9 lost, he saved countless games for other pitchers. Jim took part in 74 games, none complete, and finished 62, both major league records. He had the distinction of being the first relief pitcher ever voted his league's Most Valuable Player prize.

Konstanty had no particular speed, but it was uncanny how he could step in and choke off the most spirited enemy rallies as though he lowered a curtain. He attributed his uncanny 1950 success to his wife, Eddie Sawyer, and Andy Skinner, an undertaker in his home town of Worcester, New York. Mrs. Konstanty bolstered him mentally when he thought of his mediocre days in Cincinnati; Sawyer prodded him into a new confidence, but the undertaker's role was most unusual. Skinner was a sports fan, but particularly a Konstanty fan. During the off season he would accompany Konstanty around the country as Jim refereed basketball. But they would talk mostly baseball, and Jim's pitching problems.

Skinner was a fine bowler and had made quite a study of the spin a bowler can get on a ball. He got Konstanty into a gymnasium, put on a mit, and gave Jim some of his theories on how to impart some of the bowling spin on a baseball, especially when thrown from the side of the alley. Konstanty was vitally interested, and an apt pupil. He saw that his practice pitches were doing things they never did before. Out of Skinner's winter coaching, and lots of practice, Konstanty developed an excellent so-called "palm ball," slider, change of pace and curve. The palm ball was used against left-handed batsmen, the slider and curve against the righthanders. Konstanty also moved from one side of the rubber to the other according to the man at bat; he tossed the ball from difficult angles, used a big full wind-up, and as his 1950 control was well nigh perfect, he was always catching the batter off stride.

Prof. Skinner spent as much time with Konstanty in 1950 as his undertaking business would permit. And if he couldn't catch Jim in Shibe Park, the Polo Grounds or Ebbets Field, he would study his games on television. Then he would advise, correct the big pitcher's faults, restore his confidence. "Jim is like a bull in a China closet," Skinner often said. "He must be calmed down, made to think."

The Whiz Kids led for 101 days of the 167 that made up the 1950 National League race. Twice in May they led the pack for a week; they slumped to third in June, but in July the Kids whizzed in front again, and with the exception of a few days in late July they held the lead for the remainder of the season. While the first half of the race saw the Phillies in a close struggle with the Dodgers, Cardinals and Braves, from August 8th until a cave-in in the last week of the season, their lead fluctuated between five and seven games.

As the Phillies moved into the last month of the season, everything was going swimmingly. They went into September with a seven game lead, and most everyone expected them to clinch the flag by the middle of the month. But they ran into an unheralded squall around Labor Day. On the holiday, they labored in vain and dropped two to the Giants. September 5th was an off day, but they lost a second double header to the Dodgers on the 7th and a single game on the 8th. That shaved the lead to four and a half games, but by September 15th it was back to seven and a half. It still was seven and a half on the 20th, with only eleven days to go. And Brooklyn then was nine games behind!

Then, almost without warning, Sawyer's well-oiled pitching staff ran into serious difficulties. It started with the loss of Curt Simmons to the Army. Fearing Curt might be drafted, the Phillie management had suggested to the twenty-one-year-old southpaw wonder, and to another bonus pitcher, Charlie Bicknell, that they enlist in the Pennsylvania National Guard. In that way they expected to lose these boys for only two weeks of summer training. Curt took his two weeks of summer training beginning with July 27th, and then the Army suddenly had other ideas for the young southpaw. The Keystone Division became one of the first National Guard outfits to be called into Federal service. On September 10th, Simmons was put back in khaki and soon was on his way to occupation duty in Germany.

The loss of Simmons on the home stretch shook the morale of the entire club. Then Miller, who had broken in with eight straight victories, hurt his arm, and Bubba Church was out for eight days after being struck in the face with a line drive September 15th. Neither pitcher was of much use after these injuries. To make matters worse, Andy Seminick, hard-working first string catcher, suffered a painful ankle injury when Monte Irwin, big Negro outfielder of the Giants, slid into him at home plate. Though the game Seminick was out only briefly, he limped through the closing league games and the World Series. He shot Novocain into the ankle to ease the pain. After the Series, an X-ray showed a bone separation in the ankle.

However, as the Phillies moved into the week end of September 23-24 still seven games to the good, no real alarm was felt. People were saying, "No club can blow a seven game lead in nine days." Philadelphia went on with its World Series preparations, and Eddie Delaney was busy with his World Series press box chart. Stan Baumgartner was proudly wearing his Phillie cap, and Frank Yeutter had shaved off his mustache. Though it made him look absolutely naked, Frank vowed he wouldn't let it grow again until the Phillies clinched the pennant. He still shudders at the thought of how close he came to going mustacheless for the remainder of his days.

It was a bit of a shock when the Dodgers, who suddenly had caught fire, took the week-end games by scores of 3 to 2 and 11 to 0. They were managed by Burt Shotton, Phillie chieftain for six years in the Baker-Ruch period. The Whiz Kids salvaged two out of three from a Brave series, September 25th and 26th, and as the Phillies moved over to New York for their final two series—one at the Polo Grounds and the other at Ebbets Field—they still were cushioned by a four game lead. But the two-day session at the Polo Grounds almost proved fatal, as the Giants swept two successive double headers by scores of 8-7, 5-0, 3-1, 3-1. Roberts dropped one of the 3-1 decisions. In the same two days, the Dodgers gained an even split in a pair of double headers with Boston, closing the gap to three games. At this stage the Phillies couldn't do any worse than finish the regular season in a tie with Brooklyn.

As the Whiz Kids idled on Friday, September 29th, they sadly clung around their radios and television sets and listened to the rampant Brooks smack down the Braves in both ends of a third double header. With two days left, the Phillies now had their lead chopped down to two games. It was shaved down to one as they fell, 7-3, before Erv Palica in the Saturday game at Ebbets Field, September 30th.

As a result, all the chips were on the table in the final game of the regular season in Brooklyn on Sunday, October 1st. If the Phillies won, they would win the flag by two games; if they lost, they would be forced into a two-out-of-three play-off series with the red-hot Dodgers. Most of the writers felt the young Phillies had choked, and that if it went into a play-off series, the Whiz Kids would be dead ducks.

Eddie Sawyer put it squarely up to Robin Roberts, who was making his third start in five days. "It's all up to you," said Eddie. Roberts pitched with all the brilliance, cunning and *sang-froid* of a Christy Mathewson. His opponent was Brooklyn's big Negro hurler, Don Newcombe. Oddly enough, each stalwart right-hander had won 19 games and was gunning for his twentieth victory. It was Robin's sixth attempt to nail down No. 20. The better-than-capacity crown of 35,073 saw a never-to-be-forgotten struggle. The Phillies put a run under Roberts in the sixth on singles by Sisler, Ennis and Jones, but Peewee Reese, the Brooklyn shortstop-captain, tied it in the Dodger half with a freak home run which lodged in a wire screen between the scoreboard and the fence. In ninety-nine times out of a hundred, the ball would have rolled down and been held to a double. For the remainder of the game, the fans could see that silly ball stuck in the screen.

It looked like curtains for the Phillies in the ninth, but Roberts gave a fine example of his magnificent courage. He walked Cal Abrams as a starter, and a single by Reese sent the outfielder to second. Duke Snider whipped another stinging single to center, and Brooklyn's third base coach, Milt Stock, third sacker on the 1915 Phillie champions, waved Abrams home with what would have been the winning run. But Richie Ashburn, playing shallow, made a beautiful beeline throw to Seminick at the plate and nailed Abrams by feet. Reese and Snider each moved up a base on the throw, and Roberts still was in plenty of hot water. Sawyer ordered an intentional pass for dangerous Jackie Robinson, and stout-hearted Robin did the rest. He got rid of Carl Furillo on a pop foul to Waitkus and retired slugging Gil Hodges on a soft outfield fly which Ennis collared.

Their cause saved by Richie's great peg and Robin's pinch-pitching, the Phillies tore into Newcombe like a pack of hungry wolves in the tenth. Roberts started off one of the most memorable rallies in Phillie history with a single. Waitkus followed suit, and Ashburn—trying to sacrifice—bunted into a force play. Then Dick Sisler hit a ball which brought mingled feelings to his illustrious father, George, head scout of the Dodgers. Son Richard's powerful thrust landed well into the left field stands for a home run, as three happy Whiz Kids danced around the bases to give the Phillies a 4 to 1 triumph and their first pennant since 1915. Dick's clean-up wallop was his fourth hit of the nerve-tingling contest.

There was such chagrin in Flatbush over the loss of the game—and the pennant—that the two ex-Phillies, Manager Shotton and

Coach Stock, were severed from the Brooklyn payroll, Shotton for blowing the pennant to a supposedly inferior team and Stock for sending in Abrams in the ninth inning, when the Dodgers had none out.

The new Phillie pennant-winners almost hit the .592 percentage of Pat Moran's 1915 champions right on the nose. The club wound up with 91 victories, 63 defeats and a percentage of .591.

Apart from the pitchers, Roberts, Konstanty and Simmons, the leading contributor to the pennant was Del Ennis. The native son was the team's big power man; Del hit .313, led the league in runs batted in with 126 and was well up in homers with 31. Richie Ashburn, at .303, was the club's only other .300 man. However, big Seminick took part in 130 games, batted .288, smote 24 home runs and was an inspiration to the entire team. With Waitkus' return to first base, Dick Sisler went to left field where he hit a sturdy .296. Waitkus, after a winter of recuperation at Clearwater, recovered nicely from his shooting and hit .284. Both Puddin' Head Jones and Granny Hamner were timely hitters and played brilliant ball in the field, while Mike Goliat proved an acceptable second baseman. Swish Nicholson suffered from diabetes, and the Phillies got special permission to have Jack Mayo, brought in from Toronto as a September replacement, declared eligible for the World Series.

2

Philadelphia was pretty well steamed over its 1950 World Series, the first in the Quaker City since 1931 and the first involving the Phillies in 35 years. Unfortunately, the unsentimental Yankees, chronic American League champions, were not interested in helping to write a fitting climax to Eddie Sawyer's success story. Most of the shops on Chestnut Street had baseball displays in their windows, many of them digging up pictures of the 1915 champions or placing Pat Moran's old stars alongside pictures of Sawyer's young Whiz Kids of 1950. But alas, the World Series was over almost before Philadelphia realized it!

The Yankees, winners in fifteen of these events, gave the Phillies their cruel four-straight treatment. And to make it worse, the Yankees were managed by Casey Stengel, the Phillies' former clownish outfielder who was so happy to escape from Baker Bowl in 1921.

Yet the Whiz Kids were not disgraced. If they went down in straight games, they went down fighting and lost the first three by only one run. Going back to Pat Moran's Series of 1915, it made seven straight one-run blue ribbon defeats for the Phillies. The absence of Simmons hurt. Everywhere people were saying: "If only the Army had permitted Curt to stay a few weeks longer, things would have been different."

There were a dozen requests for every seat at Shibe Park for the first game, October 4th, but because of a mixup in holding out tickets for favored baseball people, there were 2,000 vacant seats, and the attendance was 30,746. That annoyed a lot of people whose applications had been returned. Those who got in saw a great ball game in which the Whiz Kids were nosed out, 1 to 0.

In selecting his starting pitcher, Sawyer threw almost as big a surprise as did Connie Mack when he pitched Howard Ehmke in the first game of the 1929 Athletic-Club Series. With Roberts having pitched the last tough game of the regular season, Simmons in the Army, and Church and Miller still licking their wounds, Eddie pitched his crack "fireman," Jim Konstanty. It was Jim's first starting assignment as a Phillie. With any kind of hitting behind the Syracuse collegian it would have been a great move, but the Phillies could garner only two hits off Vic Raschi, the big New York righthander. Konstanty gave up only four himself before making way for a pinch-hitter in the eighth, but he yielded the game's lone run in the fourth inning. The Yankee's Doctor Bobbie Brown, who has a World Series batting average of .439, rammed a double down the third base line, advanced to third on a long fly by Bauer and came home after Coleman flied deep to Sisler.

Robin Roberts got his World Series baptism in the second game, October 5th, before a full house of 32,660, and acquitted himself nobly; but the gallant Robin succumbed in ten innings to the Yankees' clutch pitcher, Allie Reynolds, by a 2-1 score. The The Whiz Kids got seven hits this time to ten for the Bronx Bombers. The Yanks scored in the second on a walk to Coleman and singles by Reynolds and Woodling. It needed a lucky hop to give the Phillies their tying run, and first of the Series, in the fifth inning. After Goliat opened with an infield single, Waitkus' roller hit a hard piece of dirt and jumped over Second baseman Coleman's head just as Gerry prepared to field it. It went for a single, and Goliat sprinted to third, from where he scored on Ashburn's liner to Woodling. Konstanty in the first game and Roberts in his contest held the big Yankee gun, Joe DiMaggio, hitless until the Clipper came up in the tenth. It was too good to last. DiMaggio, first up in the extra inning, emerged from the spell the Phillie pitchers had wove over him by lining a home run far into the upper left field stands. And that was it!

Moving over to Yankee Stadium, New York, for the third game, October 6th, the Phillies almost got away with it; they went into the eighth inning leading by 2 to 1, but tainted New York runs in the eighth and ninth enabled the American League champions to finish ahead, 3 to 2. This was the real heartbreaker for the Kids, as they outhit Stengel's players, ten to seven. Desperate for pitchers, Sawyer pitched his southpaw veteran "Three and Nine" Ken Heintzelman, who did remarkably well until his control deserted him in the eighth. Ken's Yankee opponent was a fellow southpaw, Eddie Lopat.

The Yanks scored a two-out run in the third when little Phil Rizzuto walked, stole second, continued on to third on Seminick's bad throw and scored on Coleman's single. After blowing several scoring chances, the Phillies tied in the sixth on Del Ennis' double to left and Sisler's single, Georgie's only run batted in of the Series. The Whiz Kids shot into the lead in the seventh on Hamner's single, Seminick's sacrifice and Goliat's sharp single to center.

Many in the crowd of 64,505 showed their pleasure when old man Heintzelman retired Pinch-hitter Woodling and Rizzuto, the first two men to face him in the eighth. Ken seemingly had the situation well in hand. Then everything went sour. He first walked Coleman and then Berra and DiMaggio on eight consecutive poor pitches. That filled the bases. Sawyer had no alternative but to call in the hard-worked Konstanty. Big Jim did his bit, but Granny Hamner didn't. Tough Bobbie Brown, batting for Bauer, grounded to Granny, who fumbled, and let in Coleman with the tying run. With the bases still full, the Fireman blew down big Johnny Mize on a foul to Jones. Poor Granny; he hit a double and two singles, and should have been the hero of a Phillie victory. He actually wept over his error in the clubhouse.

The Phillies then went down in the ninth. After a parade of pinch-hitters, Russ Meyer came up as the Whiz Kids' ninth inning pitcher and Jim Bloodworth, veteran American League discard, as the second baseman. This time Reliefer Meyer got the first two men out before trouble started. Woodling punched a tricky grounder which squirted away from Bloodworth for an infield single. Rizzuto also got a single on a liner Bloodworth dove for and couldn't hold. Then Coleman, a pest for the Phillies all through the Series, shot a single to left center and Woodling crossed with the winning run.

Disaster overtook the Phillies in the fourth game played at the Stadium on a Saturday, October 7th. The best crowd of the Series, 68,098, saw the Phillies bow out, 5 to 2. This was the only one that wasn't close, as the Phillies scored their two runs in the ninth after Gene Woodling dropped a fly which would have ended the game and given Whitey Ford, Yankee rookie, a shutout.

Still pressed hard for pitchers, Sawyer now took a gamble on Bob Miller, his young sore-armed righthander. Bobbie retired only one batter in the first inning. Woodling reached base on Goliat's fumble, took second on Rizzuto's infield out, and scored on Berra's single. The gnomelike Berra ran all the way from first to third on a particularly wild pitch. DiMaggio brought Berra home with a double to right. That was all for Miller, and Konstanty made his third appearance of the four games.

The rubber arm which had held up during 74 league games and three in the World Series finally gave out in the sixth, when the Yanks scored three on hard hitting. Berra banged a home run into the lower right field stands. DiMaggio was hit and scored on Brown's triple to deep center. The Doctor tallied a third run on Bauer's long liner to Sisler. Robin Roberts eventually finished the game on the mound for Philadelphia.

Young Whitey Ford, a New York boy who had a 9-1 American League record after joining the Yanks in midseason, held the Phillies in check until the ninth. Jones opened with a single and Ennis was hit by a pitched ball. Sisler hit into a force play and Hamner fanned for the second out. Ford's shutout looked to be in the book when Seminick sent Woodling far back for his long fly. But after Gene got his hands on the ball he let it drop, as the two runners on base scored. Mayo ran for Andy, and Goliat kept the rally going with a sharp single. That was enough for the discreet Stengel, who promptly called in Allie Reynolds, second game winner. The part Creek Indian struck out Stan Lopata, who batted for Roberts, sending the Phillies crestfallen back to Philadelphia.

The Welcome Travelers radio program of Omaha, Nebraska, brought old Grover Alexander, sturdy stalwart of Pat Moran's team, to New York for the games in Yankee Stadium. Grover sat sadly in the big Yankee press box, watching the Phillies lose the third and fourth games. "They don't hit any better than they did in 1915, when we lost those four games to the Red Sox by one run," he commented. Grover lived just long enough to see the Phillies in a second World's Series. He died at St. Paul, Nebraska —his birthplace—on November 4, 1950, a month after the second Series game. Grover was sixty-three.

Philadelphia fans weren't too hard on the club for their four straight downfall. Phillie partisans realized it was a young club that had been through much in the latter part of the league season. Philadelphia writers also pointed out that with a hit here or there, each of the first three games might have resulted in Phillie victories. And the players had considerable balm to carry them through the winter. Each of the thirty-two men voted a full share of the Series melon drew checks for $4,081.34. Not too bad for players who in 1947 had been tied for last place! And if the Phillies hit only .203 in the Series, their shattered pitching staff held the powerful Yankees to .222. If the Phillies, who hit 125 National League home runs, collected none in the Series, the Yankees, who bagged 159 in the American League, exploded only two.

Grannie Hamner was by far the Phillies' most effective batter, getting a triple, two doubles and three singles in 14 times at bat for .429. Jones and Waitkus each cracked out four hits and batted .286 and .267, respectively. But from there down, the averages were reminiscent of the 1915 team's figures against the Red Sox: Goliat, .214; Seminick, .182; Ashburn, .176; Ennis, .143; Sisler, .059. The man whose homer won the pennant in the final league game in Brooklyn had only one single in 17 times at bat, the blow which scored Ennis in the third game.

3

When the Whiz Kids won their 1950 pennant, many thought it meant the start of a string of Philadelphia championships. The Phillies were a young club, and one which figured to get better as the men grew older and more experienced. But the slump which gripped the Phillies in September, 1950, and prevailed through the World Series, still was with the club in 1951. While many thought Brooklyn would beat them out for the 1951 pennant, there was scarcely a sports writer in the country that didn't pick them for a high first division berth. Instead, the Phillies crossed everybody by limping home a mediocre fifth. Then some of the scoffers labeled the Whiz Kids the Wuz Kids.

The club never got going. It got off to a mediocre start, languished in seventh place as late as June 11th. Eddie Dyer cajoled, coaxed and scolded his players, but to no avail. They did improve in midsummer, and in latter July and the first fortnight of August the Phillies ran third to the Dodgers and Giants. No one expected them to do any worse than that. But after getting five games above the .500 mark (57-52) on August 11th, the club went into reverse and in September slumped to fifth place. They eventually wound up with 73 victories, 81 defeats, and a percentage of .474. They were 23½ games behind the champion Giants, and 3½ behind the fourth place Braves. Making the descent especially painful for the owners was a 279,377 attendance drop from the 1950 peak. The club matched its slide from first to fifth in the standing with a similar plunge to fifth in the important turnstile department.

By a strange freak of the schedule, for the third straight fall the Phillies were in a terrific extra-inning struggle with the Dodgers on the last Sunday of the season. This one concerned Sawyer's players only indirectly, but it meant everything for the Brooks. They had to win to stay in the race and earn the right to play the rampaging Giants in a play-off series. The game was played at Shibe Park, September 30th, and the fans didn't know which way to root. The scoreboard showed early the Giants had won a 3-2 quickie from the Braves. So if the Phillies won, the Giants were in, and many of the fans hated the Giants since the McGraw days.

It looked like early curtains for the Dodgers when the Phillies smacked Preacher Roe, their 22-3 pitching darling, for a 6-1 lead after three innings. It still was 8 to 5 after five, but the Dodgers tied with a three-run rally in the eighth. From there on, the battle became hotter with every play. The Phillies seemed to have the game won in the twelfth, when with the bases full and two out, Waitkus apparently whacked Don Newcombe, the sixth of seven Brooklyn pitchers, for the winning hit. It was a low liner a few inches off the ground, and was on its way to the outfield when Jackie Robinson, Brooklyn's great Negro second baseman, speared the ball while making an amazing diving catch. In clutching the ball, Robby rammed his elbow into his solar plexus, knocking himself out temporarily, but instinctively held onto the ball. Jackie was sufficiently recovered by the fourteenth to tag Robin Roberts for a home run, giving the Dodgers the game, 9 to 8. It put them into the play-off series, but it only delayed their demise by three days, as the Giants turned them back, two games to one.

All during the contest Del Ennis had a chance to break up the ball game with a timely hit. He came up repeatedly in the clinches, but left a slew of Phillie runners on the bases. And there was one of the big reasons for the Phillies' 1951 decline. It had been going on like that all through the season. In one year the big Philadelphia boy's batting average dropped from .311 to .267; his home run production fell off from 31 to 15; and his runs-batted-in skidded from 126 to 73. Andy Seminick also slumped from .288 to .227, with his RBIs falling off from 68 to 37.

If the clean-up hitter failed, so did the great relief pitcher of 1950, Jim Konstanty. Even Andy Skinner, the Worcester, New York undertaker, couldn't find the answer. Big-spectacled Jim just couldn't get them out any more. Maybe Eddie Sawyer had overworked him the year before when he pitched Jim in 74 league games and three of a four-game World Series. Konstanty again took part in 58 relief jobs, but with far different results. From a gaudy 16-7, .696 showing in 1950, he descended to a sorry 4-11, .267 job in 1951. Konstanty got into so much trouble that the club engaged Andy Hansen, a Giant discard, to rescue Jim.

The team continued to feel the after effects of the loss of the brilliant southpaw, Simmons, to the Army. It was a psychological blow to the club's morale, as well as the actual loss of the Egypt boy's stout left arm from the firing line. Bob Carpenter explained it by saying: "When Simmons left, the Phillies changed from a confident team which felt it could win at any time, into a frantic group which thought it had to score many runs to win, and as a consequence became paralyzed at bat."

The team also was getting away from Eddie Sawyer. A year before, they had gone to their understanding manager with their troubles, their hopes, their ambitions, their desires. Eddie had been almost a father confessor to the Whiz Kids. But this was changing. Sawyer said later that the men were inflated after winning the 1950 pennant; that they used their money to buy cars, homes—to live the "Life of Riley"—that they thought they again could win the pennant by merely appearing on the field.

One of the latest big bonus boys also was showing little. He was Tom Casagrande, paid a fat $40,000 after he was graduated from Fordham in 1950. The Phillies first experimented with him as a first baseman—a possible replacement for Waitkus—as all reports had it that Tom was a dangerous clouter. The experiment failed when Casagrande failed to hit like a first baseman, and he wasn't exactly Hal Chase on first base. Then Tom went back to pitching, hurled a one-hitter for Wilmington, and later was advanced to Baltimore. Tom then pouted over a salary dispute, but finally agreed to go to the club's farm in Schenectady. He still is a Phillie possibility.

While most of the team fell down in 1950, Richie Ashburn had a magnificent season. Many in Philadelphia felt he was deserving of the National League's Most Valuable Player prize. He hit a formidable .344, a figure topped only by Stan Musial, the perennial batting champion. Richie led the National League in hits, 221; outfield putouts, 538; and was second in stolen bases with 29.

Robin Roberts also had another grand season. In 1950, he was the first Phillie pitcher since Alexander to win 20 games. He showed that was no freak, nor accident, by hanging up a 21-15 mark with the 1951 fifth-placer. And for the second successive year, Robin had the distinction of drawing the opening pitching assignment for the National League stars in the midsummer All-Star game.

Bubba Church, one of the coming youngsters of the 1950 champions, was another bright spot on the staff. He looked as though he had it, winning 15 games and losing 11. On the other hand, Bob Miller, who looked so good before his 1950 arm injury, was almost a complete washout. While Miller was credited with two victories against one defeat in 17 games, he had a horrendous earned run mark of 6.88, and was shunted back to Wilmington.

CHAPTER 25

Steve O'Neill Comes on the Scene

1

THE season of 1952 promised to be a big year, possibly another pennant-winning campaign for the Phillies. Curt Simmons returned from overseas shortly before the start of the regular season, and the Simmons return was expected to work magic. It again gave Sawyer his vaunted right and left-handed "One-Two" punch in the pitching department in Roberts and Simmons.

In the previous winter, the club had made another big deal with the Reds which supposedly added much needed strength. It brought back recollections of the big swap engineered by Horace Fogel with Garry Herrmann and Clark Griffith in the winter of 1910-11. To get Second baseman Connie Ryan, Catcher Forrest "Smoky" Burgess and Pitcher Howie Fox, Carpenter and Sawyer gave up Dick Sisler, hero of the 1950 pennant-winning game; Andy Seminick; Eddie Pellagrini, a reserve infielder; and Niles Jordan, a rookie southpaw pitcher. The club especially needed Ryan for second base, as Mike Goliat, after being fined for training violations, was released to Baltimore in midseason of 1951. Fox, in the past, had shown considerable promise in Cincinnati, and it was thought he would click and prove a winner with the Whiz Kids.

Yet the Phillies were anything but a happy, harmonious family at their Clearwater, Florida, training camp. Feeling that the 1951 cave-in was due to indifference and the players having too many outside interests, the club embarked on its so-called "austerity" program. It called for no wives at the camp, no autos, no swimming in the gulf, no golf, no card playing, no nothin'—that is, nothin' but baseball. There still is some doubt as to where the idea of the austerity program originated, but it was launched and enforced by Eddie Sawyer, and the players held him responsible for it.

The austerity program quickly backfired. The club had a disconsolate bunch of young men on its hands. Many of the players brought their wives to Florida and housed them in nearby resorts. They obeyed the letter of the law by sleeping in the hotel, but that was all. It was said, but never confirmed by the top brass, that three or four of the leading players revolted and went to the front, demanding a less exacting rigor, but Sawyer kept his icy hand on the proceedings. Third baseman Willie Jones broke the curfew hour and was fined $300. Several of the players held out and reported from one day to a week late. The players lacked spirit and hustle. In contrast to 1950, when they were unbeatable in the Florida Grape Fruit League, they won only half of their training games.

However, when they whipped the St. Louis Cardinals decisively on their trip north, it looked as if the program might pay off. But once the regular season started, things went from bad to worse. The club that was expected to be a contender dropped slowly down the ladder, fell below the .500 mark, and never could put together a winning streak of even minor proportions. After a fairly good start at bat, the men slumped in hitting all along the line: Richie Ashburn fell over 100 points below his .344 of 1951; Willie Jones couldn't get himself above the .250 mark; Del Ennis hung around .260.

Howie Fox, of whom so much was expected, bogged down completely. Russ Meyer ran into hard luck and lost several tough close games for the lack of a hit or a damaging miscue by his mates. Carl Drews, a former Yankee from whom much was expected, pitched especially well but was the victim of home run pitches and won only three games of his first eleven. Konstanty, the sensation of 1950 who lost his touch in 1951, was of even less use at the start of 1952. Roberts, after a sensational start, failed to win a game for an entire month and Simmons, who was expected to breeze through the league, had his bad days with his good ones and became an "in and outer." Church, 15-game winner of the year before, got into his manager's doghouse before the season opened and did little pitching; and when he did go to the mound, Bubba was completely ineffective.

In desperation Sawyer arranged an early season deal with Cincinnati in which the Phillies regained the services of Outfielder Johnny Wyrostek and acquired Pitcher Ken Peterson for Bubba Church. Wyrostek immediately was installed in right field, while Peterson was sent to Baltimore. The deal, however, did not give the club the spark it needed. Attendance began to slump even worse than in 1951 and President Bob Carpenter began to worry. He decided he would see for himself what was wrong and joined the club at Cincinnati on the second western trip. He watched the team drop a dismal double header to the Reds and then moved on to St. Louis.

The climax came the next night, June 6th. Curt Simmons was pitted against Vinegar Bend Mizell, crack Cardinal rookie, and the Phillies took a 2-0 lead in their sixth inning. But the Cards came back to go in front, 4 to 2, in their half on whoozy Phillie playing. The Phillies tied it at 4-4 in the seventh, but in the St. Louis half Stan Musial walked with one out and Enos Slaughter hit a pop-up in back of second base that Carpenter thought Granny should have caught. However, the shortstop circled around and missed the ball, Musial going to third. Stan scored the winning run a moment later.

It was the spark that set off a powder keg. Immediately after the game, Carpenter asked Sawyer if it would be okay if he (Carpenter) talked to the boys. Sawyer said: "Sure, it's all right with me."

"Maybe I can pep them up," added the young president.

Traveling secretary Frank Powell then called a meeting of the regulars in Carpenter's hotel suite at 1 A.M. Everyone but Hamner was there. Granny, who started the 1952 season as team captain, was not invited.

There have been numerous versions of what went on, some

rather spicy. It was said that one player asked to be traded and two or three spoke belligerently to their boss. Carpenter himself said, "I praised them; I gave them hell; I patted them on the back, and I picked them apart."

The only announcement of any change was that Gran Hamner had been relieved of his captaincy. About this same time, Cy Perkins was detached from coaching duty and made a personal intermediary between the players and Sawyer. If they had any gripes they could make them to Cy, who would pass them along to the manager.

Carpenter did make one significant statement the night after the meeting, saying, "If we don't win from now on, we won't draw flies when we get back to Philadelphia." He denied, however, that he had any managerial change in mind. "Sawyer can't hit, field and pitch for the players," he said. "I have no changes in mind until the end of the season."

It looked for one day as if the president's meeting had changed things for the better when the next day the Phillies, with Roberts on the mound, defeated Gerry Staley, the Cardinal ace, 4-3. But the reformation lasted for only twenty-four hours. The Phillies dropped the final contest in St. Louis and then lost three straight to Chicago, giving them the woeful record of two won and ten lost on the western trip. One had to go back to the worst Baker or Nugent teams to match that record.

When the team returned to Shibe Park, the men played in the same listless fashion and another climax was reached when they were thrashed by the Athletics, 4-2, in a charity exhibition game on June 26th. This was the last straw for Carpenter, for the next day he got busy on the long distance telephone.

He called Joe Cronin, general manager of the Red Sox, and got permission to talk to Steve O'Neill, erstwhile American League catching great and former manager of Cleveland, Detroit and the Red Sox. O'Neill, whose entire major league career of four decades was in the American League, was scouting for the Red Sox. At the very threshold of his playing career, he was the property of the Athletics.

Carpenter and Steve came to terms over the phone. That night the Phillies, with Curt Simmons in rare form, trounced the Giants, 6 to 0, but Carpenter stuck to his decision—a new manager.

In the sixth inning, Frank Powell notified the press that an important announcement would be made immediately after the game. Frank did not give anyone an inkling of what the president had in mind. Somehow the possibility of Sawyer being fired had faded into a haze in the writers' minds. "A big deal, Frank?" someone quipped, but Powell merely smiled it off.

The writers and radio representatives gathered to wait for Carpenter in Sawyer's office. When Sawyer was not around, they began to smell a little mouse. Apparently Sawyer was out, and a new manager was about to be named. They speculated on the names of Rogers Hornsby, recently let out by the Browns, Billy Southworth, and many others; no one even thought of Steve O'Neill.

Eventually Powell led the way to Carpenter's office beneath the stands. When the door was closed, the young president said in a hushed voice, "Eddie Sawyer has resigned. We have been talking it over for some time and he feels it would be for the best interests of the club." It was evident that it had been a difficult moment for Carpenter; he was emotionally upset and his decision had not been a pleasant one. Sawyer was the second manager he had fired in midseason in his comparatively short tenure.

Bob added, "Sawyer will be retained in an advisory capacity—to evaluate the farm systems of other clubs." Eddie still had two and a half years to go on a three-year contract.

The writers then asked for Sawyer. Eddie took the blow like the real thoroughbred that he is. He showed little outward sense of emotion, of the disappointment and chagrin that must have been tugging at his heartstrings as he seconded what Carpenter previously had said. Later, however, he was reported to have said to his men in the clubhouse, "This is the first time a manager ever was fired after his club won a 6-0 shutout."

A group of players who had remained loyal to Sawyer throughout said, "It was we who should have been fired, Skip, not you."

O'Neill took charge the following day, June 28th, the Phillies in sixth place with a record of 28 won and 35 lost. That night with

Robin Roberts on the mound they defeated New York, 7-2, lost the following night, then moved to Brooklyn to win three out of four. And from then on, the progress steadily was up.

When O'Neill took charge he notified the men that the only restrictions on their actions would be proper living and a sensible curfew; that wives would be permitted on trips and could go on spring training. He took the curbs off card playing, tossed the morning and night check-offs out of the window, showed his usual friendly attitude to the press and did not frown on his men's talking to radio sportscasters and writers.

Whether or not the managerial change was justified, the change in Phillie morale, spirit and the players' attitude was instantaneous. One player remarked, "I feel as if the load of a hundred years has been lifted off my shoulders."

The club began to move and in the final three months of the season played the best ball in the two major leagues. After O'Neill took charge the Phillies won 59, lost 32, and moved into the old fourth place groove with a satisfactory percentage of .565. They missed third place by only a game, and were nine and a half behind the leading Dodgers. Despite their poor start they lost only one of their year's series, to the Cardinals, ten games to 12. Oddly enough the 12-10 combination was a favorite with the 1952 Phils; they beat both the first place Dodgers, second place Giants, fifth place Cubs and sixth place Reds by that margin. They won three double headers from the Brooklyn champions, and even more important, their .648 percentage under O'Neill was better than the pennant-winning percentages of the Dodgers and Yankees, 1952 major league champions.

Richie Ashburn batted over .300 from the time big Steve took charge. Del Ennis made a great comeback and slugged his way into the 100 RBI class with 107. Gran Hamner became the best shortstop in the National League, and after he was moved to the fifth spot in the batting order kept pace with Ennis in runs batted in. He was the National League shortstop as the N. L. Stars won an abbreviated All-Star game in Shibe Park, July 8th. Eddie Waitkus made the finest comeback of all. He played like the Waitkus of 1950, fielded spectacularly and developed a power punch that even surprised O'Neill. "Waitkus played terrific ball for me," said Steve.

Connie Ryan surprised everyone by playing more innings than at any time in his major league career. "And I didn't feel tired at the finish," said the New Orleans Irisher. "Steve made playing baseball fun."

Only Willie Jones at third base did not have as good a year as had been anticipated. Puddin' Head got into a hitting rut in the spring, when things were going badly, and never got out of it. However, unlike many players whose batting slumps affect their entire play, Willie's fielding was as adroit as ever.

One of the big surprises was the fine work by the two catchers, Smokey Burgess, obtained in the Seminick-Sisler trade, and the Detroit bonus boy, Stan Lopata. Burgess won the first-string berth by a narrow margin and hit .294 in 109 games. Before Burgess came to Philadelphia, he was dubbed a fair hitter but a guy with a "broken" arm, who was likely to throw the ball anywhere. But before the season was a few weeks old he showed himself to be a splendid thrower, a fine handler of his pitchers and a dangerous clutch hitter. Lopata improved day by day, whenever he was employed, and showed something of his long anticipated promise. Someday he will release his great hitting potential.

O'Neill also gave Mel Clark, Ohio University Bachelor of Science and rookie right fielder, an opportunity to show his wares. Clark, a right-handed hitter, alternated with Wyrostek in right field, playing solely against left-handed pitchers until a double header in Chicago, August 24th. Mel made five hits in six tries against right-handed pitchers that afternoon, and after that he played regularly until forced out by a leg injury. Clark finished the year topping the club in batting—.335 for 47 games—and batted safely in 17 consecutive games before being sidelined by the injury. When both Clark and Wyrostek were incapacitated, old Bill Nicholson did a fine job in right field in the last month of the season and still sprayed out an occasional homer.

The work of the pitching staff was sensational. Roberts truly was Robin the Magnificent, a present-day Grover Alexander. After losing four successive games from May 21st to June 20th,

Robin went on a sensational winning splurge. He won four before Max Lanier of the Giants beat him, 2-0; then copped nine in succession before he was stopped by Warren Hacker of the Cubs, 3-0; and followed this with eight straight, which carried him to the last day of the season. That gave him 21 victories in his last 23 starts.

He pitched 30 complete games, and finished with 28 victories against 7 defeats, his third straight season in the 20-victory class. When he defeated Brooklyn, September 24th, for his 27th victory, he became the first National League pitcher to reach that total since Bucky Walters, the former Phillie, won 27 for the Red champions of 1939. And when he hung up his 28th at the expense of the Giants on the final Sunday, September 28th, it made him the first 28-game winner in the two majors since Dizzy Dean of the Cardinals turned the trick in 1935. In pitching 330 innings, Robin issued the amazingly low number of only 45 bases on balls. Robin also defeated the Brooklyn Dodgers, 1952 National League champions, six times in as many attempts.

Curt Simmons, after a midseason letdown, found himself again at the finish, got back into his groove and blanked the Giants and Dodgers, the two top teams, in his last two starts. He had a 14-8 record, led both major leagues in shutouts with 7 and showed the form he displayed in 1950 before being called into service.

Karl Drews, the ex-Yankee, proved a fine pitcher and with a few breaks in one-run games could easily have been a 20-game winner. Russ Meyer also hurled excellently all season. Roberts, Drews and Simmons all finished with earned run averages of less than three runs, and Meyer wasn't far away. For the third straight summer a Philly pitcher had the honor of starting for the National League in the midsummer All-Star game, all of them resulting in N. L. victories. This time Curt Simmons, then red-hot, got the nod from Manager Leo Durocher. Curt did his bit, pitched three scoreless innings and got credit for the National League's five inning victory.

O'Neill also gave a young righthander from Yonkers, New York, Steve Ridzik, an opportunity to show his stuff, and the Polish boy showed enough to warrant the belief that he would be a regular on the 1953 staff. After pitching a no-hitter against the Cardinals in spring training, Steve saw little action until O'Neill took over. Perhaps Steve O'Neill liked the boy's name. Konstanty, the reliefer, also perked up, and O'Neill got two complete games out of him in the late season.

2

It was a happy group of players and writers who said goodbye to Steve O'Neill after the close of the 1952 season. All thought a job had been well done, and there was not one in the party who did not believe the Phils would be strong contenders all the way in 1953. Everyone felt the O'Neill gait of .648 could be carried into a new season. Even with their bad 1952 start, the final percentage of .565 was only 26 points under the pennant-winning percentage of 1950. And there was a distinct feeling that .565 could easily be excelled.

"I would like to have just one more power hitter who would turn our two-run innings into four-run explosions," said O'Neill. "We could use one man who would put over the knockout punch after the others had staggered the opposing hurler. With such a hitter, we'd really be set. As it is, this is a fine club; I'm proud of every man on it."

Bob Carpenter took the cue and began looking for that additional power hitter. But most of the Phillies—Roberts, Simmons, Ashburn, Hamner, Jones, Clark, Lopata—are still young. Not as young as the fast-running 1950 Whiz Kids, but at their peak, or just under their peak. The Phillies' splendid organization functions 365 days of the year, twenty-four hours of the day. The young millionaire who owns the club is willing to get his money at the gate. Phillie fans no longer need go to bed with the dread feeling that by morning a Robin Roberts has been sold to the New York Giants and a Richie Ashburn to the Chicago Cubs. The policy of the club still is to develop its own or buy experienced players on the market. If trades are made, there will be no cash involved. They will be made only to strengthen some position. With two pitching stoppers of the caliber of Robin Roberts and Curt Simmons, a protracted stay in the first division is almost a certainty. And another quick pennant is a distinct possibility. As Phillie pitchers have helped spark the National League to three successive All-Star victories, it may even be that in a World Series in the immediate future the two great sharpshooters, Robin Roberts and Curt Simmons, will pitch the National League out of its World Series doldrums.

Index

Compiled by Bonnie Hanks